ROMANTIC REVELATIONS: VISIONS OF POST-APOCALYPTIC LIFE AND HOPE IN THE ANTHROPOCENE

Romantic Revelations: Visions of Post-Apocalyptic Life and Hope in the Anthropocene

CHRIS WASHINGTON

UNIVERSITY OF TORONTO PRESS
Toronto Buffalo London

© University of Toronto Press 2019
Toronto Buffalo London
utorontopress.com

ISBN 978-1-4875-0450-2

Library and Archives Canada Cataloguing in Publication

Title: Romantic revelations : visions of post-apocalyptic life and hope in the Anthropocene / Chris Washington.
Names: Washington, Chris (David Christopher), 1980– author.
Description: Includes bibliographical references and index.
Identifiers: Canadiana 20190091053 | ISBN 9781487504502 (hardcover)
Subjects: LCSH: English literature – 19th century – History and criticism. | LCSH: English literature – 18th century – History and criticism. | LCSH: Apocalyptic literature – History and criticism. | LCSH: Romanticism – Great Britain. | LCSH: End of the world in literature.
Classification: LCC PR468.A66 W37 2019 | DDC 820.9/145—dc23

This book has been published with the assistance of Francis Marion University.

University of Toronto Press acknowledges the financial assistance to its publishing program of the Canada Council for the Arts and the Ontario Arts Council, an agency of the Government of Ontario.

Funded by the Government of Canada
Financé par le gouvernement du Canada

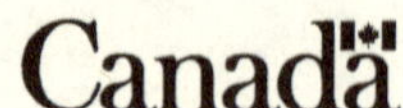

Contents

Acknowledgments

To my great and supportive colleagues at Miami University of Ohio, where this project began: Laura Mandell is as generous a scholar as you can imagine. Mary Jean Corbett and Tobias Menely were incisive and amazing readers and believers throughout. Thanks go as well to Miami University for its generous scholarship and travel-funding support over the years.

To my friends in graduate school, Adam and Erin Burkey and Joshua Miron, who listened to me for endless hours and who, during every hour, made my thinking better. Everyone should have the chance to have such friends.

Several other institutions have supported this project over the years. I benefited enormously from a post-doctoral position at the University of Southern Mississippi and the intellectual fellowship of the English department there. As a visiting professor at Loyola University New Orleans, I had the encouragement, intelligence, and friendship of colleagues there who made this an immeasurably better book. In particular Rian Thum, Laura Murphy, Tim Welsh, Chris Schaberg, and John Sebastian. To Rian, you know what you mean. I would say thank you but you know it is not enough. It might be that there is a lot of false coin out there, but not yours. Thank you for your truth and for always being true. You are my friend.

While at Francis Marion University the conviviality and support of the English faculty have made this book's final entrance into the world a pleasurable experience. Francis Marion also provided me with several summer research grants that were crucial to the book's completion. My endless gratitude to the various members of the department and the provost's office. You are both gems, Chris Johnson and Beckie Flanagan, as former and current chair respectively.

To the whole National Endowments for Humanities summer crew of 2013, fearlessly led by the inestimable Stephen Behrendt. We read, we thought, we wrote, and discussed our projects endlessly. To the whole crew: your taste for, shall we say, a grape truly burst against your palate fine – if not a tater tot – is what allowed me to write the Percy Bysshe Shelley chapter, let alone to soak up all your brilliant Romanticist knowledge. Thank you. I can only feebly hope I can contribute back as much as you gave me.

The list of others to thank is too long to print, and this is no joke. I want to name just a few who took time out of their lives to inspire mine. Alan Vardy, Anne C. McCarthy, David Collings, Joel Faflak, Jared McGeough, Aaron Ottinger, Devoney Looser, Ron Broglio, Brian Rejack, and Andrew Burkitt all read various drafts of parts of this manuscript and my book prospectus and all were instrumental in providing advice and encouragement without which the book would not otherwise be. I can only bow my head to you all and wish that I can be there for you as you were for me. My thanks are truly inexpressible. Perhaps I might try the next time we see each other at a conference.

David Sigler has been a constant presence in my life since I met him at the NEH summer seminar, often telling me just the right thing in just the right way that would allow me to hear it and follow it. He has had a rough time. He is a true gentleman and scholar, and I owe him much more than a pair of Morrissey socks. My debt to him can only be measured by what I cannot repay, in the terms of hospitality I set out in this book.

Speaking of things I don't deserve, I have been blessed to find a truly great reading and writing Romantic group: Suzanne Barnett, Ashley Cross, Michael Gamer, Yohei Igarashi, and Kate Singer. No page of this manuscript has not benefited from your enormous erudition, generosity, and professional advice. If I have put that in the backwards negative grammar structure, you all know why. I will never learn.

I have had the chance to present various parts from this work over the years at conferences where I encountered fascinating interchanges of ideas and received most welcome and helpful feedback. I was bowled over to get the chance to be on a 2016 MLA panel sponsored by the John Clare Society. It allowed me to completely finalize my Clare chapter. In 2015, Evan Gottlieb and Alex Dick gave me the opportunity to be a part of their amazing double panel at NASSR. I talked about my "The Last Man" chapter and got the rare coolness of continuing to work out my ideas with a highly engaged audience. I presented part of the "Mont Blanc" chapter at the 2014 International Conference on Romanticism in Minneapolis, a conference that proved a blessing in other ways as I met a host of scholars there who changed my life incomparably for the better.

To all of the scholars who contributed essays to *Romanticism and Speculative Realism,* a volume I co-edited with Anne C. McCarthy, you all showed me new ways of thinking about both words in that title, and that thinking is on every page of this book.

Thanks to the great crew of editors and production people at the University of Toronto Press. Thanks specifically are due to my editor, Mark Thompson, for believing in the book from the first. And to the last. And for three anonymous readers who provided invaluable feedback and recommendations that the book be published—which was also invaluable. And thanks to Barbara Porter and Angela Wingfield for their expert copy editing.

To Suzanne Barnett for her unwavering support and patience and kindness and endless readings and brilliance. Thanks specifically, too, to her, for a brilliant suggestion at a key moment that gave the book the energy and inspiration to start again and cross the finish line.

And, ah, that heroic eaver of all those sheaves, Steve Lusher, I will not even pretend to have the words. Your presence continues to make my life more present, your life continues to inspire mine. Thank you, buxxcy.

To my family for their unceasing support over the years, and especially my singular mom, who makes every day possible: I am nothing without her, nor, indeed, is anyone.

And for Kate Singer, the future of theory, who, in all of the ways that really matter, actually wrote this book. Of course your miracle puts a "u" in it. Thank yuu for being mine. If there is any hospitality to come, it is only your super-star, which I watch on my VCR.

Portions of this book have been previously published in the following journals, which I thank for their permission to reprint. Part of the introduction appeared in *Literature Compass* 12, no. 9 (2015), 448–60. Part of chapter 3 appeared in "Byron's Speculative Turn: Visions of Posthuman Life in *Cain,*" *Essays in Romanticism* 22, no. 1 (2015), 73–95. Part of chapter 4 appeared in "John Clare and Biopolitics," *European Romantic Review* 25, no. 6 (2014), 665–82.

ROMANTIC REVELATIONS: VISIONS OF POST-APOCALYPTIC LIFE AND HOPE IN THE ANTHROPOCENE

Introduction

There Is a Light That Never Goes Out?

When Elizabeth Bennet memorably tells Darcy that he is "the last man in the world whom I could ever be prevailed upon to marry," we do not immediately associate these words, or this novel, with a genre that would only be invented two years later in the famous ghost-story-writing contest of the Shelleys and Byron, but nonetheless they capture the same political contours of post-apocalyptic fiction.[1] Later, when Elizabeth and Darcy embower themselves in Pemberley's paradise of wedded bliss at the novel's end, they write themselves not into a community of last men and women but into a fairy-tale happy ending that ensures humans will continue to exist, directly opposite the extinction of the human species we see in Byron's "Darkness" (1816) and Mary Shelley's *The Last Man* (1826). Yet as Elizabeth's words intimate, she and Darcy could have remained forever frozen in lastness, unable either to exist or to become extinct, their views of each other as different – even, as we will see, nonhuman – thwarting the production of new forms of life and love. In that scenario they would be similar to the creature in *Frankenstein* who is alone with no hope of life with the human species and yearns instead for that paradigmatic Romantic paradise – a return to a Rousseauvian state of nature – in the wilds of South America with another creature like him, a situation that can lead to future life. The courtship comedies of Austen and the creature's imagined paradise remind us, then, that lastness is always a possibility when we seek to make a common cause, a common life, with others like and unlike us.

Such instances of lastness trace a dilemma that what I call "post-apocalyptic Romanticism" forces us to confront when these texts deposit us back into the state of nature (since all societal institutions have fallen), and we face the stark political choice of forming new social contracts for living on or giving in to the inevitability of species extinction. It is a choice, as I show in this book, between social-contract democratization and libertarian do-it-yourself, conservative anarchism, both choices that pollute the environment and kill off humans, ultimately terminating any chance for a human paradise on earth. In its Romantic articulation the aporia of lastness returns us to the beginning and the end, times without origin (*an-arche*), a solitary firstness and lastness from which all creatures can, theoretically, make life. Precisely because we remain stuck in this state-of-nature aporia of existence and extinction, *Romantic Revelations* contends that we are not yet even alive. And while the loneliness of the creature indelibly haunts Romanticism as he recedes into the vanishing point of the Arctic, "lost in darkness and distance," *Romantic Revelations* shows that Romantic writers invent the post-apocalyptic genre not to advocate extinction and exclusion – of the creature, of humans – but rather to design an ontologically radical social contract that includes both the human and the nonhuman, bringing all creatures in from the cold.[2]

Responding to the climate-change events of 1816, "the year without a summer," the proleptic prophecies of Mary Shelley (*Frankenstein*, *The Last Man*), the abyssal portraits of Percy Shelley ("Mont Blanc," *Prometheus Unbound*), and the cosmic ("Darkness," *Cain*) and comic (*Don Juan*) eschatologies of Byron coalesce into a cataclysmic end-times episteme. But if, as Michel Foucault asserts, the biopolitical imperative of the Enlightenment is the continuation of the human species, then post-apocalypse Romanticism challenges us to rethink what life, broadly understood, is, or could be, when human beings enact their own potential obsolescence.[3] Rather than indulge in a *sentiment des ruines*, an eighteenth-century passion for a sentimentalized lost world, the Romantics think within the ashes of posthuman history to theorize life and the hope of life in the darkness they find themselves unexpectedly straggling through. In doing so, they establish communities for living with human and nonhuman others in the Anthropocene. Indeed, one of the primary aims of this book is to illustrate how post-apocalyptic Romanticism exemplifies how hope of and for life can only emerge precisely when there is no hope. Just as Darcy's hopelessness in Elizabeth's feigned denial of their future-to-come "taught [him] to hope," in order for hope to be, it must emerge from and exist despite its inexistence, despite hopelessness, or otherwise it is not hope (251). Percy Bysshe Shelley's Demogorgon nicely captures this in his exordium at the end of *Prometheus Unbound*: "to hope, till Hope creates / from its own wreck the thing it contemplates" (573–4). Hope only occurs in its extinction, in hopelessness.

While we do not of course associate the lightness, brightness, and sparkle of *Pride and Prejudice* with post-apocalyptic texts – after all,

Elizabeth and Darcy achieve their happy ending while in *Frankenstein*'s upside-down fairy tale the creature's one-person species is vanquished – it nonetheless depicts the same central paradox of such texts that *Romantic Revelations* takes as its subject. As I will endeavour to show throughout this study, post-apocalyptic Romanticism is ultimately about happy endings. True, post-apocalyptic texts are often characterized by what many see as their incessant and irrepressible nihilism, texts that predict a future planet inhospitable to human life and to the meanings we attach to and derive from that life. Anne Mellor's reading of *The Last Man* captures this nihilism: "if the human race can be eliminated, as it is in [Shelley's] novel, then the very concept of meaning is, finally, meaningless."[4] But given that the basic plot of such texts eradicates humankind and its works, readings like this tend towards an uncritical anthropocentric immersion in the text, a version of Jerome McGann's "romantic ideology," manufacturing and perpetuating the nihilism they purport to discover as a primordial Romantic energy.[5] Contra such readings, *Romantic Revelations* demonstrates that these texts work counter-intuitively and paradoxically, facing down extinction as the limit of life to show that it is this very extinctual limit that makes life possible, both in the now and in whatever future may come. It is by revealing life's possibility within the crucible of extinction that post-apocalyptic Romanticism engenders hope rather than despair, hope unbound rather than the giddy accelerationism of some contemporary schools of thought that clamour for an end to all human things.[6] Furthermore, post-apocalyptic Romanticism equates nihilism with its avowed opposite, the paradisiacal Romantic fantasies that foresee a forthcoming perfected world in which humans reign as sovereign lords over the earth and the nonhuman creatures on it, what we might refer to as anthropocentricism with a vengeance.

But to demonstrate how post-apocalyptic Romanticism responds to this anthropocentric vengeance, it is important to delineate at the outset that Romanticism distinguishes between the apocalyptic and the post-apocalyptic. Forty years ago, when M.H. Abrams wrote "that in the early 1790s Wordsworth, together with Blake and a number of other contemporaries rejoiced [...] that the revolution of their epoch would issue in an earthly paradise," he defined the period in a way that continues to hold both overt and clandestine sway over how we conceptualize Romanticism.[7] Abrams links Wordsworth's and Blake's belief in an immanent earthly paradise to literary apocalypse, drawing on its Greek etymology as *apocalypsis*, which means "revelation," and its biblical heritage, to define apocalypse as "a prophetic vision, set forth in arcane and elaborate symbols, of the imminent events which will bring an abrupt end to the present world order and replace it by a new and perfected condition of man and his milieu."[8] Romanticism is configured as a revelation of, a return to, earthly paradise. More recently, Morton Paley has also identified a Romantic belief in a millennial period, however secular, that follows the revelation of revolutionary apocalypse.[9] While we may be tempted to view Abrams's thesis askance, as somewhat old fashioned and out of fashion, in reality it remains a through line in how we read Romanticism, a thesis covertly updated and rebooted as the decades have slipped by, reappearing by a kind of legerdemain in green Romantic writers and writers of the Romantic disaster who see the period as redemptive and revitalizing.[10] And while it is true that Romantic disaster can, as post-apocalyptic Romanticism does, reject "false redemption," it nonetheless, as Jacques Khalip and David Collings write, positions itself as "endemic to the human itself," even though, as Collings puts it, disaster "enables and potentially undermines human flourishing."[11] But, as Khalip says, "disaster narratives … are too frequently conjured as pertaining specifically to the human in whose perspective they are composed and which they in turn confirm."[12] Post-apocalyptic Romanticism, however, seeks to avoid this exclusively human perspective. In doing so, we can see it responding to Khalip's question concerning what he refers to as "hope without a hope" – "Can or should there be hope after extinction?"[13]

Romantic Revelations finds, as I said, hope possible only as it emerges from that which makes it impossible, the extinction of hope, a non-dialectical affirmation of post-apocalyptic Romanticism's quest for life amidst the ash. There is, in other words, hope after extinction precisely because we are not yet extinct because, post-apocalyptic Romanticism argues, we are not even yet alive. And while apocalypse is also closely linked with burgeoning democratic ambitions in the period, as illustrated by Steven Goldsmith, such a straightforwardly hopeful politics is theorized as immanently utopian and human, a kind of flip-side version of the creature's imagined paradise.[14]

Romantic Revelations examines how Romanticism nurtures a darker, post-apocalyptic vision of a world of barren landscapes under blackened skies, a place where human institutions like governments have dissolved and the species is mournfully disappearing from the face of the earth. As I argue, post-apocalyptic Romanticism dissociates itself from the idea of an earthly paradise peopled and ruled by human sovereignty by cleaving the classic apocalyptic Romantic merger of subject and object, human and nonhuman. *Romantic Revelations* finds itself agreeing with Claire Colebrook's theoretical expansion of what theory can be in the age of the posthuman. For her theory would reorient itself as a "theory that opened itself to the thought of extinction."[15] This theory would avoid the humanism that she argues remains firmly rooted in posthuman theory to the extent that "all social, political, ethical, and aesthetic considerations appear to be singularly concerned with developmental narratives of human fruition and democracies-to-come in the face of annihilation."[16] However, post-apocalyptic Romanticism departs from Colebrook's argument in that it imagines a democratic politics with a nonhuman twist. It conceives of the possibility of a viable democracy-without-the-demos on a world without us.

Recognizing that the world is without us in that it exists before us and will exist after us, post-apocalypse Romanticism, in my account, urges us to forgo an obsession with our finitude that prevents us from living. Post-apocalyptic Romanticism therefore refers to both a concept and a state of being that emerges once we move beyond finitude; it is not simply, that is, something that follows apocalypse. Unlike extinction, which, as Khalip notes, "finds itself more often than not repeating the knowledge of inception that rhetorically pushes it to invest in the allegory of origination in spite of itself," post-apocalyptic Romanticism encompasses times that take place when the human species seems precarious (Shelley's *The Last Man*), on the verge of the social scene's eruption from the state of nature (Byron's *Cain*), and even extends into possible future worlds unknown (Shelley's *Frankenstein*; Austen's *Pride and Prejudice*).[17] Post-apocalyptic Romanticism is a temporal contretemps; it is not located anywhere, before or after, but conceptually everywhere already in the Anthropocene.

There is, of course, a historical component to apocalyptic Romanticism that must be taken into account. Before 1816, the so-called year without summer, the period displays a vision of apocalypse as Abrams explicates it, a recurrence to earthly paradise – what the creature in *Frankenstein* yearns for when he informs Victor that he and his "Eve" will venture to the wilds of South America to live in their own newly made paradise. The early Romantic writers appear to be especially susceptible to the visionary company – the French Revolution, Pantisocracy, utopian Grasmere collaborative poetics – that soothsaying apocalypse foretells in its predictive model of an intermediation of mind and world that will correspondingly lead to a new-found valley of milk and honey.[18] Wordsworth's "Prospectus" to *The Excursion* neatly encapsulates the tableaux of a mind-world union.

> Paradise, and groves
> Elysian, Fortunate Fields – like those of old
> Sought in the Atlantic Main, why should they be

A history only of departed things.
Or a mere fiction of what never was?
For the discerning intellect of Man,
When wedded to this goodly universe
In love and holy passion, shall find these
A simple produce of the common day.
I, long before the blissful hour arrives,
Would chaunt, in lonely peace, the spousal verse
Of this great consummation: – and, by words
Which speak of nothing more than what we are.
Would I arouse the sensual from their sleep
Of Death, and win the vacant and the vain
To noble raptures; while my voice proclaims
How exquisitely the individual Mind
(And the progressive powers perhaps no less
Of the whole species) to the external World
Is fitted: – and how exquisitely, too,
Theme this but little heard of among Men,
The external World is fitted to the Mind;
And the creation (by no lower name
Can it be called) which they with blended might
Accomplish – this is our high argument.[19]

Wordsworth's speaker construes himself in a biblical fashion, the high prophet of a paradise whose time is nigh and will be eternal upon its projected landfall. His Miltonic "high argument" blends the mythopoetics of Christological earthly ascension with a green vision of renewed harmony on the planet that the marriage of "Mind" and "World" simultaneously transcends. Just as importantly, Wordsworth's high argument is also an exhortation to action, to make "the history of departed things" like Paradise reappear through the pastoral politics and poetics of the Romantic imagination: the fields of Paradise return as "produce of the common day" when we till the earth, the personal garden of our "Mind." This explication is not only how Abrams understands Wordsworth's plan but an apocalyptic view that can also be detected in Northrup Frye, Harold Bloom, Geoffrey Hartman, Paul de Man, Alan Liu, and Mellor, to name only a few of the agenda-setters of Romanticism over the last decades.[20]

More importantly for this book than the apocalyptic millennial dimensions, though, Wordsworth's game plan also instances, as we will see in greater detail further on in this introduction, what speculative realism calls "correlationism," the Kantian belief (which Quentin Meillassoux identifies as actually beginning with Berkeley) in the subjective mind's phenomenal structuring of the objective world. This same correlationism carries over in the listed scholarly treatments of the era, treatments that validate McGann's romantic ideological critique that what is supposedly present in Romanticism gets unwittingly internalized in scholarly assessments of it, reproducing the object of critical analysis as the critic's analysis. Abrams, indeed, describes this apocalyptic tradition explicitly in terms that mirror the post-Kantian philosophy speculative realism critiques: "The tendency in innovative Romantic thought … is greatly to diminish, and at the extreme to eliminate, the role of God, leaving as the prime agencies man and the world, mind and nature, the ego and the non-ego, the self and the not-self, spirit and the other, or (in the favorite antithesis of post-Kantian philosophers) subject and objects."[21] The justly famous Simplon Pass episode of *The Prelude* (1850) strikes the same notes: once Wordsworth crosses the Alps, "Imagination … That awful Power rose from the mind's abyss," a movement in a mind-world progression that culminates when "the unfettered clouds and region of the Heavens, / Tumult and peace, the darkness and the light – / Were all like the workings of one mind, the features of the same face … Characters of the great Apocalypse, / the types and symbols of Eternity, / Of first and last, and midst, and without end" (lines 592–3, 634–40).[22] Wordsworth's poetic ambition to merge mind and nature in a mutual embrace of spiritual and sexual ecstasy – the same fantasy of most contemporary environmental and eco-theory systems of thought – is the subject-and-object dilemma resolved by a fusion of Kantian transcendentalism and green-theory ecological earth-saving. We can detect a similar urge in Blake: "I will not cease from Mental Flight / Nor shall my sword sleep in my hand / Till we have built Jerusalem / in Englands green & pleasant Land" (8–12).[23] Apocalyptic thinking is characterized not only by a vision of a New Jerusalem manifesting and expanding across the globe but also by the methodological mechanism of its foresight: wedded bliss derives from the commingling of subject and object (mind and England, for Blake), the human and nonhuman, a flattening of distinctions that clears the dance floor for Hymen and the reproductive human sovereignty over the earth's futurity his garlanding two-stepping moves propel.

But even when critics like Goldsmith – who link, as I do in this book, the formal aesthetics of apocalypse to politics – decisively push back against Wordsworthian dreams of transcendence and apolitical apocalyptic strands and striations running in Romantic studies, they tend to con-fuse the apocalyptic and the post-apocalyptic. They often correlate the mind and world, the subject and object, in that it is only in the former apocalyptic case that the two are irrevocably connected.[24] And so for all of the environmental and political potency it is possible to leverage from Wordsworth's hopeful dreams of Elysium, Wordsworth and his powerful critics are certainly not the enemy here (if there is an enemy in this book, it is, as Pogo says, us).[25] This book instead argues that these visions are Romanticism's own poetical version of an opium-induced fantasia, a smacked-out Edenism diverging from the historical and philosophical reality of, say, the Industrial Revolution and the French Revolution that engenders the climate-change disasters and accordant politics of the geological period of the Anthropocene. This assuredly, pleasantly druggish myopia is what Coleridge's dulcimer player and wailing demon lover's hortatory imperative "Beware! Beware!" declares: avoid the dipsomania that comes with having fed on "honey-dew" and having "drunk the milk of Paradise" (line 54).[26] A form of ideology, being drunk on Paradise, bedevils Romanticism to the extent that, like the seductive Satan in its midst, the mirage of the light-dappled, harmonious garden imprisons us by means of the flame-wielding angels of our own anthropocentric cunning. If it is Paradise, after all, why work so hard to lose it, as the Shelleys do, and why work so hard to love beyond its lastness (since nothing follows from perfection), as Elizabeth and Darcy do?

Exploring and explaining the full implications of post-apocalyptic Romanticism is the subject of this study, which amends and extends the critical conversations of the last half-century that have defined Romanticism as a fertile and enduring environmental and apocalyptic field where, in Jonathan Bate's words, "poetry is a place where we can save the earth," the place where humanity can reverse its own planet-imperiling footprint.[27] Emphasis on Romanticism's ostensible back-to-nature environmentalism has obscured, I argue, the very real nightmares and hell-scapes through whose charnel ground the later Romantics mournfully slough. Apocalyptic understandings of the period do not fully grasp the full-throated challenge that post-apocalyptic Romanticism poses to some of the most fundamental tenets of Romanticism. In its sceptical posture towards Romanticism, post-apocalyptic Romanticism and its writers diverge from Romanticism by dint of their self-reflexive distancing, while simultaneously this exercise of self-negating irony proves post-apocalyptic Romanticism to be Romantic in its very heart. Post-apocalyptic Romanticism, as I develop it here, heeds Coleridge's last call for non-alcohol vis-à-vis the politics of paradise, an abstention that is akin to the deconstructive double-speak of sobriety in Orrin Wang's terms – a rejection of sensation, an "abstaining from all that Romanticism offers" that "also allows the very notion of Romanticism" – but it is also an abstention drunk on its own affective doubleness, its own joy sprung from bursting despair's grape against its palate fine.[28]

It is in this fashion that post-apocalyptic Romanticism vastly complicates the environmental-saviour complex associated with Romanticism, by developing what is at once a diagnosis and a critique of said complex that I call "extinctualism." But let me be clear up front about what extinctualism is not. It does not recall us to an anthropocentric idea of an exclusively human-centred extinction of the species, nor does it invoke the dread imagery of futuristic end-of-the-world scenarios where human life is a condition whose preciousness we must spotlight. Instead, the term conceptualizes the mental paradox that defines our relation to the world in the Anthropocene. Extinctualism is both the condition of our euphoric ecstasy in contemplating our own doom and our concurring refusal to concede that such a ghastly end for our species is possible. We might think of extinctualism as a kind of Derridean erasure in that humans, in marking themselves out as infinite, re-mark, in the same gesture, their species as finite, erasing themselves at the very moment they prophesy immortality. In this sense, extinctualism reflects current beliefs about climate catastrophes, beliefs that are imperfectly held together in the geological term *the Anthropocene*. The term is almost a self-contained rhetorical example of antanaclasis, when the same word is used in quick succession to signify completely different things (think of all the "wills" in Shakespeare's sonnets). We use *anthropos* to name the period that began in the Romantic era because it establishes how humans acquired the technological capabilities to master and control the atmosphere and the biosphere of the earth in such drastic fashion that it jeopardizes our survival. In this sense, the word provides a snapshot of our finitude as a species. Simultaneously, the Anthropocene, as a documented geological timeline with no end in sight, suggests our human infinitude, our ability to harness the natural world to our species' sustainability if we so choose, in such a fashion that we become this infinite timeline.

In this paradoxical, hand-in-hand face-off of finitude and infinitude, we find extinctualism. Extinctualism is our worry about our own finite end that is likewise grounded in our self-denial that such a thing could ever happen because of our infinitude: "we will solve climate change somehow, one day, in the future"; "if we caused it, we can solve it." The reductive simplicity of extinctualism clarifies rather than stymies the profound implicate of hopefulness and hopelessness such thinking bounces between: "we're all going to die, therefore we must act," versus, "humans are the masters of the universe and cannot die." An easy example of this simplification that captures the wobble between believing ourselves both finite and infinite is the pop-culture philosophical commonplace conundrum: if a tree falls in the forest but no one is around to hear it, does it make a sound? Deceptively simple, and easily dismissible, it is also a quintessentially Romantic question – even, as I want to argue in this book, one of the most fundamental Romantic philosophical questions what with its focus on the epistemological and ontological division between the human subject and the nonhuman object.

In fact, the question is a rephrasing of Percy Shelley's famous question in "Mont Blanc" (1816) that asks, in its apostrophe to the seemingly mute mountain, "and what were thou/and stars, and sea, and earth/if to the human mind's imaginings/silence and solitude were vacancy?"[29] This apostrophic, seemingly unanswered, query, like the forest-tree riddle, speaks to how humans ontologically understand their orientation in relation to the natural world, even as it suggests the contradictory possibility of a certain primordial or a priori unknowability in this regard. Mary Shelley poses the question differently and yet still more ecologically straightforwardly in *The Last Man*:

> will the mountains remain unmoved, and streams still keep a downward course towards the vast abyss; will the tides rise and fall, and the winds fan universal nature; will beasts pasture, birds fly, and fishes swim, when man, the lord, possessor, perceiver, and recorder of all these things, has passed away, as though he had never been?[30]

This book will return, in chapters 1 and 2, to the Shelleys' two formulations of post-apocalyptic Romanticism. For the moment I want to outline the broader stakes the question in its various permutations articulates. The fallen-tree question, a bite-sized candy version of the Shelleys' questions, asks whether humans are necessary for the world's survival or whether the world might not just be better off without humans after all. This question, in its Romantic manifestations, is the problem this book will seek to answer. For all its seeming simplicity, then, our folk rewriting of these thorny Romantic questions into a one-line extinctualism enviro-riddle invokes some of the most notoriously difficult philosophical problems regarding epistemology and ontology in the world of Romantic and post-Romantic modernity that I have touched on so far: the environmental devastation wrought by humanity on nature, the phenomenological complications of mind and world, the eschatology of human finitude versus the world's infinitude, and the revolutionary politics driving unrealized egalitarian dreams-to-come.

On the one hand, these questions are epistemological in so far as they raise the hoary philosophical issue of whether our representational apperceptions of the world phenomenologically capture the world as it is, that is, capture the Kantian thing in itself (*ding an sich,* a term that Kant uses interchangeably with "noumenon"). On the other hand, appended to this concern, the questions ontologically wonder whether or not the world actually exists if the speaker of "Mont Blanc," say, is not present to experience the world's independent "silence and solitude" that are "vacancy" (how does the speaker know about this vacancy in her own absence?). Even more problematic, from an anthropocentric perspective, is the chiasmus of the human and the nonhuman: if it is true that the world might not exist unless the human subject's interaction with it brings it into ontological being, it follows therefore that the human might not exist either if there is no nonhuman world. Or alternatively we might say that the human and the world are irreconcilably, materially riven, with human extinction apprized as the all-but-inevitable result. In their most militant anti-anthropocentric mode, these questions *speculate* (we will come back to this important word below) that the earth may well outlast the human perishables its gradual cooling and heating will chill to the bone and roast on the open fire ("all hearts were chill'd into a selfish prayer for light" and "forests were set on fire," "fell and faded," Byron writes in "Darkness" [lines 8–9, 19–20]).

Romanticism's darkest fear raises its head in tremulous recognition of these latter-day possibilities. Rather than a predicted apocalypse of peace and plenty, this subject-object rift glimpses a post-apocalyptic, second Fall, except that this one pitches us forward directly into the End of Days. For the subject who stumbles out of the philosophical mazework of these questions into the real-world sunless sky is confronted by an uncaring yet cognitively concussive world where the decease of that world entails human species annihilation while, concurrently, the erasure of humanity signifies an a-referential vacuity, neither sound nor fury, neither a burn out nor a fade away. Navigating through these texts' philosophic arguments, tropological experiments, and representations of humanity's end, *Romantic Revelations* traces how Romantic authors think through the duelling double bind of self-doubt and stubborn self-assurance concerning survival that is extinctualism, even as they do not indulgently luxuriate in it. Rather, they find that their collapse into despair and hopelessness evades extinctualism's aporia and forges in its stead a hopeful posthuman social contract. Such an impossible future incorporates both human and nonhuman life, a radical new politics that can help us to find forms of "living on" (a phrase I develop below) in the Anthropocene.

At its core, then, this book examines how post-apocalyptic Romanticism interrogates whether the most basic assumption of classical humanism, the so-called Copernican turn that locates humanity at the centre of the world, remains credibly viable in the face of contrariwise evidentiary catastrophes that climate change supplies. Exemplified by their shift to post-apocalyptic writing in 1816, extinctualism undercuts whatever anthropocentric notions the Romantics may have harboured, resulting in a plague of self-doubt about the value, utility, and purpose of the egalitarian aesthetic innovations, utopian political revolutions, and societal reformations that the Romantics wanted their writing to enact and forward. Bereft of a locative cosmic position, adrift in an ocean of falling stars (*disaster*, from the Latin for "diseased star," literally means "fallen star"), the Shelleys and Byron experience the full force of extinctualist jitters – that humanity amounts to a meaningless, though briefly destructive, geological indenture (or perhaps a Tasmanian Devil–shaped hole in the earth's crust) on the spatio-temporal timeline of a completely expressionless, emotionless world. We cannot, they realize, make the universe turn its smile upside down, since it literally could not care less. Post-apocalyptic Romanticism thus confronts us with the possibility of this world without us, in two registers: a future world literally devoid of human beings and a world existing outside of and beyond us. In this latter regard, post-apocalyptic Romanticism demonstrates that, since the world and humans are distinct entities, we have *always already been inhabiting this world without us*. Instead of collapsing in a helpless meltdown as a result of this blasted assessment about their own insignificance, thinkers of post-apocalyptic Romanticism seize on this insight to instigate new forms of life, of "living on," on this nonhuman world without us.

The present study therefore exhumes Romantic mind-world, subject-object phenomenology to highlight that it is more crucial than ever to engage with the subject-object dilemma because it governs how we think politics and the political in relation to climate change on and alongside this world without us. *Romantic Revelations* claims that, despite recent work on ecology and animal studies in the period, the vitally urgent ontological ramifications of the nonhuman and its consequences for thinking through anthropogenic climate change remain overlooked in critical studies of Romantic politics.[31]

I should be clear, then, about what I mean by "nonhuman" and "politics." "Nonhuman," in this book, collects and at times syncretizes more than "animal" or "nature" (terms whose erasure at the hands of Derrida and Tim Morton render them less than helpful) and instead confects animals in all of their plurality; nature in the diffracted forms of trees, winds, rivers, light, sun; and the world as both the planet Earth and the conceptual, phenomenological shaping that worlds us.[32] For that matter, I use the singular "nonhuman" only as categorical convenience; like "the animal" that elides the multitudinous plethora of animals, as Derrida recognizes, the nonhuman, more properly speaking, consists of "nonhumans," all of which are radically distinct from each other.[33] But "nonhuman" connotes a temporal signification as well, as we will see shortly, marking a distinct infinitude that humans do not possess, but which, as seen above, the world might. Politics will, differently, be initially understood as shaped by its Enlightenment heritage revolving around social-contract debates that resurface in subtle, obvious, and sometimes just plain strange guises in post-apocalyptic Romanticism. It is the nonhuman, in all its signifying and ontological capacities, I argue, that actualizes post-apocalyptic Romantic political responses to ecological and climatic catastrophes that occur in aesthetic, social, material, and affective registers in the later half of the period. Politics, in other words, is not solely a human affair. Thus this book moves away from Aristotle's, and Giorgio Agamben's, distinction of *bios* from *zoe* that informs biopolitics and towards what Nicole Shukin calls "zoopolitics," a politics that encompasses all living forms.[34]

For the destructive climate-change events of 1816 instigated by the nonhuman, the volcano Mount Tambora, undeniably alter how the Romantics thought about the environment and the end of the world and the anthropocentric politics augured by both.[35] Late Romantic texts like *The Last Man* that explore post-apocalyptic worlds thus remind us that classic Romantic subject-and-object concepts like "the imagination," "the mind," and "the world" are matters of life and death, and that these same metaphysical, historical, and climatological issues continue to vex us today as we grapple with the challenges of climate change. All of these concepts are also wrapped up in anthropocentricism, the belief that humans are sovereigns over the world, and it is this ideology that post-apocalyptic Romanticism deconstructs. Lionel Verney, the "last man" of Shelley's novel, has already perfectly articulated the problem of anthropocentric politics when he voices the question that tasks us to consider whether or not the streams, birds, fish, and other nonhuman life will continue on with their own habits, their own lives, once humanity is gone. To invoke it again:

> will the mountains remain unmoved, and streams still keep a downward course towards the vast abyss; will the tides rise and fall, and the winds

> fan universal nature; will beasts pasture, birds fly, and fishes swim, when man, the lord, possessor, perceiver, and recorder of all these things, has passed away, as though he had never been?

While his question, in one direction, sets up a human and nonhuman conflict, in the other direction, it suggests that the creatures' lives will continue unaffected, even as it sets out the impossibility of this possibility through the mantel of human lordship and sovereign rule in its next clause. The text's doubled consciousness, of a world indifferent to humanity and of a world impoverished without humanity, establishes an ironic affirmation – precisely through its ironic duplicity – of the human–nonhuman split. In answer to Verney's question, *Romantic Revelations* demonstrates that, for the Romantics, the earth is necessary for human survival, but in the event or advent of global disaster, humans are not necessary for earthly survival. Human irrelevance, *Romantic Revelations* posits, is the conclusive result of humans' inability to relinquish their own sovereignty over the world and make common cause, not only with each other, as humans fail to do in Byron's "Darkness," but with nonhuman life, with this world, and the other beings on it, that live without us on this world without us. The "without" of a world without us here, therefore, takes on another denotation in addition to its articulation above as a world that exists independently of us: nonhumans do not depend on their interconnection with us for their existence.

In thinking through this division of subject and object, post-apocalyptic Romanticism, as in Verney's question, theorizes a new type of Romantic ironic thinking about existence and extinction that I term "the post-apocalyptic sublime." It is unlike Edmund Burke's aesthetic sublime, which concerns the finite mind's contemplation of the world's infinitude. In Burke's contemplation, the terror the subject experiences when the mind's limitations are juxtaposed with infinity give rise to an unaccountable pleasure that is also, Burke tells us, derived from and antagonistic to our sense of species self-preservation.[36] Burke's sublime therefore wishes to safeguard the human species from its extinctual fears and the pleasure it takes in them; it proves to be another example of anthropocentric politics and extinctualism in that the infinity it finally contemplates is human infinity. The post-apocalyptic sublime does not attempt to think human infinitude but rather the infinitude of the whole, nonhuman world; in Burkean discussions of the sublime (and, as we will see below, Kantian discussions), we have always been concerned with human notions of infinity in relation to a world connected to us. Nor is the post-apocalyptic sublime what John Keats referred to as Wordsworth's "egotistical sublime," the notion that the world is subordinate to the mind.[37] The post-apocalyptic sublime instead confronts the human mind with the reality that the human mind only faces true annihilation if it fails to understand its own finitude and simultaneously accepts the potential infinitude of the nonhuman world. This problem of infinitude spills over on to and influences political conceptions, as Anahid Nersessian shows. Nersessian, quoting Hegel, argues that the political left – exemplified by Judith Butlers' exhortation to "demand the impossible" – has confused the finite as the real in favour of utopian dreams of infinitude.[38] Countering this leftist call to impossible action, Nersessian urges a Romantic "adjustment" that revises utopia, paradoxically, as a "doing with less," transforming utopia into the possible while alleviating it of its totalitarian need for perfection (*Utopia, Limited*, 3). Nersessian's limited utopia performs a valuable reminder of how both liberal and conservative politics occlude ontology when they think in utopian terms: "what has been lost in historical evaluation of Romanticism as a utopian literature is precisely loss itself, or rather the ability to receive loss as an ontologically positive entity integral to the material makeup of the world – to any world, including the better world called utopia" (5). Despite this useful reminder, my book diverges from Nersessian's in the sense that she sees last-man texts differently than I do here. She sees these texts as part of a utopic continuum in which humans can take action, do more with less, in the in-between of utopia and extinction. "Doing" is where post-apocalyptic Romanticism departs from limited utopia in that it does not want to do more with less but rather to not do at all – what I call, echoing Derrida, "passivity without any passivity."

For all that the Romantics are aware that the earth may outlast humanity, the post-apocalyptic sublime is, as I said above, counter-intuitively productive as it foregrounds the conditional limit that allows for life's possibility. To put it another way, if we cannot accept human species extinction, then we cannot formulate solutions to massive, Malthusian, planetary-scale events like the food-and-water disruptions and shortages of 1816. The post-apocalyptic sublime grounds us in a generative attitude of hopelessness, the realization that we cannot survive, which results in the acceptance of our finitude, in the process deleting our anthropocentric notions, our sovereign demands, about the world and ourselves. But this acceptance occurs by means of a passivity without any passivity, a not-doing wherein what does do is the nonhuman other – and in which our sovereign, drunk-on-the-milk-of-Paradise beliefs become moot.

Despite the phrase's Derridean ring and Levinasian evocation, what I mean by "passivity without passivity" can be fruitfully articulated alongside the Romantic interventions of Anne-Lise François and Jacques Khalip. François presents us with a kind of passivity, a "'making little happen' as an alternative to the overly narrow definitions of action as production and articulation associated with Western modernity's ideology of improvement," to indicate how "thought and desires to which we cannot or will not give consequence or empirical result" retain an affirmative and contented content.[39] For her, it is imperative to think contra conservationist thinkers who advocate "doing nothing" or "as little as possible" to allow for a non-negative prospect of living with those acts – which we commit every day – that are uncountable as prescriptively ethical because of their "secrecy or unwitnessable nature," the acts we make in private but do not broadcast; hence her title, *Open Secrets*.[40] Khalip's notion of Romantic anonymity, meanwhile, thinks through how "non-identity promises ... a suspension from prescriptive *doing*" that is akin to François's but departs from recessive action in that, for him, actions are not exactly an open secret, because not hidden but instead "are neither empirically demonstrable nor conceived to be intentional."[41] Passivity without passivity shares a certain adherence to the similar logic underwriting François's open secret and Khalip's anonymous life; yet it departs from these concepts in that it is neither a response (as an open secret might be) nor an action (through which non-identity's will-less-ness dissociates the self from the self). For passivity without passivity is an ethics that takes its viability through a response that is non-responsive to human needs, to any account of our agency or subjectivity, a doing that does, that acts, but acts through a volitional non-acting on behalf of the other whose needs come first in this state of our lastness. Aporetically, it places human needs last, that is to say, places them post-apocalyptically since, when we choose novel paths to make common cause with creatures like us, we let those creatures and nonhuman others set the terms of the debate – the logical end-point to action on a world that is without us. As the choice has already been, genitively and ablatively speaking, made for us by us we must now stop choosing and acting in order to give that which is exterior, anterior, and posterior to us – the world, creatures – a chance.[42] Passivity without any passivity is a (non)-action that refuses to overdetermine our place on a world without us, refuses to be aggressive in hierarchizing the world on human terms and privileging our lives over the lives of the other. But the final turn of the lastness screw of passivity without passivity is that we are, ourselves, the other just as much as the other.

In this sense, rather than some natural contract with the world *pace* Michel Serres that retains anthropocentrism by refashioning humans as "legislators" (and here we must think of Shelley's famous "poets are the legislators of the world" as well) working on behalf of the Earth, for post-apocalyptic Romanticism, "legislation" cannot proceed from top-down human doing.[43] The great irony of post-apocalyptic sublimity, then, is that in depowering us of action, of sovereign trickle-down power, by forcing us to accept our own finitude, it allows us to accept what comes after human finitude: *life*. Whereas Ray Brassier argues that we are already dead, *Romantic Revelations* rebukes and denies such thinking.[44] Timothy Morton, similarly rejecting Brassier's thanatopolitics, claims that hyperobjects have ended the world, but only in the sense that there is no longer any meaningful concept of the world available to us in so far as the world means it exists for us and therefore "end-of-the-world" scenarios do not help us to live today.[45] This book departs from both philosophies. Instead, I argue throughout the book that, stuck within the cocoon of infinitude, we have, as the Romantics knew, never yet been finite, never reached chrysalis, and so *have never yet been alive*. Given this butterfly effect perhaps it is no wonder that so much modern post-apocalyptic literature focuses on the walking dead. Post-apocalyptic Romanticism stirs us to life for the first time.

While such is decidedly not the argument of Quentin Meillassoux's book *After Finitude: An Essay on the Necessity of Contingency* (2008), the touchstone of speculative realism and jumping-off point for its twisted sister, Object-Oriented Ontology, *Romantic Revelations* nevertheless dialogues with this burgeoning philosophy, finding, like other Romantic scholarship, that the connections between the two fields prove mutually illuminating concerning matters of human and nonhuman ontology.[46] However, my interests in this book are not speculative realism per se but rather the conceptual and theoretical ontological concerns that pre-exist this philosophy in Romanticism. Nonetheless, I want to rehearse the highlights of Meillassoux's argument to diagram the points of convergence and divergence between speculative realism and post-apocalyptic Romanticism. Meillassoux's book, a dense but lucid philosophical proof, provides the architectural apparatus for this multidirectional, proliferating school of speculative thought. The spectre haunting modern thought, according to Meillassoux, is what I mention above, "correlationism," which confuses and entangles ontological problems with epistemological problems, much like the question at the end of "Mont Blanc" does. Another way to put this is that correlationism entangles the subject and object, when in fact, as Meillassoux, like the Romantics who precede him, shows, the subject and object are really separate types of -ologies. Meillassoux defines correlationism as "the idea according to which we only ever have access to the correlation between thinking and being, and never to either term considered apart from the other. We will henceforth call correlationism any current of thought which maintains the unsurpassable character of the correlation so defined."[47]

For Meillassoux, correlationism explains philosophical thinking since Kant, who distinguishes between the phenomenal world that humans know by means of sensory perception and the noumenal world, a world beyond, and unknowable by, human sensory perception. According to Kant, because the thing in itself is not fully knowable, all that presents itself to human perception are instances of a transcendental world outside us. For Kant, human thought is thereby characterized by a fundamental finitude, a proposed limitation Meillassoux disagrees with, hence the title of his book *After Finitude* (and where Meillassoux and I diverge on thinking about finitude since it is thinking finitude that allows us to think about life). In contradistinction to Object-Oriented Ontologists Graham Harman and Morton, Meillassoux only finally offers that an escape from correlationism is impossible even if, as he believes, this mental confinement need not ultimately constrain the mind from accessing the noumenal, the world outside of us.[48] Yet, at book's end, Meillassoux postpones explicating how this cognitive afterness can occur.

Despite the book's cliffhanger ending, Meillassoux's account of Kantian correlationism diagnoses how humanistic thought, at its own expense and ultimately its own peril, thinks that its own scientific insights are independent proof of the fact that the world exists for us. In Meillassoux's narrative, correlationism runs aground on the knowledge afforded by modern science, that is, the empirical evidence of a world beyond the correlate of human subject/nonhuman object dualism. Specifically, modern science inaugurates a genuine caesura between thinking and being that throws into relief what Meillassoux terms "ancestrality": "any reality anterior to the emergence of the human species – or even anterior to every recognized form of life on earth."[49] Science, indeed, does make statements about life before and after human being on Earth. The problem of ancestrality highlights how, for epistemology and phenomenology, there can be no objects, laws, events, or world that can be thought without these things being correlated to a subject who thinks. But if such epistemological claims are true, then it makes no sense to talk about neutrinos, dinosaurs, and starlight because we only have evidence of them after the fact and hence they are not correlated – they exist independently of the mind. And yet we do speak with certainty about them. In other words, epistemology and phenomenology both want to make truth statements about whether or not humans accurately perceive the world as it is, whereas science wants to make it possible to make statements about the world as it is, independent of us. But because science makes ancestral statements that cannot be verified by us – or else they would be correlated – ancestrality reveals an aporia that exists in both philosophy and science: our inability to account for a world outside of us without, paradoxically, accounting for it. This is what Meillassoux calls the "correlationist circle," and the only way to counter it, according to Meillassoux, is to admit the possibility of what he describes as "contingency," the idea that foundational reasons for reality are never given or verifiable. Meillassoux argues that, since the laws derived by science cannot be demonstrated to be necessary, they remain only facts, examples of what Meillassoux calls "the Principle of Factiality": "the absolute absence of reason for any reality … the effective ability for every determined entity, whether it is an event, a thing or a law, for it to appear or disappear with no reason for its being or non-being."[50] Scientific laws, because they are contingent and can change, are therefore factial rather than necessary; indeed, the laws of physics discovered by Newton have been revised by Einstein's theory of relativity, itself now challenged by quantum mechanics. In Meillassoux's formulation, factiality, or contingency, by identifying the gaps and paradoxes of the correlationist circle, can perhaps allow us to see beyond the circle, beyond the Kantian mind-world problem, and begin to figure out how to see the ontological world as it is.

Speculative realism therefore seeks to prioritize ontology over epistemology. What Meillassoux calls "the arche-fossil" – "material indicative of an ancestral reality anterior to terrestrial life," such as "an isotope whose rate of radioactive decay we know, or the luminous emission of a star that informs us as to the date of its formation" – is an example of this prioritization.[51] By engaging in prehuman discourses, scientific statements about isotopic decay and star luminescence make claims about (and within) a posthuman discourse about being divorced from thinking, ontology divorced from epistemology. The arche-fossil disturbs human conceptions of temporal finitude because it takes account of the genuine "temporal discrepancy between thinking and being." It registers deep, cosmic time and therefore raises futural and telluric implications "about possible events that are ulterior to the extinction of the human species."[52] Meillassoux calls this temporal disruption of the human-world-correlation "dia-chronicity."[53] Since it unhitches the two halves of the correlation (human thought and the world) from each other, it is a diachronic, real-world temporality "indifferent to our existence" and hence concerned with the ontology, rather than the epistemology, of a literal posthuman future state.[54]

In my terms, then, Meillassoux's book becomes not just about the titular *After Finitude* – the mind's ability to think beyond the limits of Kantian finitude – but also about real after-finitude, a post-apocalyptic state that takes place ulterior to human finitude. But, as is readily evident, a certain bleakness develops from this diachrony as it pitches humans headlong into a heedless future, leaving them waywardly floating in a temporal sea, disinterested in their continued existence.

My book intervenes precisely here in this thinking, following the Romantics who think life after finitude, life as taking place only after we accept our finitude, to render a genuine posthuman politics for life in this after-, rather than last-, ness. We might think of this project in terms of Eugene Thacker's summation of speculative realism: "to think a concept of life that is itself, in some basic way, unhuman, a life *without us*."[55] Only, unlike Thacker, who thinks that "life and the living have little to do with the human," the Romantics, as I trace their thinking, find that life's variations and variegations are inclusive of the human and the nonhuman, even though, as I said above, humans are not yet alive; so, life is inclusive, too, of accepting extinction (and not extinctualism), the dead or the not yet living, what it means to live otherwise.[56]

As I develop it in the chapters of this book, what I term the post-apocalyptic sublime fosters a new version of Romantic irony that offers an alternative to correlationism when dialogued with Derrida's notion of *l'avenir*, the impossible future that can always unexpectedly arrive and that, because of its contingency, structures the present. Romanticism has already anticipated, and thought beyond, the discourses of deconstruction and speculative realism – but only when both are thought together, a move anathema to many speculative realists.[57] Via this Derridean speculative realist lens that I have developed here, then, the impossible future that might arrive is what Derrida calls a "living on" without "us," a life without humans positioned as subjects ineradicably tethered to the world.[58] These paradoxes of Romantic irony open on to Derrida's "democracy-to-come," a hoped-for, still-to-be-defined democracy that will unexpectedly emerge as, and precisely because it is, impossible.[59] Derrida's democracy-to-come is radically paradoxical: it is impossible in that it will never arrive, because the future will never arrive because the future is always already here, advancing into each moment that passes away. To borrow from *The Last Man*, "already the to-morrow is come."[60] This arche-materiality of the structure of time's succession is what Derrida means by "living on"; since the future's intractable entrance into the present actually creates the present, we are perpetually living on in the present. In my reading of the era, Romanticism thus becomes a staging ground for competing theories of telluric temporality and human finitude. But Derrida's democracy-to-come, for all its explanatory power, remains anthropocentric, as my reading of Shelley's *The Last Man* demonstrates in chapter 2. In Romantic apocalyptic literature, time paralyses us, perpetually resituating us within the confines of subject-object correlationism. The post-apocalyptic time that is present in the works of the Shelleys adheres to a hard-nosed realism that recognizes the present as a period of potentially true end-of-the-worldness for us in which subject and object are radically, ontologically differentiated. Thus, Romantic post-apocalyptic time, by restraining us to the present, sets us free from false narratives of the future that create false hope and inhibit action; everything will perhaps not work itself out. To quote from another species-extinction fable, *The X-files*, we must "fight the future" – but it is a fighting by means of a version of a passivity without passivity, a not-doing, as I discuss in Byron's *Cain* in chapter 3, in which humans learn to "sacrifice" sacrifice, to stop the senseless mass putting to death and carnal consumption of animals. Realizing how to fight is the final piece of the puzzle regarding our passivity without passivity. Coming to grips with the ironic working of its ironic temporality, I want to argue, post-apocalyptic Romanticism and its sublime tropology allows us to think living on because, even though post-apocalyptic Romanticism's setting is the Last Days, it is actually about the days of our lives now rather than later.

Romantic Revelations derives from the post-apocalyptic sublime's ironic thinking a politically temporal insight: although post-apocalyptic Romanticism appears socially, politically, and climactically allegorical – as if it is sketching possible futures – it is actually a realist narrative of our current socio-political reality in the long durée of the Anthropocene.[61] Post-apocalyptic Romanticism, though ostensibly about the end of humanity, replays, in grim terms, classic Enlightenment debates about egalitarian principles that undergird constitutional democracies meant to preserve and extend life – Foucauldian biopolitics, in other words.[62] Such debates pivot on what thinkers like Thomas Hobbes and Jean-Jacques Rousseau term "the state of nature," a pre-modern time period that witnessed the formation of human societies and governmental institutions; in this way the state of nature prefigures Romantic and post-apocalyptical modernity.[63] Life in such a time, as Hobbes wrote, was "poor, solitary, nasty, brutish, and short," or, as he put it elsewhere, a "*bellum omnium contra omnes*" (a war of all against all).[64]

For Hobbes the solution was, of course, a strong monarchical head of state who could restrain humans from their natural disposition to wantonly slaughter each other into extinction. Rousseau, in contrast, developed an in-theory more egalitarian social-contract society to ward off this multidirectional, all-consuming war. In other words, debates over proper governance in the state of nature staged a battle between libertarian anarchism and social-contract democratization (correspondingly, conservative and progressive politics), the very reality depicted in post-apocalyptic literature in which humans struggle to survive by either banding together or getting their war on.[65] "In popular terms," as Jared McGeough writes, "anarchy readily calls to mind a Hobbesian nightmare in which an absence of authority collapses the social order into a war of all against all," but he also reminds us that there are many forms of anarchism.[66] To be clear then, "libertarian anarchism" as I use the term equates to this state-of-nature situation and not to, say, a Godwinian political anarchy that fears government encroachment on the individual. Despite this anti-governmental strain in Godwin's work that would seem to comport him with this Hobbesian nightmare version of anarchy, Godwin ultimately falls on the progressive side of this debate since he champions the individual as duty-bound to serve justice vis-à-vis other people, and decries the selfishness of the individual in the war of all against all that continues to define conservative thinking.[67]

As Byron and the Shelleys demonstrate, these competing Enlightenment visions of humanity's end continue to hold political sway in post-apocalyptic futures because they return us, unexpectedly, to the past, to the state of nature, a premodern social imaginary wherein societal and governmental institutions did not exist, just as they have fallen to dust in these post-apocalyptic futures that are our present. The post-apocalyptic sublime proves doubly ironic, then, since the "post" only recalls us to the past, which is already present since it is already recessed in the pastness of its own assumption of progressive forward movement: the future. In this we can hear something similar to Jerome Christensen's claim that Romanticism is a type of non-conservative anachronism, aware that "history is what happened, not what had or has to happen."[68] Developing this temporally scrambled, post-apocalyptic state of nature, *Romantic Revelations* explicates how Romantic authors forge a revolutionary posthuman politics that writes a third type of social contract (in contrast to Hobbes's and Rousseau's political visions of life), one that does not, as I said at the outset, exclude nonhuman life (as do these other, still-competing social contracts that dominate contemporary politics). It is, rather, the nonhuman that actualizes this politics.

Throughout *Romantic Revelations* I show how post-apocalyptic Romanticism drafts this new posthuman contract that is not only socially but also ontologically, temporally, and politically radical. As Foucault influentially argues, the eighteenth century witnesses a governmental shift in power relations, wherein biopolitics is the dominant mode of human ontology – humans begin to conceive of themselves as a specific, distinct species. Biopolitics instrumentalizes and routinizes the wholesale industrial slaughter of animals for food, and the world as fuel, as a means of feeding and maintaining humans as a species. Post-apocalyptic Romanticism resists this form of biopolitical power that converts animals into biocapital whose very beings are subordinate to human life's continuance. Instead, John Clare, whose poetry I examine in chapter 4, finds value in animal and other nonhuman life because these creatures exist on their own terms that do not have to be human terms – just as Shelley finds dissymmetrical and uncommon worth in the differences between humans and *Frankenstein*'s creature. For these Romantic writers, biopolitics runs hand in hand with anthropocentrism – the idea, to repeat, that humans are sovereigns over the world and masters of the universe, the same belief that drives global capitalism. However, rather than collapse the differences between human and nonhuman, post-apocalyptic Romanticism proliferates difference in its rewriting of the social contract. In this way, post-apocalyptic Romanticism also differentiates itself from apocalyptic Romanticism because, as Steven Goldsmith notes, apocalypse is a literary tradition that erases difference and generates what Luce Irigaray refers to as the heterogeneity of "the Same."[69] Post-apocalyptic Romanticism's social contract is underwritten by Derridean "hospitality," an ethical commitment to respect the other, not on the basis of its social similarity to the human but, rather, for the difference and strangeness arising from the other's ontological distinctness.[70]

While Peter Melville has alerted us to the importance of hospitality for Romanticism, I take up hospitality differently than he does by thinking through the question that Derrida claims Levinas – from whose work Derrida develops his notion of hospitality – cannot.[71] When pressed on whether an animal or nonhuman has a face and can thus be open to hospitality and to ethics, Levinas claims that he does not know – an uncertainty Derrida ultimately shares.[72] In my final chapter I explore how, for Mary Shelley and Jane Austen, species distinctions are often used to brand humans as nonhumans, as "monsters," thus creating human categories that also get expelled from social-contract incorporation. To counter this problem, Shelley and Austen push hospitality further still than Derrida does, into a radical rethinking of love that, by ignoring species boundaries, acknowledges – but, more pointedly, accedes to – the right to life of other ontologies beyond the human. Whereas in the post-apocalyptic world of Byron's "Darkness" "no love was left," Shelley and Austen reimagine a form of love that is the binding agent of such worlds (line 41). Merging the social and ontological into a posthuman political contract, post-apocalyptic Romanticism deconstructs the idea of human sovereignty that underwrites politics and replaces it with an ethically supple egalitarianism for "living on" in the Anthropocene.

By thinking through the paradoxes of extinction as both life's limit and its perpetuation, the Romantics envision a politics whose hospitality and responsibility maintain all life without eradicating the living difference between life forms. Unlike some current speculative realists, biopolitical theorists, and posthumanists, the Romantics do not clamour for a flattened ontology or even for what we call democratic equality but, rather, for a notion of being-with (*mitsein*) whose social contracts guarantee equality precisely on the basis of a hospitality that reaches out to the other across lines of difference and inequality. As I read it, post-apocalytpic Romanticism theorizes a social contract that radicalizes and revises the term so that it hinges on difference and non-mutuality. In this sense "social contract" is essentially Romantic in that it captures its own ironic radicality in so far as there is nothing social (in the human sense) nor contractual about this new community of those who have nothing in common. It would be easy to claim another paradoxical deconstructive manoeuvre here. Perhaps, ultimately, that is what this new contract amounts to because its warrant in these Romantic writers is that we have a tendency to look for social incorporation, to acceptance and assimilation, like the Borg in *Star Trek*, when, as post-apocalyptic Romanticism argues, we should think in terms of rejection. For maintaining and respecting difference requires its increase, its multiplication rather than creating a monopolistic homology. The acceptance of difference demands accepting rejection for the possibility of difference to be accepted. Working out this paradox at the heart of hospitality, the heart of this Romantic social contract between the human and nonhuman, is the problem undertaken and answered by Shelley and Austen in their theorization of love in the Anthropocene in my fifth chapter.

What this book finally wants to argue, then, is that the Romantic period, which continues to haunt us because we remain stubbornly stuck in subject-object dualism, offers two competing dynasties, the legacies of which will govern human survival. On the one hand, there is the Romanticism defined by a subject-object apocalyptic conjunction closely related to the symbolic, associational representations that designate "nature," for example, as a stand-in for empirical factitiousness. On the other hand, we can identify an ironic, post-apocalyptic Romantic mode that, because it operates synchronically, deposits us firmly in the present. It refuses to operate as a dream switch fantasizing about a vaguely sketched, always redeemable future, even as it provides for us a crucially important distance from ourselves as anthropocentric masters of the universe. The former, apocalyptic version of Romanticism deals in idealism and parable, a teleological utopian paradise; the latter, post-apocalyptic Romanticism beholds contemporaneous disaster ironically, without looking away, and makes legible the consequences of a world without us by forcing us to peer deep, deep into its peerlessly ironic eyes. Nor is this estimation simply a replication of a commonplace chestnut about dystopian science fiction, namely, that the scientized fiction and the fictionalized science of science fiction teach us about the present by imagining the possibilities of an abominable future. Rather, it is that post-apocalyptic Romanticism denies that any strictly human, anthropocentric future whatsoever is on the horizon. Whatever future, that is, present, will be, will be posthuman. For if the architecture of a post-apocalyptic world will be, as climate-change predictions suggest, an endless hell of unimaginable nightmares of the sort Byron foresaw in "Darkness," when all of the fallen trees are burnt in a "selfish prayer for light," then perhaps it is time, as we stand on this terrifying threshold, for a post-apocalyptic Romanticism that divests us of such selfish sovereignty and helps us to accept the nebulous darkness (line 10). For only in the hopeless darkness of the present day is there hope, perhaps even light. Now is the time, considering the time we may have left, we've been waiting for.

1 The Mind Is Its Own Place: What Percy Shelley's Mountain Did Not Say

What are men to rocks and mountains?

Elizabeth Bennet

In the final doomed month of his life, Percy Shelley's thoughts remained vexed on the subject of Elysium, regarding it as an astral ameliorative towards which the metaphoric ships of his sad, unrealized passion for Jane Williams might sail in "Lines Written in the Bay of Lerici" (1822). Overlapping this lyric's sweetly depressing encomium, he ruminates on an abyssal descent into abstraction, dissolution, and nothingness in *The Triumph of Life* (1822), a poem whose trajectory deviates from the hopeful mental and material millenarianism so powerfully realized and celebrated by the earlier *Prometheus Unbound* (1820).[1] In what follows I read this face-off in Shelley's work – between a transcendent, peaceful apocalypse and a desolate, disturbing post-apocalypse – as Shelley's intervention into his, and therefore our (because it is the Anthropocene), contemporary end-of-the-world predictions and prophecies about humans' ability to survive into the future. Deeply invested as it is in phenomenal problems of the subjective imagination and its connection to the objective, material world, Shelley's writing theorizes what I have been calling the post-apocalyptic sublime. As I have developed it in my introduction in relation to speculative realism's critique of the Kantian sublime, post-apocalyptic sublimity enacts a temporal divorce of the paradigmatic, Romantic, hoped-for marriage of the human mind and the natural world, while nonetheless realizing that a wholesale divorce of subject from object is neither possible nor desirable. If speculative-realist accounts declare that the ontological world is indeed without us, residing independent of humanity, this does not necessarily mean that we are not with the world but rather that subject and object are not, as has commonly been thought since Kant, irreducibly connected.

So far in this book I have pressed into service Quentin Meillassoux's speculative-realist account of post-Kantian modernity – the dehiscence between "thinking and being" in the form of the "arche-fossil" that evidences visions of life anterior and ulterior to humankind – with Derrida to help explain how certain tendencies of late Romanticism reframe our contemporary condition as post-apocalyptic rather than immanently paradisiacal, which has been the abiding narrative of redemptive Romanticism.[2] These traditional understandings of the Romantic sublime and the apocalyptic remain within the Kantian territory Meillassoux and other speculative realists critique. Romantic apocalypse adheres to a Kantian framework that argues that the world's existence – and this begins with Berkeley, as Meillassoux notes – depends on human phenomenological perceptions to structure the conditions of the world. Meillassoux calls this interdependence between mind and world the correlationist circle: there appears to be no way to talk about a world independent of a human thinking subject, and hence humans remain trapped within their own mental "finitude," the limitations of the human mind that foster an anthropocentrism that, I have been arguing, proves inimical to human life itself. This anthropocentrism, which underwrites Romantic apocalyptic narratives, surprisingly and counter-intuitively amounts to a disguised and revisionary form of climate denialism because it creates anti-realist narratives that link the human mind to the world's survival contrary to all current climate-change science that informs us that the human might end despite our wishes otherwise. Put simply, such discussions about the future are a brand of what I call in the introduction "extinctualism" in that they both valorize and contribute to the hastening end of human life since they are a curious kind of deferral of our present predicament.

Indeed, humans can end, and the world can end, but the end of the former does not necessarily entail the end of the latter. The Chorus of Spirits in act 4 of *Prometheus Unbound* gives voice to this classic correlationist problem of paradise and Romantic anthropocentrism:

> We come from the mind
> Of human kind
> Which was late so dusk, and obscene, and blind,
> Now 'tis an ocean
> Of clear emotion,
> A heaven of serene and mighty motion. (IV, 93–7)[3]

The chant ends apocalyptically: "And, beyond our eyes, / The human love lies / Which makes all it gazes on Paradise" (act 4, lines 126–7). As harbingers "from the mind / of human kind," the Chorus's prophecy represents a form of correlationism, since the mind, configured as explicitly "human," recreates the world as "Paradise." But like all good prophecies, such a proleptic, yet immanent, vision – one that would embower us like grateful supplicants in this new paradise – sketches a fictionalized future not necessarily moored in, and perhaps even adrift from, the contemporary time in which the prophecy is foretold.[4]

As deeply invested as it is in climatological events, Shelley's work highlights this problematic facet of Romantic apocalyptic prophecy: that it is another version of a sublime transcendentalism that allows us to indulge in projected futural fictions and speciesist biopolitical fables about our surviving on, perhaps forever.[5] But if we follow Shelley's thinking on poetry, prophecy, and temporality (poets were originally prophets, he says) in "A Defence of Poetry" (1821), then the future is always already here since it grants structure to the present moment. As witnessed by his famous pronouncement in the "Defence," Shelley's temporal *poiesis* anticipates both Paul de Man and Derrida: "Poets are the hierophants of an unapprehended inspiration, the mirrors of the gigantic shadows which futurity casts upon the present."[6] What Shelley develops in the "Defence," in "Mont Blanc" (1816), and ultimately in *Prometheus Unbound* is a version of what de Man called "Romantic irony," a temporal severance of subject and object that deposits us firmly in the present. However, Shelley's temporal ontology is also a form of what Derrida calls "the future-to-come" (the archi-trace structure of temporality): each moment that passes away does so in the present and thus is past even as it gives way, at and in that same moment, to the future. Constantly arriving, the future can never arrive even as it structures and affirms the present by means of its deferral. The consequences of Romantic irony's temporal structure for Shelley are such that, in a poem like "Mont Blanc," which manifests this subject-object catastrophe against the backdrop of 1816's climate-changing "year without a summer," irony deconstructs Romantic apocalyptic prophecies that allow us to place our hopes in a future paradise we will one day miraculously reach. Seen in the light of the future's shadows, irony thus divorces the present from the future even as, again, the future structures the present's sun. Shelley's comments on the fiction of a futural afterlife in an early essay on speculative philosophy, "On a Future State" (c. 1811–13), bear this out: "This desire to be for ever as we are; the reluctance to a violent and unexperienced change, which is common to all the animated and inanimate combinations of the universe, is, indeed, the secret persuasion which has given birth to the opinions of a future state."[7] But like Derrida, Shelley believes that the future is a time that can never arrive, because it is always deferred, a shadow rather than substance (to repurpose the opening of "Defence"), an indication that the sun shines another day, casting yet more shadows, and that this is not the Last Day but merely today – and so it is also the Last Day. To engage in prophesying about the future – to be, as we saw in the introduction, without a sense of living on, without a sense of the here and now – makes one, de facto and de jure, a false prophet, a hierophant of the shadows of a fake futurity. Shelley's poets are quite different: they are temporal ironists, refusing futural projections, and living, and living on, firmly in the present, learning how not to die but to live on in the Anthropocene.[8]

Shelley's poetic visions – which so often present themselves as lights shining through the darkness visible of penumbral caves and hidden temples, celestial spheres and the unknown, river-riven pathways of love – reflect the counter-clockwise paradox of modern temporality in which the future is already gone even while it remains what we talk about when we talk about climate change. His work offers a curious corrective by forcing us to look at the real world around us and thus to look past any human survival, miraculous or otherwise, in the future – and hence to look past anthropocentrism and towards what Meillassoux calls "the great outdoors," or, as I have been terming it in my revision of Meillassoux, a world without us.[9] My own embarkation point in this chapter into Shelley's work is "Mont Blanc," where, amidst the snow-covered landscapes, the aesthetico-political apogees of *Prometheus Unbound* meet the exploratory rambles in speculative philosophy of his early essays and the later "Defence." This confluence, which merges high-minded hope and terrified scepticism, forsaken speculation and frightened enlightenment, clarifies the temporal and climatic stakes that thrum through the bloodlines of his poetry.

But to follow this syncopated rhythm in Shelley, we first have to work through Shelley's Kantian tendencies as manifest in his early speculative-philosophy essays and in *Prometheus Unbound* and its apparent affirmation of apocalyptic temporality, a time of the subjective imagination harnessing the world's ontology to the mind's will. Methodologically, of course, this process carries certain dangers, admirably articulated by Cian Duffy: "commentators routinely read and assess pre-Kantian texts in broadly Kantian terms."[10] This retroactive reassessment, Duffy claims, has contributed to the Kantian inflections of "the Romantic sublime," a theoretical sublimity that resolves itself into an idealist transcendentalism that ignores the historical and cultural contexts in which Romantic texts were written.[11] Yet, while Duffy's point about the tunnel vision of Kantian-inflected retrospective reading is well taken, his claim that "Mont Blanc" is not transitional at all – that is, endemic of "Shelley's movement from empiricism to idealism" – seems to me correct even as it ignores the very real Kantian-like crossroads that the poem stands colossally astride. We might say, to borrow from Robert Frost's familiar, darkly deep, choose-your-own-adventure poem, that two roads did indeed diverge on the snowy summit of "Mont Blanc," one Kantian and one post-Kantian, and Shelley continued along the speculative path of his earlier essays, the one less travelled.

More than repurposing the energies of the Romantic sublime into a progressive, revolutionary politics, "Mont Blanc" examines Kant's assertion that we do not have access to the thing in itself, and rejects it as crucially missing the point. It thus speaks directly to whether the human mind is fundamentally limited or, as Meillassoux puts it, defined by its "finitude." On Meillassoux's reading, Kant thinks we cannot know the thing in itself but only instances of a transcendental world outside us. Kant therefore thinks human thought in terms of finitude, an idea that "Mont Blanc" recontextualizes in terms of the climate-change fears that emerge in the background of the poem's composition during the Anthropocene. "Mont Blanc" shows how the imagination's finitude reveals the limits of human finitude, and suggests instead that human annihilation is at the heart of Shelley's metaphysical and poetical imagination of the imagination. In doing so, "Mont Blanc" revises traditional conceptions of the Romantic imagination along a post-apocalyptic trajectory that theorizes human life as expendable, but whose expendability clears away the life-occluding Kantian philosophical groundwork underwriting modernity. Shelley, on my reading, accepts that an ontological real world outside of us exists, a world that we may only ever glimpse or never glimpse at all. Indeed, as "Mont Blanc" demonstrates, our failure to access epistemologically or to verify the world's existence provides evidence of a world without us. By venturing down the post-Kantian road less travelled, Shelley wilfully barrels into a blizzard of delusional human optimism and potential human extinction.

Hypotheses like mine are iconoclastic within Shelley criticism.[12] And no doubt Shelley's intentionally provocative idealism, radical atheism, and negative theology – the triple-threat vehicles for his vision of a forthcoming, peaceful, millenarian utopia-to-come – would seem to be scandalized by the thesis that I have advanced. Unlike Mary Shelley in *The Last Man* (1826) and Byron in *Cain* (1821), Shelley does not appear to endorse or encourage the possibility of a posthuman world (outside of, perhaps, whatever exactly happens at the end of *The Revolt of Islam*).[13]

If one typical way we understand Romanticism is as a *time* underlying and allowing for possible utopian futures, then Shelley, as I read him, becomes something of a curator of the post-apocalyptic present, of the ontological politics of today. He becomes, differently, a deflationary prophet urging us to tend to our own time instead of messing about in the hypotheticals of future existence even if, living as we do now in a world without us, we must remain in contact with that world precisely through our speculative non-knowledge of it. Despite the ostensible, even obvious, impetus driving towards a posthuman world in Mary Shelley's and Byron's later climate-change texts (the subject of my next chapters), it is Shelley's script-flipping in "Mont Blanc" that accretes this speculative thinking. It does the initial theoretical heavy lifting, ultimately paid off in *Prometheus Unbound* and "A Defence of Poetry," by trumpeting a post-apocalyptic Romanticism whose triumph is the belatedly necessary severance, and therefore paradoxical entanglement, of mind from world, subject from object.[14] On my reading, then, Shelley's post-apocalyptic Romanticism embraces, in order not to becloud, the complicated dying-off spiral its own time period torques into industrial, capitalistic, climate-changing motion.

If the climate-change storm cloud of the nineteenth century imperils, and it does, then it does so hand in hand with what Steven Goldsmith calls a Romantic aestheticization of an apocalyptic ideology that, as I argue, retains for humanity a subject position as cosmic overlord.[15] This investment in our overlord status takes centre stage in Shelley's understudied, somewhat scatter-brained, early essays on speculative Kantian problems. Written in the dying throes of his infatuation with George Berkeley (whom, it is important to remember, Meillassoux identifies as the originator of correlationist thought), Shelley claims in "Speculations on Metaphysics and Morals" (c. 1811–13) that "a catalogue of all the thoughts of the mind and of all their possible modifications is a cyclopaedic history of the Universe."[16] The assertion's bold non-ambiguity affects a Kantian posture; the mind's thoughts (if one can put it that way) not only can but do index external reality, which means that no clear-cut division predominates between mind and world. But inextricably tying the mind to the universe, or more accurately configuring the mind *as* the universe, as Shelley does here, raises a host of perplexing problems about the future of humanity. If the mind is indeed unlimitedly capacious enough in its encyclopaedic scope that it encompasses the universe, as Shelley claims, then it follows from this premise that the external world of the universe will persist only so long as humanity endures. Shelley's later repudiation of Berkeley notwithstanding, the ideology emerging from the Berkeleyan thesis Shelley does retain – that nothing exists but what we can perceive – spells out the stakes that persist throughout Shelley's mature work.[17] Not only are mental and mortal life placed under the headman's axe, but both the world and life itself, as in Byron's "Darkness," are pressed down on the block alongside condemned humanity.

And yet Shelley's mature literary work itself seems invested in living over dying, in fecundity over decomposition, wellsprings rather than droughts. Both *Prometheus Unbound* and *Epipsychidion* (1821) feature denouements cast in the mode of Elysian, even Edenic, paradise (in contrast to shorter poems like "Ozymandias"). But even if these poems do ultimately valorize their own superficial paradisiacal visions – and I argue that they finally do not – they do undoubtedly feature the same "involving and involved" mind-world (to borrow a wonderful Shelleyan phrase from *Prometheus Unbound* [IV, 241]) as do the early philosophical essays. In the preface to *Prometheus Unbound* Shelley explicitly confirms his ambiguously dualistic purpose: "the imagery which I have employed will be found, in many instances, to have been drawn from the operations of the human mind, or from those external actions by which they are expressed."[18] Alan Richardson's helpful characterization of Shelley's lyrical drama as "mental theater" is indicative, like Shelley's own prefatory discussion, of his continued belief, hearkening back to "Speculations on Metaphysics and Morals," in the human mind's epistemological capability not just to capture the world but to see, and consider, itself as the world.[19] "The "external actions" of the world are physical representations of internal thoughts, hence Richardson's apt term "mental theater." In the mental theatre of *Prometheus Unbound*, the real world appears to be enveloped in an anthropocentric construct called the imagination, voiding the objective world as immaterial, one more aspect of the mind, as if what exists exists because the human mind grants, or can even deny, the world ontological being.

If we take Shelley's claim in the preface literally, then the magnificent and magniloquent vision of act 4 of *Prometheus Unbound* applies to the external, material world only in so far as that world is what we might call an "imaginative apocalypse" that returns us to the temporal belief in an apocalyptic paradise-to-come, a humanist belief in anthropocentrism.[20] Hugh Roberts's examination of Shelley as responding to and developing Lucretius's atomism in *De rerum natura*, and of Shelley as something of a chaos theorist burdened by intimations of entropy as a result, aids in unravelling Shelley's claims about mind/world irreducibility.[21] Although he does not use this language, Roberts reads this passage on wrecks and ruins in act 4 of *Prometheus Unbound* as atomistically posthumanistic in its outlook: "the 'mortal, but not human' past revealed by the Spirit's probing beams takes us out of this static, mythic chronotope and throws us into a torrent of entropic chance, with the clear implication that we shall be, for some future age, as inexplicable a remnant of the past as these wrecks and fossils are to us."[22] When entropy occurs, theoretical physics informs us, life lurches backward along the terminal velocity of a past that unspools like threads being steadily pricked out as time, literally, flies by and is undone. On Roberts's reading, this means that future reassessments of the disappeared human species will autopsy said species as mere material, bone and ash, a transitory life form naturally evanesced while the world spins ever onward, indifferent (much like Byron's *Cain*, as we will see in chapter 3).

In *Prometheus Unbound*, the second of Panthea's and Ione's shared mystical visions seems to bear out this entropic posthumanism. "The deep music of the rolling world" sounds to Panthea and Ione, but this sonic symphony proves synesthesiastic as "two visions of strange radiance" appear (IV, 186, 202). In the first, Panthea sees a familiar Shelleyan chariot speeding the glowing white Infant with eyes "of liquid darkness" across the landscape of the ruined world, waking "sounds as sweet as a singing rain of silver dew" (IV, 235). In the second, Ione describes the densely multitudinous Orb that appears, with "ten thousand orbs involving and involved" inside it, carrying the sleeping Spirit of the Earth (IV, 241). Out of this shoot "vast beams like spokes of some invisible wheel" that "make bare the secrets of the Earth's deep heart" (IV, 274, 279). While with the release of Prometheus and the fall of the tyrant Jupiter the Earth itself is freed from its former enslavement, the "secrets of the Earth's deep heart" that these two ecstatic visions excavate appear to be the charnal grounds of entombed remains that are not human. Humans will, as in Roberts's reading, become part of this ground-up bone-yard, a remnant of a past that the world has passed by.

Yet the ecstatic jubilation experienced by the Earth after Jupiter's fall and Prometheus's and humans' sovereign ascension, juxtaposed against these images of Earth's desolation and decay, seems to adhere to an apocalypticism that rejects such a life-defyingly bleak version of posthumanism:

Panthea:
And from a star upon its forehead, shoot,
Like swords of azure fire, or golden spears
With tyrant-quelling myrtle overtwined,
Embleming Heaven and Earth united now,

Vast beams like spokes of some invisible wheel
Which whirl as the Orb whirls, swifter than thought,
Filling the abyss with sun-like lightenings,
And perpendicular now, and now transverse,
Pierce the dark soil, and as they pierce and pass,
Make bare the secrets of the Earth's deep heart;
Infinite mines of adamant and gold,
Valueless stones, and unimagined gems,
And caverns on crystalline columns poised
With vegetable silver overspread;
Wells of unfathomed fire, and water springs
Whence the great Sea, even as a child is fed,
Whose vapours clothe Earth's monarch mountain-tops
With kingly, ermine snow. The beams flash on
And make appear the melancholy ruins
Of cancelled cycles; anchors, beaks of ships;
Planks turned to marble; quivers, helms, and spears,
And gorgon-headed targes, and the wheels
Of scythèd chariots, and the emblazonry
Of trophies, standards, and armorial beasts,
Round which Death laughed, sepulchred emblems
Of dead Destruction, ruin within ruin!
The wrecks beside of many a city vast,
Whose population which the Earth grew over
Was mortal, but not human; see, they lie,
Their monstrous works, and uncouth skeletons,
Their statues, homes and fanes; prodigious shapes
Huddled in gray annihilation, split,
Jammed in the hard, black deep; and over these,
The anatomies of unknown wingèd things,
And fishes which were isles of living scale,
And serpents, bony chains, twisted around
The iron crags, or within heaps of dust
To which the tortuous strength of their last pangs
Had crushed the iron crags; and over these
The jaggèd alligator, and the might
Of earth-convulsing behemoth, which once
Were monarch beasts, and on the slimy shores,
And weed-overgrown continents of Earth,
Increased and multiplied like summer worms
On an abandoned corpse, till the blue globe
Wrapt Deluge round it like a cloak, and they

Yelled, gasped, and were abolished; or some God
Whose throne was in a Comet, passed, and cried,
"Be not!" – and like my words they were no more. (IV, 270–318)

According to this vision, the former inhabitants of Earth, who were "mortal but not human," have been abolished either by the Earth itself ("a blue globe") or by some unknown god (IV, 297). Although the passage frames these inhabitants' mortal dissipation in post-diluvian terms, which recalls the biblical deluge, it nevertheless also imagines beyond that account to the possibility of extinction wherein the Earth's sovereigns are replaced by the apparently natural phenomenon known as "mother earth." In his 1813 work *An Essay on the Theory of the Earth*, Georges Cuvier had already postulated that floods led to the formation of new creatures even as old species went extinct.[23] In other words, the passage hovers clearly over a post-apocalyptic abyss that figures paradise as nonhuman in orientation. And yet, in Earth's almost drunken speech post-vision – "The joy, the triumph, the delight, the madness!" (IV, 319) – following this frightening narration of "ruin within ruin," love, theorized as appended specifically to humans, becomes the linchpin that holds the universe together. In fact, "Hate, and Fear, and Pain [...] Leave Man, who was a many-sided mirror / Which could distort to many a shape of error / This true fair world of things – a Sea reflecting Love," which elevates humanity as the apotheosis of life (IV, 381–4). Synecdochically, "Man," here an unfortunately gendered stand-in for the whole species, loses its distortionary power when "Hate, Fear, and Pain" depart and grant to humans a world that is a mirror-like sea of irreducible love – a boon presaged by Asia's light. The post-apocalyptic potentiality of the world-historical cataclysm becomes itself transformed, then, parallel to the human species' conversion: the catastrophic events usher in revelation (*apocalypsis*) of a world whose regal human sovereigns are freed from a negative thanatopolitical reality and who reign in peaceful harmony.[24]

In positioning humanity as inheritors of paradise, the dramatic action of the play performs a type of recuperative humanism antagonistic to post-apocalyptic schemas; anthropocentrism remains, therefore, to put it somewhat tautologically, the centre of the world. If we take seriously Shelley's claim that his lyrical drama depicts the actions of the mind, then the perfectibility of the world envisioned by Promethean and human ascension is a natural telos of the mind and the world, and, also, of the Fall, as the Satanic school, ironically, puts humanity on a road that, long and hard out of hell, leads up to light. The mind-world connection proves deep, necessary, and irreducible. Indeed, Demogorgon, the nebulous primordial energy that has proven so non-amiable to interpretation, reappears in the concluding stanzas precisely to detail how humanity has been freed from its "dark slavery," to borrow a phrase from "Hymn to Intellectual Beauty" ("Man, who wert once a despot and a slave, – / A dupe and a deceiver, – ; a Decay"), just as an encyclopaedic list of other entities has also been freed: the Earth, the Moon, "the Kings of suns and stars / Daemons and Gods / Aetherial Dominations," the dead, genii, and the spirits (IV, ii, 549–50). As Stuart Curran claims, "the Promethean entourage presides over the second awakening of the human imagination."[25] However, in what proves a crucial decentering of the human imagination, Demogorgon presents love, and not the human imagination, as the revolutionary force that can revision, reshape, and heal the world: "Love, from its awful throne of patient power / In the wise heart, from the last giddy hour / Of dread endurance, from the slippery, steep, / And narrow verge of crag-like agony, springs / And folds over the world its healing wings" (IV, ii, 557–61). By casting down Jupiter, the mind has freed itself from the shackles of hate, fear, destruction, and woe. But what Prometheus represents, finally, is the will of the human mind's imaginings to fulfil its own self-prophecy even as the poem, in contrast, privileges this other, affective, non-imaginative, non-mental force called "love" as necessary to the world's survival. We can see, then, a deep Kantian conflict emerging in the poem between, on the one hand, a human-mind correlation and, on the other, a free-floating affect that belongs to the world and not humanity.

Shelley's stated philosophical and literary tastes in his preface to *Prometheus Unbound* pay off this conflictual reading of the play, in which the Miltonic power of mind overmasters material reality and even eschatological theology – a conflictual reading that only finds its resolution through the speculative-realist leverage provided by the ironic snowy cataracts of "Mont Blanc." He writes, "for my part I had rather be damned with Plato and Lord Bacon than go to Heaven with Paley and Malthus."[26] In stating this preference for speculative philosophy over a theoretical history associated with end-times disaster, Shelley casts his work as invested in debates over immanent catastrophe, the Malthusian theories of population surges and food shortages, and with teleological humanism, the Paleyesque belief in human purpose and progress that unearths divinity in the natural world. However, preferring damnation to salvation, as Shelley does, has the funny consequence of casually standing apocalyptic Romanticism on its head, just as Marx claimed to have done to Hegel, by positioning hell as conditionally more desirable than paradise. But despite what Shelley's protestations against the Malthusian apocalyptic and the Paleyan teleological indicate, *Prometheus Unbound,* as a narrative of radical redemption and paradisiacal accomplishment rather than ecclesiastical lamentation and damnation, appears to invert Shelley's stated Platonic lake-of-fire preference as it suddenly becomes possible to go to heaven with Plato or to hell with Malthus (as Plato represents transcendent paradise and Malthus post-apocalypse) – just the opposite of what Shelley claims that he would rather do because of its paradisiacal end. As with these messy contradictory inversions involving a pagan humanism triumphing over the religious orthodoxies of hell-fire, Shelley's lyrical drama also belies his other claim in the preface that he offers no "reasoned system on the theory of human life."[27] The gods in the drama, as warring representatives of the human psyche, stage a battle between assured conservative social stasis and the unpredictable vicissitudes of democracy: Jupiter, the backward-looking tyrant, is dethroned, so to speak, by the forward-looking egalitarian energies represented by Promethean humanism. The result of said encounter introduces a theory of life contingent on the odes to love that close the play, odes that seek to imbricate nonhuman love within a belief in the universal goodness of humanity and its rebellious, restorative drive to liberate itself from its own self-delusional anthropocentric phantasms. Witness Demogorgon's final speech: "Gentleness, Virtue, Wisdom, and Endurance, / These are the seals of that most firm assurance / Which bars the pit over Destruction's strength … These are the spells by which to reassume / An empire o'er the disentangled doom" (IV, 562–5, 568–9). Invoking traits both mental and moral, Demogorgon locates sovereignty over mortal destruction as a capacity at one with the fortitude of human kindness, right-thinking rectitude, senescent surety, and inherent stamina.

This theory of life positions humanity – and essentialist qualities ascribed to humanity – as the universe's fundamental force of motricity in that the physical world, trending so close to a posthuman future with its "earth-convulsing behemoths," literally becomes the product of human thought: an instance of Kantian correlationism. Thus, the metaphor of the sea reflecting back love for humanity, and thence onto the twisted, blasted landscape of the wrecked and doomed world, liquefies into an expansive ocean encompassing the whole globe. It seems that Shelley, at least in 1819 when he was writing *Prometheus Unbound,* saw the world through apocalyptic eyes and as a result experiences the revelation of the kingdom to come of human felicity, absent the sociopolitical strife imposed on the world by a divine godhead. However, as I will return to below, this reading of the play, though imminently plausible, is itself phantasmatic, the idealist stuff dreams are made on, because it overlays a speculative palimpsest that turns out counter-intuitively to champion Jupiter – or at least his representation of an ironic subject-object disjunction – as its heroic exemplar. The drama's instructions to transgress the normative belief systems of the time – the socio-political order – are self-reflexive: the drama, and any ethico-politics it purports to support, contradictorally risks becoming itself tyrannical if it is not read as a speculative what-if rather than an idealist what-is: "And if, with infirm hand, Eternity, / Mother of many acts and hours, should free / The serpent that would clasp her with his length; / These are the spells by which to reassume / An empire o'er the disentangled doom" (IV, ii, 565–9). Idealism endorses the completion of a teleological, or apocalyptical, history, an endorsement that the play's final lines reject as a form of bad-faith historicism and quaint anti-realism; perfect liberty is never perfect if only for the simple reason that liberty demands the possibility of future usurpation by tyrannical regimes. Free will is the freedom to destroy free will. The ouroboros, having never left, always returns by remaining right where it is. Indeed, even a kind of Marxist social democratization, perhaps the nearest historical characterization of what the play finally anticipates and envisions, can become (and perhaps simply is) a socio-political regime that violently brooks no dissent, a danger that the twenty-first-century neoliberal, democratic, global order surely goes on to bear out in a remarkably twisted, bloody perversion of its underlying politics.

"Speculations on Metaphysics and Morals," and the similarly minded "On Life (1812–15)," though written earlier, reveal the full contours of *Prometheus Unbound*'s human-imagination/ontological world dilemma. In "Speculations on Metaphysics and Morals," Shelley claims that "the great science which regards the nature and operations of the human mind is popularly divided into moral and metaphysics."[28] Within this schematic division Shelley privileges morality and says that "metaphysical science will be treated merely so far as a source of negative truth."[29] Drawing on his reading of Berkeley, Shelley writes, "It is an axiom of mental philosophy that we can think of nothing which we have not perceived. When I say we can think of nothing, I mean, we can imagine nothing, we can reason of nothing, we can remember nothing, we can foresee nothing."[30] Shelley's adherence to this Berkeleyan creed cements the genealogical link between Shelley's speculative philosophy and speculative realism, for Meillassoux claims that correlationism began, not with Kant, who only finalized epistemological investigation over ontological speculation as philosophy's principle purpose, but with Berkeley.[31] Berkeleyan belief leads Shelley to a specifically correlationist claim, one that explicates his initial assertion that nothing exists but as it is conceived:

> But, it will be objected, the inhabitants of the various planets of this and other solar systems, and the existence of a Power bearing the same relation to all that we perceive and are, as what we call a cause does to what we call effect, were never subjects of sensation, and yet the laws of mind almost universally suggest, according to the various disposition of each, a conjecture, a persuasion, or a conviction of their existence. The reply is simple; these thoughts are also to be included in the catalogue of existence; they are modes in which thoughts are combined; the objection only adds force to the conclusion, that beyond the limits of perception and thought nothing can exist.[32]

In renewing his assertion that nothing exists beyond human perception, Shelley circumscribes the universe within the sphere of the mind even as he delimits the circumference and extensionality of the mind. Thoughts about the existence of alien others on distant planets, while external to the human mind, are nevertheless, when thought of by the mind, "modes in which thoughts are combined." Hence, for Shelley, speculation on metaphysics entails only Kantian speculation about the finitude of the human mind. Shelley's subsequent definition of metaphysics drives this point home: "metaphysics may be defined as the science of all that we know, feel, remember, and believe inasmuch as our knowledge, sensations, memory, and faith constitute the universe considered relatively to human identity."[33] Meillassoux identifies the post-Kantian metaphysical problem par excellence as one in which it is thought impossible to speak speculatively beyond the terms and limits of an anthropocentrism that fundamentally connects mind with world but that also sees the mind as finite. According to Shelley, it is precisely the mind-world connection itself that is the object of speculation: "[Man] is not a moral and an intellectual – but also and pre-eminently an imaginative being. His own mind is his law; his own mind is all things to him. If we would arrive at any knowledge which should be serviceable from the practical conclusions to which it leads, we ought to consider the mind of man and the universe as the great whole on which to exercise our speculations."[34] Given the orientation of mind to world, as that "in which to exercise our speculations," Shelley appears to fall neatly into the correlationist circle Meillassoux explicates.

"On Life" features the same Berkeleyan claim that "nothing exists but what can be perceived" and covers much of the same ground as "Speculations on Metaphysics and Morals" but appends crucial insights on the phenomenal-material nexus. Shelley writes: "Life, and the world, or whatever we call that which we are and feel, is an astonishing thing. The mist of familiarity obscures from us the wonder of our being."[35] Life's conditions, according to Shelley, are such that humans stand arrested before it, unable to comprehend it fully because even as it mesmerizes, it also mystifies. Part of life's obscurantist function stems from the human inability to penetrate the familiar features of the world despite that life and the world and "whatever we are and feel" are conflated. Humans have become accustomed to the "mist of the familiar," "the scenery of this earth, the mountains, the seas and rivers, and the grass and the flowers," Shelley claims, and hence they do not see "the wonder of our being" (Shelley makes similar arguments in "A Defence of Poetry" that are important to my reading of that essay below). Interestingly, Shelley does not argue that our representations obfuscate reality; rather, it is the repetitious nature of phenomenality, wherein we recurrently perceive the same things, that initiates an over- rather than a de-familiarizing process in which human awe (what we might otherwise call the sublime) gets enveloped by an obscuring brume. It is not epistemological access that obscures; the sheer nature of phenomenality rebuffs both material access and existential wonder. The world, in Shelley's analysis, may or may not exist independently of human thought, but we have, quite literally, lost sight of it and ourselves as a result of our complacent ontological blindness that sinks us into an unproductive ecological stupor – rather like the utopian delusions to which *Prometheus Unbound* occasionally gives voice.

Speculative philosophy clears this ontological obscurant mist by eradicating "error" and erasing the mind's baleful blindness; it "leaves, what is too often the duty of the reformer in political and ethical questions to leave, a vacancy."[36] Vacancy will be important shortly in my discussion of "Mont Blanc," but it is worth noting here that the vacancy referred to occurs in the mind; speculation clears the mist that obscures the world from human perception by creating a mental blank spot in the mind that allows it to see clearly. This allows for a proper consideration of human ontology in relation to the world so long veiled:

> [...] man is a being [...] incapable of imagining to himself annihilation, existing but in the future and the past, being, not what he is, but what he has been, and shall be. Whatever may be his true and final destination, there is a spirit within him at enmity with nothingness and dissolution (change and extinction). This is the character of all life and being. – Each is at once the centre and circumference; the point to which all things are referred,

> and the line in which all things are contained. – Such contemplations as these materialism and the popular philosophy of mind and matter, alike forbid; they are consistent only with the intellectual system.[37]

Whereas above the phenomenal-material junction prevented humans from basking in existential delight, here, in a rather astonishing turn of events, materialism is equated with annihilation and extinction. Humans can only imagine their continued existence, can only imagine the past and the future but not the present – an assertion that directly endorses redemptive Romantic apocalypticism over Romantic post-apocalypticism even as it also, paradoxically, sets materialism, the notion of a world beyond us and so without us, into affirmative post-apocalyptic motion. The mind's incapability to imagine extinction, thus, on the one hand, affirms Shelley's belief in Plato and Bacon over Malthus and Paley, a belief in apocalypse as a paradise rather than as a catastrophic extirpation or a naturally occurring end of the human species. And yet, Shelley's Berkeleyan position (which he asserts once again in "On Life"), that "nothing exists but as it is perceived," seems to contradict this assertion that humans cannot "imagine their own annihilation" since on Shelley's logic the human imagination must reach the limit of its perceptual capacity when confronted with its own extinction. This paradoxical incapacity, in turn, affirms that the crux of Shelley's poetics is human annihilation, the post-apocalyptic, which necessarily connects us to larger fears about human survival in the Anthropocene.

Shelley's contention that every human is "the centre and circumference" of the universe, a classically humanist anthropocentric position, only emphasizes how the posthuman, post-apocalyptic organizes Shelley's work. For on Shelley's account it is the post-apocalyptical impossibility – the impossibility of imagining annihilation – that causes the imagination to seize up (since it is impossible to imagine), which means that the post-apocalyptical, in arresting the mind from considering its own destruction, thereby foresees and enacts that very destruction of the mind even as it makes the imagination possible by also providing its limit. As the post-apocalyptic is the limit of the imagination, and since nothing that cannot be imagined can exist, if a mind imagines the post-apocalyptic, then, by Shelley's logic, the mind's destruction has already occurred even as this destruction *engenders imagination*. To put it in terms that revise the Kantian sublime, the mind proves finite because it cannot imagine humanity's own finitude, but, just as significantly, humanity cannot imagine human infinity (because that is the limit of the imagination), living beyond annihilation, either. Humans remain stubbornly within the present since surviving in the future, like not surviving in the future, is impossible for the mind to imagine. All that is left is the present world, whose existence we do not doubt even as it is nevertheless a world encrypted by our phenomenal attempts to perceive it. To put Shelley's thought in the more typical Derridean formulation of which it is redolent, imagination's possibility is made possible only because of its impossibility, its own potential, but always recurrent, extinction. And "Mont Blanc," as we will see, places the logic of these metaphysics in dialogue with the historical problems of climate change.

For the moment, though, it should be noted that the consequences of this deconstruction indicate the heart of Shelley's post-apocalypticism. For if it is impossible on Shelley's theoretical post-apocalypticism, therefore, to think about ontological extinction because human species death is unimaginable even as that is what makes possible the imagination in the first place, then it also becomes impossible to think about solutions to the climate-change problems of "the year without a summer" during which Shelley writes "Mont Blanc."[38] Grappling with confusing and often contradictory metaphysics against the backdrop of the historical climate-change consequences of Mount Tambora's 1815 eruption, Shelley's poetics remind us that understanding deconstructive concepts like "the imagination," "the mind," and "life" are historical, philosophical, and climatological issues that continue to be misunderstood, continue to plague us in the real-world present.

"Mont Blanc" foregrounds these phenomenal and ontological issues concerning human extinction by depicting the human mind confronted by the sublimity of nonhuman agency that reflects back its own telluric mortality and assured doom. As I discussed in my introduction, the literary, historical, and climatic touchstone of 1816 poses troubling questions about contemporary "green" narratives that link Romanticism to a paradise to come on earth. When confronted by the disastrous, threatening weather events of 1816, unlike the time periods in which "Speculations on Metaphysics and Morals" and "On Life" were written, historical materiality rudely intrudes on the metaphysically idealistic, yet strangely speculative, tendencies of those essays. Shelley poses his most intricately complex, troubling question about the world at the end of "Mont Blanc." Apostrophizing the mountain in the final lines, the poem famously asks: "And what were thou, and earth, and stars, and sea / If to the human mind's imaginings / Silence and solitude were vacancy?" (lines 142–4).

As Shelley scholars and Romantic critics in general have long recognized, the question's bald, metapoetic rhetoricity seems self-consciously to call for and deflect easy answers.[39] In enacting its own perpetually deferred answer (hence it is a question of temporality), however, it also invokes a host of other questions. For one, as an apostrophe to "thou" amidst "earth, and stars, and sea," the question positions the mountain as a synecdoche that contrasts with the natural features of the world, from global generality ("earth") to expansive astrology ("stars") to boundless hydrology ("sea"), while also appearing to be representative of them. For another, is the human mind to be read universally here? Is "imaginings" to be read as "imagination" in the expansive yet generalized sense? Or even in the sense with which Shelley uses it elsewhere, say, in "A Defence of Poetry"? How is "silence" to be understood in an apostrophe, which, by its very nature, implies voice? If "the Power is there," as well as "the fields, the lakes, the forests, and the streams," not to mention various animals, referenced in stanza IV, then how does "solitude" enter the picture? If the speaker is indeed alone amidst impressive natural surroundings, does this not invoke a nature/human split that undoes the apparent force of at least one reading of the question, namely, that the human mind in fact constructs the natural world around it and so is indubitably linked to it? And in doing so, does it not also anthropomorphize the mountain and, as such, neuter it of the awe-inducing, nonhuman power that apparently induces the poem in the first place? And what of "vacancy," a word that invokes *oikos*, place, space, emptiness, air, breath, mastery, freedom, liberation (and hence revolution), and even, with the Latin dative, temporality? For that matter, does "thou" even refer to the mountain? And all of these questions do not even approach the issue of contextualizing the question within Shelley's larger poetic and prose corpus (think of the positive "vacancy" of "Speculations on Metaphysics and Morals" above), let alone in relation to his extensive knowledge of geology, natural history, mythology, philosophy, and physics.[40]

What does seem clear, however, is that no matter how one parses the poem's recalcitrant question and its elusive answer, the question traverses the epistemological and ontological correlationist circle that Meillassoux identifies as modernity's foundational formula for thinking about human thought and its connection to the world. The two most obvious possible answers to the question demonstrate the correlationist heart of it. On the one hand, to affirm that "to the human mind's imaginings / Silence and solitude" *are not* "vacancy" locates within the human mind a generative capacity intimately tied to its contemplation of the natural world. That is, the rhetorical force of the question can be read as claiming that the topographical elements of land, sea, and air are indeed meaningless unless supplied with meaning, and even existence, by the human mind's contemplation of them in "silence and solitude." On the other hand, to affirm that "to the human mind's imaginings / Silence and solitude" *are* actually "vacancy" denies to the mind the creative faculty – the imagination – to construct or discover purpose in the external world. In the former, anthropocentric answer, the mind is indeed the encyclopaedia of the universe of things (recalling Shelley's comments in "Speculations on Metaphysics and Morals"); in the latter, non-anthropocentric answer, it is but one "of the everlasting universe of things." Therefore, as many critics note, the question further puzzles by invoking material and phenomenal issues it resolutely leaves unresolved; but, whether affirming or denying the mind's status as creative agent, the question, if such it really is in the final analysis, posits the mind-world correlation as the problematic matrix by which other existential and metaphysical conflicts are set at loggerheads with each other.[41] And yet, all of that said, there is a still more fundamental, important difference between the two answers in that they alternately cast the poem as posing either an epistemological or an ontological problem. Affirming that the mountain is a construct of the human mind raises epistemological problems as to the accuracy of human understanding of that world. Conversely, denying a correlate between the human mind and the world suggests that a world exists separately and independently from the human mind. On this schema, the human mind no longer centres the universe. Hence, the possibility of a posthuman future arises.

In other words, as I suggested at the outset of this chapter, the question opens an aporia in Shelley's work whose solution, in effect, determines whether Shelley's poem is apocalyptic – the Romantic belief in an earthly paradise – or post-apocalyptic – a world in which humans are already or soon to be extinct, but a world that is nonetheless hopeful in the unrelenting horror and weirdness of its realism. This mortal dilemma, so masterfully presented by "Mont Blanc," is, as I've been arguing, the unresolved heart of Shelley's lifelong ambition to ground a reformation of human life and society in a poetical theory of the human imagination that paradoxically unveils the possibility of a world without us.

Many readers, quite understandably, have attempted, like backpacking explicators, to back-track through the snow-covered, mountainous terrain of the poem on a quest for in situ textual clues and dispositive interpretive evidence. In what follows, I follow in the footprints of my fellow critics but do so within the explicatory framework I have elaborated above, of Shelley's poetics as riddled with post-apocalyptic, rather than apocalyptic, anxiety and energy. The poem is something of a Möbius strip in that the epistemological and ontological confusion that closes it also opens it:

> The everlasting universe of things
> Flows through the mind, and rolls its rapid waves,
> Now dark – now glittering – now reflecting gloom –
> Now lending splendour, where from secret springs
> The source of human thought its tribute brings
> Of waters, – with a sound but half its own.
> Such as a feeble brook will oft assume
> In the wild woods, among the mountains lone,
> Where waterfalls around it leap for ever,
> Where woods and winds contend, and a vast river
> Over its rocks ceaselessly bursts and raves. (lines 1–11)

It is difficult not to read this watery salvo on metaphysics as nakedly correlationist, with the universe flowing through the human mind and the human mind recursively re-entering the universe, a kind of materialistic cybernetic loop. Instead, the first stanza counter-intuitively problematizes the relation of mind and world, when the simile compares the mind to "a feeble brook." The movement of waters here corkscrews in several directions: "the everlasting universe of things" flows into the mind, but the mind, acting as an estuary, brings its "tribute" to this larger river of cosmic water. Hence, logically, the cycle is circular as the universe pours into the mind, which apparently allows for the "secret springs" to propel its own trickle back into the universe as river. This cycle bogs down in murkiness, however, when one contemplates what and where the "feeble brook" is in relation to the raucously echoing landscape of "the wild woods." If the "feeble brook," amidst the "ceaselessly" bursting and raving "vast river" of the Arve is truly feeble, then is it drowned out by this larger, noisier, stronger back-drop of the ravine? Or is the human mind, quite simply, feeble? Or enfeebled by the material world? Or, as Earl Wasserman suggests, is the mind representative of an individual mind that, logically, seems small in comparison to the rest of the "One Mind"?[42] What is remarkable here is that all three of these scenarios ultimately arrive at the same place: the mind – whether individual and hence dwarfed by the universe, drowned out by transcendental forces beyond its compare, or simply too enfeebled to interpret its cosmological insignificance – is subordinated to the universe of which it is a part. But mental subordination to the universe, for all of its explanatory attractiveness, only is definitive, ironically, in the incomplete satisfaction it offers since its human-world dialectic bivouacks it between the alternative encampments of apocalypse and post-apocalypse.

The mitigating arbitrator of these competing camps is the "Power" that has famously flummoxed interpretations of the poem. Stanza II begins the long apostrophic style that characterizes much of the rest of the poem, but it also begins with an odd, critically overlooked word, "thus" (12). This apostrophe and logical connector perplexes since the Ravine of Arve – the subject of the stanza and of the "thou" of "thus thou" – does not clearly enter into the metaphysical conundrums of the first stanza. By implication, then, the Ravine surely takes on material import as the "wild wood" surrounds the feeble brook, which "ceaselessly bursts and raves." There is an implication, too, of *thus thou* that translates to "thus thou art," as if the Ravine represents, outside of the context of the first stanza, a geographical fixture riven with transcendental significance by the ontological fact of its sheer being. As Anne C. McCarthy argues, the poem focuses for most of its length on the Ravine and not Mont Blanc, and so, on her reading of the poem that also draws on Meillassoux, "the Ravine of Arve reveals the possibility of a sublime whose *telos* is not stability but contingency, an undoing or suspension of *telos*."[43] "Mont Blanc," therefore, "becomes a poem about learning how to live in a world governed by contingency."[44] McCarthy's perceptive reading alerts us to the mountain's largely absent presence in the poem – a deconstructive materialism that, in my estimation, perversely and paradoxically signals the mountain's importance in relation to the fleetingly appearing Power. The Ravine, then, displaces us into the material and ontological realm that illuminates how Power operates via sleight of hand in the poem to reorient us away from the very metaphysics that the poem asserts as its ostensible topic in its opening lines.

Shelley reveals that Power, which makes its first appearance in the second stanza, actually resides (if that is the word) on or within the mountain Mont Blanc. More importantly, Power, as described here, does not cohere with its description later on in the fourth stanza:

Thus thou, Ravine of Arve – dark, deep Ravine –
Thou many-coloured, many-voiced vale,
Over whose pines, and crags, and caverns sail
Fast cloud-shadows and sunbeams: awful scene,
Where Power in likeness of the Arve comes down
From the ice-gulfs that gird his secret throne,

Bursting through these dark mountains like the flame
Of lightning through the tempest; – thou dost lie,
Thy giant brood of pines around thee clinging,
Children of elder time, in whose devotion
The chainless winds still come and ever came
To drink their odours, and their mighty swinging
To hear – an old and solemn harmony;
Thine earthly rainbows stretched across the sweep
Of the ethereal waterfall, whose veil
Robes some unsculptured image; the strange sleep
Which when the voices of the desert fail
Wraps all in its own deep eternity; –
Thy caverns echoing to the Arve's commotion,
A loud, lone sound no other sound can tame;
Thou art pervaded with that ceaseless motion,
Thou art the path of that unresting sound –
Dizzy Ravine! and when I gaze on thee
I seem as in a trance sublime and strange
To muse on my own separate fantasy,
My own, my human mind, which passively
Now renders and receives fast influencings,
Holding an unremitting interchange
With the clear universe of things around. (lines 12–40)

This Power, which "comes down from the ice-gulfs that gird his secret throne," illuminates the Ravine with its lightning-like visuals, infusing the Ravine with the darting flame of its hidden fire. But Power is not the material Ravine but only its "likeness," clearly distinguishing it as different from the Ravine as a force that seems everywhere and nowhere in this passage. Given this, "his" likely refers to the as-yet-unseen mountain itself, Mont Blanc, among the other "dark mountains" despite the seeming grammatical sense that ties it to the Ravine. Power, at once associated and disassociated with the mountain, is rendered visually and sonically legible as a delocalized corporeal entity once it rains down into the Ravine: "Thine earthly rainbows stretched across the sweep / Of the ethereal waterfall, whose veil / Robes some unsculptured image [...] / Thy caverns echoing to the Arve's commotion, / A loud, lone sound no other sound can tame" (lines 25–31). Shelley personifies the Power's source in anthropomorphic and anthropocentric terms (it is made mystically regal when enrobed with an "ethereal waterfall") as part of the mountain's "caverns," thereby effectuating not an alien landscape threatening to or unknowable by humanity but a topos acting in concert with the human mind.[45] Hence, when the speaker gazes on the mountain, it leads to a trance in which the speaker contemplates "my own separate fantasy," an apposite of "my own, my human mind," which "renders and receives fast influencings, / Holding an unremitting interchange / With the clear universe of things around" (lines 36–40). Since it "renders and receives," the interchange is not passive on the part of the mind, but interactive. The subordinated mind of the first stanza, no longer enfeebled on account of its diminutive nature, has attained coeval agency with the "universe of things."

This would seem to return to a correlationist proposition, and yet there are two powers at work in the poem, of which the mountain, we discover, is the power behind the Power, a power withdrawn from human perception. Power's next appearance, in the fourth stanza, unlike its articulation as an elemental force discoverable by the mind in the second, becomes ephemeral and indecipherable: "Power dwells apart in its tranquility / Remote, serene, and inaccessible" (lines 96–7). Power is at once removed and unreachable, unlike the rocky surface of Mont Blanc personified as "the naked countenance of earth" that can "teach the adverting mind" (lines 98–100). The mind can conceive of Power but only through the medium of the mountain that reveals Power's existence even as it shields and rebuffs cognitive attempts to access that Power. As Evan Gottlieb writes, Shelley "is in the presence of something that holds at least the promise of an enlightenment or clarification that exceeds the human," even if he can only finally term this a "Power" that "remains both objectively present and impossible for us to apprehend directly."[46] In other words, the surface exteriority of the mountain discloses Power ontologically but not phenomenologically. While Power remains hidden, the material world of precipice and precariousness ushers in an almighty avalanche of destruction:

The glaciers creep
Like snakes that watch their prey, from their far fountains,
Slow rolling on; there, many a precipice,
Frost and the Sun in scorn of mortal power
Have piled: dome, pyramid, and pinnacle,
A city of death, distinct with many a tower
And wall impregnable of beaming ice.
Yet not a city, but a flood of ruin
Is there, that from the boundaries of the sky
Rolls its perpetual stream; vast pines are strewing
Its destined path, or in the mangled soil
Branchless and shattered stand; the rocks, drawn down
From yon remotest waste, have overthrown

The limits of the dead and living world,
Never to be reclaimed. The dwelling-place
Of insects, beasts, and birds, becomes its spoil;
Their food and their retreat for ever gone,
So much of life and joy is lost. The race
Of man flies far in dread; his work and dwelling
Vanish, like smoke before the tempest's stream,
And their place is not known. Below, vast caves
Shine in the rushing torrents' restless gleam,
Which from those secret chasms in tumult welling
Meet in the vale, and one majestic River,
The breath and blood of distant lands, for ever
Rolls its loud waters to the ocean waves,
Breathes its swift vapours to the circling air.

("Mont Blanc," lines 100–26)

Shelley likens the Ravine to a paradox, a "city of death [...] Yet not a city" from which "a flood of ruin," a deluge recalling Power's descent in the second stanza, pours down the mountain's peak to overthrow "the limits of the dead and living world." With the "limits" of life and death deposed, the boundaries of the world therefore become delimited, and the apocalyptic truly shifts to the post-apocalyptic: "the race / Of man flies far in dread; his work and dwelling / vanish." Whole biospheres are disrupted in a fashion that mirrors Byron's "Darkness" when the "dwelling-place / Of insects, beasts, and birds" gets swept away by the rushing torrent. But although the diluvian descent mirrors Power's in the second stanza, this reflection nevertheless does not mean that this second form of Power becomes sensationally evident. Rather, life's and death's limits are *deposed*. Power thus remains a mysterious yet structural source of life, limning life's limits even as the material conditions of Earth can perturb these limits. Mont Blanc, Shelley realizes, will outlast humanity, an enduring symbol of what climate-science theorists refer to as deep time, the transhistorical span of time from the origins of the universe that exceeds human conception.[47]

That Mont Blanc testifies to human extinction explains the two competing ecological pictures present in the fourth stanza. Atmospheric disruptions, stratospheric interference, and natural disasters, like a clenching fist, crush the delicate petals of the future's flowering and thereby return us to the reality of the present day:

The fields, the lakes, the forests, and the streams,
Ocean, and all the living things that dwell
Within the daedal earth; lightning, and rain,

Earthquake, and fiery flood, and hurricane,
The torpor of the year when feeble dreams
Visit the hidden buds, or dreamless sleep
Holds every future leaf and flower; – the bound
With which from that detested trance they leap;
The works and ways of man, their death and birth,
And that of him and all that his may be;
All things that move and breathe with toil and sound
Are born and die; revolve, subside, and swell.

("Mont Blanc," lines 84–95)

As yet, these are natural disasters rather than climate-change-related extinction events on a planetary scale – life cyclically perpetuates, birth and death revolving, subsiding, swelling, like respiration. Indeed, all things "are born and die." The poem distinguishes between these cyclic and natural phenomena when the next line introduces Power as dwelling apart from these lifelines. It is at this point that catastrophe occurs: "there, many a precipice / Frost and the Sun in scorn of mortal power / Have piled: dome, pyramid, and pinnacle / A city of death, distinct with many a tower" (lines 102–5). Rather than the sparkling ice and tufts of snow that one might find in an idyllic loco-descriptive poem, weather becomes climate as precipitous accumulation occurs explicitly "in scorn of mortal power." This accumulative snowfall proves cumulative, piling up flake after flake into a "city of death."

Confirmation of this climactic destiny arrives in the poem's fifth stanza when Power reappears as, ironically, that which cannot be seen. Whereas the fourth stanza opens with a description of the natural progression of cyclical life on earth, the fifth conceives of life and death differently:

Mont Blanc yet gleams on high – the power is there,
The still and solemn power of many sights,
And many sounds, and much of life and death.
In the calm darkness of the moonless nights,
In the lone glare of day, the snows descend
Upon that Mountain; none beholds them there,
Nor when the flakes burn in the sinking sun,
Or the star-beams dart through them: – Winds contend
Silently there, and heap the snow with breath
Rapid and strong, but silently! Its home
The voiceless lightning in these solitudes

Keeps innocently, and like vapour broods
Over the snow. The secret strength of things
Which governs thought, and to the infinite dome
Of heaven is as a law, inhabits thee!
And what were thou, and earth, and stars, and sea,
If to the human mind's imaginings
Silence and solitude were vacancy? ("Mont Blanc," lines 127–44)

An under-appreciated word in this stanza, "much," relates the changed conceptualization of life in that not all of life and death is *there*; some portion, some remainder resides elsewhere in an undisclosed, and perhaps unknown, location. Therefore this suggests, in keeping with the first stanza, that a sovereign power behind the throne exists apart from any gleanable Power: the power of the inert mountain itself, a hard reality rather than a metaphysical idealization. Capital *P* Power is thus a product of the human imagination, whereas this second power exists in the world as "the secret strength of things / Which governs," and is ungoverned by, "thought." Shelley's yoking of sight and solitude, sound and silence, scrambles any residential, terrestrial, incarnate identity that lowercase *p* power could have. This synaesthetic symbiosis effaces the power's legibility even as its presence is disclosed by the mountain's material surface and majestic sublimity. Lowercase *p* power, appropriately, yet confoundingly and contradictorily, seems to be localized, delocalized, historically situated, transhistorical, ahistorical, temporal, and atemporal.

Power's defiance of categorical understanding underscores its radical alterity, its nonhuman posthumanness that decouples it from the human imagination. Seen in this light, the mountain becomes a posthuman, ontological reservoir of desolate beauty and splendour: "upon that Mountain; none beholds them there." The presence and absence of power's nowhere-and-everywhere reality, as the poem's final question declares, embrangles the mind in epistemological uncertainties that occasion speculation on the mountain's ontology. Only the "secret strength of things," an unfathomable, unknown force of material entities with its own power ("strength"), remains beyond human conception and outlasting the human race even as it "governs" human thought by the brute fact of its recalcitrant always already dispossession of power from human thought. The flakes burning in the sinking sun, like scraps dissolving into ashes, signal the endurance of the world despite the symbolism of microscopic elements of that world disappearing in this flash of fiery light. Mont Blanc thus exemplifies the post-apocalyptic sublime: the suspension of normative rules of human sense-making about the world because the world stands beyond human sense even as that suspension allows for sense's origination. "Silence and solitude [*are*] vacancy" in the end *because* to think the power of the world, its "secret strength of things," is to think the limit of life and death, human extinction, a limit that the human imagination cannot allow us to think even as that limit allows for thought itself.[48] Speculating on the existence of a world beyond the mind's phenomenality, the poem acknowledges that its own existence – and failure of access – confirms that world's radically exorbitant ontology. Like Graham Harman's example of the Islamic cotton ball, which evinces colour, shape, and texture but never the cotton ball itself, the mountain Mont Blanc, "the naked countenance of earth," is *not* the Earth but only one of its qualities, a synecdoche that references an object never fully present to human consciousness.[49] It is for this reason that the mountain's surface itself indicates reality's radical inaccessibility and humans' eradicability. Understood thusly, within this speculative framework, the Mont Blanc of "Mont Blanc" stands as the nexus of Romantic post-apocalyptic temporal vortices, an attempt to think being outside of thought, to ground consciousness in the falseness of an exteriority hyper-aware of its own illusory and hence ironic dissimulation, what divides consciousness from the world outside it. Shelley's post-apocalyptic sublime thus forces us to confront our present-day reality as it demarcates the human from the nonhuman world, thus pressing the mind into a direct confrontation – just as the speaker faces Mont Blanc's face – with the world's independence from humanity and humanity's counter-dependence on the world.

Shelley's realization of Mont Blanc as indicative of, because indifferent to, humanity's end parallels contemporary paradoxes of human futural historicism instantiated by the climate-science prophecies with which I opened the chapter. For Mont Blanc, in contrast to us (whatever that is), "yet gleams on high." If we can find some measure of surety and security in the poem, it lies in its insistence of life as *seen* rather than *seen into*. From this angle we might further contextualize my reading by identifying it as a parallel inversion to Marjorie Levinson's now (in)famous reading of "Tintern Abbey" wherein Wordsworth, even as he sees "into the life of things," "excludes from his field certain conflictual sights and meanings – roughly, the *life* of things."[50] Here, the life of things is seen by its occlusion – even as seeing into the life of things is not permitted, precisely because of life's radically expropriated nature from human phenomenological access. We see, to put it cheekily and deconstructively, what we cannot see: a world without us.

The same invisible world without us can now be rightly glimpsed in the interstitial hurly-burly of *Prometheus Unbound*'s temporal politics. Shelley's later treatment of Demogorgon, "the Power" whose "demos" confederates it with humanity, seems somehow to solicit the human mind to aspirations of transcendence over and above itself and the world. Consider the connection between the "flakes" melting in the post-apocalyptic sublime of the sun at the end of "Mont Blanc" and the flakes associated with Demogorgon. Asia's dialogue frames the mountain of Demogorgon's reign in terms reminiscent of Mont Blanc but differentially metaphorizes the snowflakes as a mind stockpiling its wintry resources for a cold-war revolution against ideologies of mental enslavement:

> Look, sister, ere the vapour dim thy brain:
> Beneath is a wide plain of billowy mist,
> As a lake, paving in the morning sky,
> With azure waves which burst in silver light,
> Some Indian vale. Behold it, rolling on
> Under the curdling winds, and islanding
> The peak whereon we stand, midway, around,
> Encinctured by the dark and blooming forests,
> Dim twilight-lawns, and stream-illumèd caves,
> And wind-enchanted shapes of wandering mist;
> And far on high the keen sky-cleaving mountains
> From icy spires of sun-like radiance fling
> The dawn, as lifted Ocean's dazzling spray,
> From some Atlantic islet scattered up,
> Spangles the wind with lamp-like water-drops.
> The vale is girdled with their walls, a howl
> Of cataracts from their thaw-cloven ravines,
> Satiates the listening wind, continuous, vast,
> Awful as silence. Hark! the rushing snow!
> The sun-awakened avalanche! whose mass,
> Thrice sifted by the storm, had gathered there
> Flake after flake, in heaven-defying minds
> As thought by thought is piled, till some great truth
> Is loosened, and the nations echo round,
> Shaken to their roots, as do the mountains now. (II, ii, lines 19–42)

No summer soldiers or sunshine patriots, the unleashed revolutionaries of "heaven-defying minds" depend upon the mind's flaky build-up, upon the metaphysical revolutions of the mind itself expressed here as a winter wonderland of teleological purpose. Asia's poetic aria exults winter to indicate the mind's steadfastness in opposition to Paine's boastful cowards and pretentious half-termers. Shelley's metaphysics here repurpose his famous, seasonally based "Ode to the West Wind" to ask, by means of temporal paradox, whether winter, and not spring, can be far behind because winter, and not summer, is indeed coming. Demogorgon as Power is therefore a power of the mind and not of mountains, a power of metaphoric mental seasons and cycles and not of the wintry wasteland of Mont Blanc's sun-bathed, frost-blasted summit. Jupiter's fall shortly thereafter confirms how season shuffling metaphorically enacts a heroic mental reshuffling because in Jupiter's monologue the flake-as-revolution metaphor is refashioned as but another instance of human transcendence over their self-imposed mental captivity. In that passage, Jupiter's curses "Like snow on herbless peaks, / fall flake by flake, / And cling to" the ascending, unvanquishable soul of humanity (III, i, lines 12–13). To contextualize this within the spirit of the speculative-realist critique in "Mont Blanc" of Kantian metaphysics, Jupiter represents the idea that the mind is confined within a jail cell of its own making, humbly accepting, like Christ, its own finitude, whereas Demogorgon represents the mind's jail-break from this stunning finitude into the vasty wilderness of an infinity that, by its completely captivating nature, ultimately prevents human survival. As Gottlieb notes, Meillassoux seemingly shares Shelley's apparent anthropocentrism in *Prometheus Unbound*, yet here we glimpse the much more radical possibility that the poem presents us with a humanity whose realization of its own finitude allows for hope to arise from hopelessness: "to hope, till Hope creates / from its own wreck the thing it contemplates" (573–4).[51]

Such a reading would suggest, in contrast to conventional wisdom, that Jupiter is the poem's real champion of humanity since to be Demogorgon's follower would continue a walk along a pathway riven from the real-world mountain of Mont Blanc, a life invested not in its present reality but in a science-fictional future. Progress along this latter rocky edifice leads to a land of more delusions, veiling once more the familiarity of the world, and, rather than accepting human finitude, accepting that humans are *of* rather than *at* the centre of the universe of things. On this reading, Demogorgon, contrary to his meta-status as revelation of human self-deceit, becomes very much a "people-gorgon" in that he represents humanity's self-deception. This self-deceit leads humanity into further errors, further codes of, as it is put in "Mont Blanc," "fraud and woe." Read through the lens of the legislative realism of "Mont Blanc" (and, yes, I chose the word *legislative* for its resonances with Shelley's claim about poets at the end of the "Defence"),

Demogorgon is yet one more Power obscuring the real mountain and hence reality. As I argued in the introduction, and as the above reading of "Mont Blanc" exemplifies, we already live in a world without us. We just cannot see it – either the world without us or that we cannot see that we cannot see our own blindness of our own blindness.

Unveiling the familiar world obscured to us, a world without us that we live in but that exists apart from us, is the main function of poetry according to Shelley in "A Defence of Poetry." Earl Wasserman reads Shelley's appropriation of Milton's *Paradise Lost* – "'The mind is its own place, and of itself can make a Heaven of Hell, a Hell of Heaven'" – as supportive of Shelley's Berkeleyan thesis "that all things exist as they are perceived," and hence the mind and the universe are a unity, the One Mind of Wasserman's Neoplatonism.[52] However, Shelley's reference to Milton, although superficially concerned with a resultant paradise of mind-world unification, actually signals a disjunction between mind and world. The mind is, for Shelley, after all, its *own* place. It does not go for walks outdoors, which is, in any event, on Shelley's conception, outside the doors of the mind's perceptions. The Miltonic allusion thus deflates the loftiness of paradisiacal transcendentalism, endorsing in its stead a radical, posthuman speculative awareness of a world without us. Shelley's "Defence of Poetry," in fact, deepens and elaborates on his vision in "Mont Blanc" of a potentially earthly eternality that exceeds human capacity to fully master or understand, only in "A Defence of Poetry" he equates this eternality with Poetry or the Poem rather than with P/power. The irreducible "power" of the universe of everlasting things in "Mont Blanc" becomes this eternal poem in "A Defence of Poetry"; indeed Shelley invokes the term in a capacious, almost mythical fashion that captures something eternal that is always withdrawn from us. The metaphor of the ever-abundant acorn perpetually in seed captures what is a speculative-realist, object-oriented-ontology resonance of Shelley's poiesis: "all high poetry is infinite; it is as the first acorn, which contained all oaks potentially. Veil after veil may be undrawn, and the inmost naked beauty of the meaning never exposed."[53] As William Keach notes, unveiling in Shelley is always both a revelation (*apocalypsis*) and a concealing.[54] But it is also a post-revelation (*post-apocalypsis*) and a concealing. No matter how many veils are drawn down, what Shelley calls "the inmost naked beauty of the meaning" of the infinite poem (like the thing in itself) lies recessed behind yet another veil. Removing a veil reveals a veil. Meaning, and the world itself as it is, remain inaccessible.

Despite the world's inaccessibility, each veil itself reveals some new truth of the world, some new facet of the material world, even if the totality of truth will always already wear its unrepentant shroud. The poet's primary tool for investigation and elucidation is metaphor, which the poet wields, crucially, both voluntarily and involuntarily since metaphor is inseparably woven into language's semiotic fabric. For Shelley, metaphor indexes the primal distinction between reason and the imagination: "Reason is to Imagination as the instrument to the agent, as the body to the spirit, as the shadow to the substance."[55] But Imagination, more than simply being corporeality's animating agent, "respects … the similitude of things," while "Reason respects the differences."[56] *Respect*, from the Latin *respecto*, means "to look back on." Imagination, as Shelley conceives it, discovers for humans the similitude of things, not only by paying them renewed attention (the popular understanding of *respect*); it also marks that similitude only during a reconsideration, during an explicitly *specular* reappraisal. Whatever their particular differing vagaries are, in Enlightenment theories of sympathy, like those of David Hume and Adam Smith that anticipate Levinas's location of the face as the site on which ethics pivots, the common underlying factor is human sight of the human face and body.[57] Sympathetic imagination's affective affinities depend on sight, on looking – and looking back on – the face of the person one observes. The facial-recognition program of sympathetic identification is thus fraught with species differentiation. Shelley's theory of the imagination, however, crosses species borderlines: the imagination can also look at "the similitude of things" and not just the similitude of persons. In the next few paragraphs of the text, Shelley offers a Rousseauvian narrative about the "origin of man" that poetry is "connate with" and asserts that the language of poets "is vitally metaphorical." This state-of-nature narrative signals, by the word "vitally," that the real topic of "A Defence of Poetry" is life understood as not just persons but as the rocks and trees, seas and animals that the world entails. It also confirms that metaphor – making dissimilar things similar – is not a substrate of poetry but rather a critical aspect of how the poetic imagination, and the imagination in general, operates (511). Hence, poetry "marks the before unapprehended relations of things and perpetuates their apprehension."[58]

In Shelley's historical account of progress from the state of nature to Romantic modernity, human beings and the world are ontologically speaking not interdependent: humans observe the natural world's rhythm and attempt to mimic its perfect harmony. State-of-nature humanity's instinct is, however, a phenomenological yearning for ecological yield; what they see the world doing, they do. This harmony, or "rhythm," equates with the imagination's metaphoric powers of looking again – *re-specting* – at the world of things and articulating the similitude of those things.[59] But the work of poetic imagination is paradoxical in that, to demonstrate the similitude of the things of the world, poets must engage in "making familiar objects be as if they were not familiar."[60] Oddly, or at least unexpectedly, this paradoxical process is catachresis. Metaphorically making the familiar unfamiliar eventually shows how the external forces of the world cohere with the natural rhythm of the world. A poet must determine and demonstrate, to be a poet, behind volition, through metaphor, how unalike things are alike, how the external world, though to the casual viewer a chaotic mess, amounts to a veiled harmony in reality. But beyond the discovery of the world being the poet's subject and object, it seems that, at an even more fundamental level, for Shelley, metaphor's tropological pathology is that it just functions this way, metaphor as a natural process that de-naturalizes and so re-naturalizes nature. Metaphor makes the familiar unfamiliar – that *that* thing is actually like *this* thing – and the catachresis of metaphor, as Derrida pointed out long ago, also reveals how unfamiliar things really are fundamentally familiar.[61] On this reading, "poets are the unacknowledged legislators of the world" because metaphor, vital to the poet as it allows for establishing a rhythm between humanity and the world, makes legible the similitude of things through the revelation of their harmonious dissimilitude.[62] The example of Isaac Newton, the great scientist of revelation, clarifies Shelley's point about metaphor and its agent, the poet.[63] Newton's seventeenth-century articulation (what we call "discovery") of the laws of motion – his system of the world – apprehends that which has gone unapprehended earlier by human beings in a metaphoric process wherein the explication of the laws of motion makes what is familiar to the world – bodies in motion – unfamiliar in its novel explanation of them, and therefore makes the previously undisclosed reality of the world *more* familiar. Now we understand what we did not understand, even though we saw it every day. Metaphor, by means of this simultaneous process of jointure and cleavage, anchors (to mix metaphors) the division of the human subject and the external world and its objects.

Understanding Shelley's theory of metaphor is therefore crucial to understanding the post-apocalyptic energy, theory, and politics that I have unearthed in his poetics. Like Hume and Smith, Shelley identifies social solidarity as the cornerstone of civilization: "The social sympathies, or those laws from which as from its elements society results, begin to develop themselves from the moment that two human beings co-exist."[64] But sympathy, similarly to metaphor, again, "lifts the veil from the hidden beauty of the world; and makes familiar objects be as if they were not familiar," and thereby solves the mystifying problems of perceptual familiarity that over-familiarizes, as raised in the early speculative essays. In this brief excursus on morals Shelley defines love as sympathy, claiming that "the great secret of morals is Love; or a going out of our own nature, and an identification of ourselves with the beautiful which exists in thought, action or person, not our own."[65] Love, like sympathy, entails "going out of our own nature" and identifying with things unlike us, other thoughts and other people (though we will see love take on similar although also radically different contours in *Pride and Prejudice*, in my chapter 5). "A man to be greatly good," he continues, "must imagine intensely and comprehensively; he must put himself in the place of another and of many others; the pains and pleasures of his species must become his own."[66] Poets, as Shelley says, are the unacknowledged legislators, not because they make something new but because they reveal a heretofore-unknown truth of the universe. Poets help us to imagine "that which we know," as Shelley puts it.[67] If metaphor makes the familiar unfamiliar and vice versa in its catachresis, if the poetic imagination unveils eternal, natural truths of the world, thereby making the unfamiliar familiar, then Shelley's theory of sympathy here reveals the animating biopolitical context of his work: the human species and its potential, and always already, imaginative, and real, extinction. To be a poet requires imaginative sympathy, going outside of oneself and placing oneself imaginatively in the bodies of the rest of the species. This is, finally, what he calls "the poetry of life": making sense of how metaphor entangles the human species (with its finite existence) with a world that seems remote, infinite, and eternal. But, and here is the crucial post-apocalyptic move by Shelley, this is not just the poetry *of* life; poetry *is* life in the sense that poetry, or the great poem, is itself eternal, a thing beyond mortal finitude and notions of species survival and annihilation (and so Shelley means by poetry more than the mundane sense of a poet's verse but an existence that is part of the very fabric of the universe).

The workings of the eternal universe can be brought into the light, and yet the eternal itself remains incompletely knowable as individual historical epochs can never achieve progressive totalization. Shelley's discussion of erotic poetry as historically anchored "episodes" of "that great poem, which all poets, like the co-operating thoughts of one great mind, have built up since the beginning of the world," defines the poem in similar terms to Wasserman's identification of the One Mind:

> A poem is the very image of life expressed in its eternal truth. There is this difference between a story and a poem, that a story is a catalogue of detached facts, which have no other connection than time, place,

> circumstance, cause and effect; the other is the creation of actions according to the unchangeable forms of human nature, as existing in the mind of the Creator, which is itself the image of all other minds. The one is partial, and applies only to a definite period of time, and a certain combination of events which can never again recur; the other is universal, and contains within itself the germ of a relation to whatever motives or actions have place in the possible varieties of human nature. Time, which destroys the beauty and the use of the story of particular facts, stripped of the poetry which should invest them, augments that of poetry, and forever develops new and wonderful applications of the eternal truth which it contains. Hence epitomes have been called the moths of just history; they eat out the poetry of it. A story of particular facts is as a mirror which obscures and distorts that which should be beautiful; poetry is a mirror which makes beautiful that which is distorted.[68]

Yet, in the context of "A Defence of Poetry" as a whole, this passage also suggests that history provides a snapshot of the external, universal world since poets can only build up this great poem precisely from their own *present* individually couched historicity. Poets, in this sense, are the great Newtonians, standing on the shoulders of poetic giants, setting down "a system of the world" one puzzle piece at a time in their given epochs.

Even though poetry "strips the veil of familiarity from the world, and lays bare the naked and sleeping beauty, which is the spirit of its forms," it nevertheless does not uncover what lies behind the final veil, be it truth, beauty, god, or mother nature, because it is a continual process of creation and recreation – like the political epicycles that close *Prometheus Unbound*. The mind is its own place; the world is another:

> All things exist as they are perceived: at least in relation to the percipient. "The mind is its own place, and of itself can make a Heaven of Hell, a Hell of Heaven." But poetry defeats the curse which binds us to be subjected to the accident of surrounding impressions. And whether it spreads its own figured curtain, or withdraws life's dark veil from before the scene of things, it equally creates for us a being within our being. It makes us the inhabitants of a world to which the familiar world is a chaos. It reproduces the common universe of which we are portions and percipients, and it purges from our inward sight the film of familiarity which obscures from us the wonder of our being. It compels us to feel that which we perceive, and to imagine that which we know. It creates anew the universe, after it has been annihilated in our minds by the recurrence of impressions blunted by reiteration.[69]

Shelley sees the familiar as the continued reiteration of static common life, a type of veil that "obscures from us the wonder of our being," though it leaves in place our ontological knowledge of being, of existence. That is, for Shelley, we know we exist but know so without wonder, an affectless state that renders life chaotic ("the familiar world is a chaos"). In Milton's *Paradise Lost*, Chaos – a word that the *OED* says can mean to disconnect from the mind – is associated with the undefined and unbounded, the limitless (book 2, lines 890–7; book 7, lines 165–242). Chaos as Shelley conceives it functions much the same in that the familiar world is never completely knowable by the human mind even as its chaos is simultaneously productive of new discoveries since this is metaphor's defamiliarizing process at work, "inventing" – from the Latin *invenio* for "finding" – as it goes, the laws of physics. The mind is finite, whereas the disassociated world is not. But even these revealed laws are an instance of what Meillassoux calls "factiality" since they prove to be factual rather than fundamental, or transcendental, or universal; laws are *discoverable* and therefore *revisable*. Poetry's ameliorative power stems from its ability to "purge [...] from our inward sight the film of familiarity" and therefore make the world non-chaotic, make the world partially, and perhaps temporally, better understood (as in the laws of motion and gravity and Einstein's relativity). Only in this sense does poetry derive its creative forces: "it creates anew the universe" by unveiling part of the universe heretofore obscured, even as the universe itself is not ever fully knowable to us, like Mont Blanc, and even as other aspects of the world remain concealed. In its numinous quintessence and mysterious intensity the poem remains beyond full human comprehension and apperception.

Hence, even with this renewal of the universe, that which is eternal always withdraws from our full understanding since "the recurrence of ... reiteration," of "the mist of familiarity," will temporally annihilate "in our minds" whatever glimpse of the external world beyond us that we may glean. The mind's post-apocalyptic limit will always restart this reiterative destruction because annihilation itself – as shown both here and above – works paradoxically to both destroy the mind and engender imagination. The mind *is* its own place: a post-apocalyptic, fruitful wasteland. Thankfully, the mist of familiarity always descends again since it also demystifies, however partially, incorrectly, and misleadingly. Despite that "all things exist as they are perceived, at least to the percipient," all things also, like Mont Blanc and the eternal power continually walled off from human thought, exist as they are whether or not they are perceived.

The eternality of the poem, or poetry, is not, then, an aesthetic appeal to the work of art as forever endurable, nor is it a chasing after some long-sought human infinitude; the poem stands for the nebulae beyond the veil of human life, human life only visible to us by its temporized surface phosphorescence. Whatever this poem may ultimately consist of, Shelley does not undertake to say (nor, given his conception of the poem, can he); however, it is clear that, for him, life is not, as Wasserman claims, "the identity of existence and perception, the unity of mind and the universe, of subject and object," but rather the walling off of these, what were assumed to be, good neighbours.[70] Life is something that is much more evanescent and perhaps ever out of the human mind's reach, however much the mind should exceed its own grasp.

If Newton is the great alchemically minded, arcane scientist of apocalypse, then Shelley is the great poet-prophet of post-apocalypse. But whereas Newton considered himself a prophet and exegete of the future end of days, Shelley's idea of the poet, as I claimed at the beginning of this chapter, diverges from the rapturous ecstasy of thanatopolitic's doomsday predictions.[71] Much depends on what Shelley means by "the eternal," which wobbles equivocally throughout the essay, a kind of pivot that touches on, with passing hand, now the past, now the future. Beckoning us onward towards a truth – and it is the final truth because the end of both the world and truth, as Derrida says – prophets, alongside legislators, were, in antiquity, the original poets:[72]

> Poets, according to the circumstances of the age and nation in which they appeared, were called, in the earlier epochs of the world, legislators, or prophets: a poet essentially comprises and unites both these characters. For he not only beholds intensely the present as it is, and discovers those laws according to which present things ought to be ordered, but he beholds the future in the present, and his thoughts are the germs of the flower and the fruit of latest time. Not that I assert poets to be prophets in the gross sense of the word, or that they can foretell the form as surely as they foreknow the spirit of events: such is the pretence of superstition, which would make poetry an attribute of prophecy, rather than prophecy an attribute of poetry. A poet participates in the eternal, the infinite, and the one; as far as relates to his conceptions, time and place and number are not.[73]

A two-tier logic fuels this secular poetics: as its first step, poets are said to combine the qualities of both legislators and prophets, a premise recursive in the essay's famous final pronouncements. As its second step, poets as prophets are distinguished from the naïveté of religious superstition's unquestioning belief in eschatological end-points. Shelley's secularization of poetry's religiosity also evacuates it of Romantic prophecy's count-down to extinction. Poetry, in Shelley's temporalization of it, "beholds intensely the present," and when it "beholds the future," does so, crucially, in the present. Deranging the past and present does not so much scramble time as warn us of and ward off prophesying about the future. Poets cannot, do not, foretell but "participate in the eternal, the infinite, and the one," which would seem to indicate a universalist desire for temporal transcendence. Yet, since future conceptions are constrained in the present what Shelley means by the eternal is a bounded-down participatory politics (poets are legislators too) in the here and now, for there is no other time. The future only takes place in the present. Poetry is not prophecy nor about the future, but rather a running after eternity, which Shelley distinguishes from the future – and indeed even from the past because poetry and the eternal world are forever sundered. Poetry, again, can, through unveiling, surface pictures of that world – the mountainous face of the world on Mont Blanc – but never the thing in itself, the world that endures beyond human deracination. Such surfacing is what Shelley means by legislating: "poets are the hierophants of an unapprehended inspiration; the mirrors of the gigantic shadows which futurity casts upon the present; the words which express what they understand not; the trumpets which sing to battle, and feel not what they inspire; the influence which is moved not, but moves. Poets are the unacknowledged legislators of the world."[74] In Shelley's hands, time's Aionic arrow flies non-linearly, directly into the unwitting eyes of Chronos. And as the day breaks, the shadows of the future fall on the present *in* the present, and the future appears, fleetingly, before it disappears, as all shadows do in the light of the passing sun.

Like Byron, who sends Cain through a lake-of-fire phantasmagoria, Shelley's final major poem, *The Triumph of Life*, sends his unnamed narrator on an *Inferno*-esque investigation of life's spiritual provenance and cessation. Shelley's fragmentary poem refuses to offer any easy answers to its final question, "Then, what is Life?" left so tantalizingly suspended by the abrupt non-answer of Shelley's tragic demise. Indeed, it might seem, given the fairly depressing topics at hand – climate change, species death, annihilation – that post-apocalyptic sublimity represents the triumph of *apathia* over *ataraxia*, of succumbing to a mollifying indifference rather than the blissful isles of Elysium. If for Shelley this thing called the great poem, or the truth, exists in eternality, a time forever forbidden by the future's intractable coming into the present, then the answer to the

Triumph's life question may well echo forth unbidden from the depths: life is a ceaseless void whose light radiates over a kingdom of nebulous darkness. This non-rosy picture recalls the bleak brutality of Hobbes's state of nature, in which life was a zero-sum game whose victors wore the sigils of nihilism. But scenarios such as these that pit nothingness against happiness enact destruction in the very crucible of their contest. They engender the very thing they seek to forestall. They know not what they do for they do nothing. Illusions of lotus blossoms create the *apathia* that cancels action, for only in prelapsarian paradise can one be indifferent since all cares lie prostrate before apathy's glory. In contrast, for all of its apparent melancholic associations, by revealing life's heart of darkness, Shelley's post-apocalyptic sublime confronts us with a non-delinquent reality that can arrest the diseased, fallen stars of disaster in their luminescent free fall, to give ironic birth, rather, to the dancing star of hope.

2 No More Cakes and Ale, Only Oil Slicks: Mary Shelley's Post-Apocalyptic State of Nature

While the radical ontology of Percy Shelley's post-apocalyptic sublime in "Mont Blanc" offers hope for understanding the world on its own terms, it is Mary Shelley who theorizes a new posthuman politics for living on and with the world. In her novel *The Last Man* (1826) the human survivors of a devastating plague grapple with their loss of control over the world, even as animals and the nonhuman world reclaim the earth as their liberated home. By considering Shelley's *The Last Man* in the context of the post-apocalyptic political implications raised by Byron's poem "Darkness" (1816), this chapter claims that humanity is destroying itself by poisoning the earth's climate but that this leads to an opportunity to rethink how we conceive of what politics is and what it can be. Read against the back-drop of "the year without a summer," these works seek to undermine belief in our anthropocentric sense of our own human sovereignty and earthly importance. While much Romantic-era political theory presupposed that humans' abilities to reason, choose, and speak created contractual politics, Shelley reveals this anthropocentrism to be only the ruse of our own circular logic: our anthropocentric attributes justify our anthropocentric solutions. *The Last Man* decouples sovereignty from anthropocentrism because the novel views anthropocentrism as a dangerous ideological form of extinctualism whose circularity prevents thinking through problems of how to live during global climate change. Byron's "Darkness," for instance, depicts animals retaining their bonds with humans while humans accede to their Hobbesian state-of-nature, instinctual hunger for war, an earthly destruction that amounts to a nihilistic picture of sundered social covenants. *The Last Man* repairs this shattered promise of peace by rewriting the social contract to include nonhumans in any democracy-to-come. Nonhumans, it turns out, can be, if not sovereigns or even co-rulers, the creatures whose existence enacts and governs politics on the earth.

As I read it, *The Last Man* stages a pitched political battle over the fate of the earth between libertarian anarchy and progressive social contractualism, before finally identifying both politics as irreducibly anthropocentric. However, as I said in my introduction, this is not Godwinian anarchy – which shares suspicions about government with the type of anarchy I am describing here – but rather a conservative form of anarchy that celebrates the selfish desires of the individual for capitalist accumulation of goods. If anything, Godwin's interest in justice for all (even though that justice is, for him, unequally distributed) falls along the progressive axis. Yet Shelley's politics in this novel extend beyond Godwin's, in which "man is of more worth than a beast," even as they tend to agree with Godwin's assertion that "I should be content to die" if "I can promote the general good."[1] In opposition to the familiar conservative and progressive political dead ends captured in Godwin's ideas, the politics the novel proposes hinge on recognizing the rights of nonhuman others beyond our totalitarian human concepts of "rights" and "justice." To resist these conceptions, Shelley's novel crafts a social-contract theory based on hospitality that extends to nonhuman life, even if it means totally giving over one's own life for another's, instantiating a radical, unconditional opening to the other.[2] Shelley's theory of hospitality in the novel evacuates sovereignty of human power and prescribes what I have been calling passivity without passivity. Adopting passivity without passivity, humans accept their finitude and turn to care not for themselves – they stop acting on their own behalf – but for the finitude of others, the neglected, the helpless, the strange, the nonhuman: biopolitics remade as Nicole Shukin's zoopolitics.[3] This zoopolitical hospitality allows for alternative modes of not only thinking but also living, contracting to live on, with the creatures whose existence we severely curtail with our efforts to prolong our own species' existence.[4]

The year without a summer of 1816 is, of course, one of the most famous times in literary history since it witnesses the rain-soaked night that gave birth to Mary Shelley's *Frankenstein* (1818), when, feeling trapped inside their chateau by the weather, Mary, Percy, Byron, and John Polidori engaged in a ghost-story contest based on their reading of *Fantasmagoriana* (1812). Only Mary completed a full work, while Polidori coughed up *The Vampyre* (1819), a short novella-like text supposedly derived from Polidori's bewitched fascination with the real-life Byron and the darker myths in circulation about him. William and

Nicholas Klingaman's *The Year without a Summer* (2014) provides a valuable guide to how the events of that summer are closely tied to climate change, but it is Gillen D'Arcy Wood who contextualizes these events within Romanticism, and Romanticism within the 1816 climate change.[5] Mount Tambora, a massive volcano in Indonesia, erupted with such force in 1815 that "within three weeks" its "stratospheric ash cloud had circled the planet at the equator, from where it embarked on a slow-moving sabotage of the global climate system at all latitudes."[6] Using the Shelleys and Byron as his tour guides, Wood takes us on a journey around the globe, examining the climate consequences of this explosion, from China, where it created a food shortage that led to the eventual rise of opium as a national crop, to the United States – where a bewildered and beleaguered Thomas Jefferson watched his crops fail and the numbers in his ledger slowly chronicle his bankruptcy. For Wood, despite the fact that Tambora's eruption was a "natural" phenomena, it nonetheless provides one of the few world-historical examples of what massive global climate change can wreak. To this end, it becomes, as he says, "a case study in the fragile interdependence of human and natural systems ... whose downstream effects can be traced long into the nineteenth century."[7] Trapped inside the chateau with Percy Shelley's strange and horrified visions of women with eyes for nipples, the Shelley circle experienced the first effects of Tambora, internalizing, without them even necessarily fully realizing it, the harsh productions of climate change. As their last-man texts from that summer detail in harrowingly vivid word grimoires – and I include "Mont Blanc" (see chapter 1) and *Frankenstein* (see chapter 5) in this compendium – the world has no regard for the lives of humans. No wonder, then, that the Shelleys and Byron undertook a writing that fulfils the promise of ghost stories, tarrying with the lingering impressions of life after human life ends in post-apocalyptic last-man poems and novels.[8]

Last-man texts present something of an odd paradox, though, because, curiously enough, none of these texts is actually about a last man; they theorize instead what I have been calling extinctualism. Simply put, last-man texts cannot be about the last man, since last men do not, cannot, appear in these texts. The old man whom the unnamed man and boy meet in Cormac McCarthy's *The Road* (2006) encapsulates this paradox well when he asks them, "How would you know if you were the last man on earth?"[9] In truth, the theoretical last man could not know he was the last man. If the last man suspected he was the last man, he could never confirm it, could never scour the whole globe, everywhere and all at once, in order to assure his status. Confirmation of last-man status could only occur if the last man were omnipotent, omnipresent, and omniscient. But the last man would always exist, geographically and spatially, only where he is. Therefore he knows only the limit of his existence, his finitude. Hence, he could not also be omnipresent and omniscient, since he would have to be otherwise than himself if he were omnipresent and omniscient.[10] He would, in other words, need to exceed his own lastness in order to know that he was last. However, if somehow the last man could be omnipresent, omniscient, and omnipotent, then he would be God – not human at all, let alone the last of the last of them. Existentially speaking, from whichever direction, lastness is an epistemological and ontological paradox: for the last to know he or she were last, he or she would have to not know it. Only by not knowing one is the last can one be the last, which, in turn, means that one cannot be cognitively aware that one is the last. Not-knowingness, this inability to ever know for sure that one is the last, renders every one a last man or a last woman. Because to be alive means we might always become last, one of the conditions of life – arguably its primary condition – is that we are always, already, the last man or woman, already extinct. If that potential to become the last were not possible, it would mean that we were other than human, already dead, well past the point of lastness, and so not human any more. If, one day – the last day? – we were to become what we thought was the last man or the last woman, it is only because we have that potential, that knowingness of what a last man or a last woman is, and that is what allows us to reach the not-knowingness of last human status. Paradoxically, this last-human status, even though we can never know that we are the last human, is based on an epistemological reification, the certainty that we are the last human – lastness bred from our very existence. To put this in Derridean terms, it is the last man's conditional impossibility of unknowing that makes possible the very possibility of its knowingness.[11] We are, as I said at the outset of this book, not yet alive because we remain, epistemologically and ontologically, trapped within extinctualism. Lastness represents how the limit of life is extinction, even as this limit is what allows for life at all since we rely on it for the notion – the very idea of the idea – that we may live. We are always, already, last before we are last.

These romantic last-man texts are not about the last human then but rather, I think, about the political quandary of liberalism and conservativism that situates us within the last-human space that the post-apocalyptic sublime opens up for us to think within. As I argued in the previous chapter, Shelley's "Mont Blanc" provides a powerful example of the post-apocalyptic sublime. The mountain, Mont Blanc, existing independently of humanity, captures the world's potential infinitude while the mind contemplating the mountain remains limited by its own finitude. The post-apocalyptic sublime enwraps us in the temporal paradox that we can only grapple with the climate-change disasters hurtling at us in a fistful from the future if we accept our own finitude in relation to a world that might go merrily spinning on indefinitely once we are gone. Percy Shelley ultimately leaves us in a familiar posture, standing before the mountain, thoughts of our own possible extinction flowing through our heads, a useful mindset to have found given that it reintroduces us to the real world from our previous *Matrix*-like, Romantic apocalypticism that believed we are the centre of the world when, as Shelley demonstrates, we are not even, so to speak, necessarily part of *that* world.

Enter Mary Shelley's novel on post-apocalyptic politics. Her novels and stories abound with parables of extinction, human efforts to circumvent that eventuality with immortality cocktails and magical elixirs of eternal life, philosopher's stones, and references to the arcane writing of the alchemists Paracelsus and Agrippa. But no matter what fantastic forms or improbable proportions extinction and infinitude take in her work, she remains constantly interested in lastness, and particularly in lastness as the conditional that underlies life itself. Lastness, for Shelley, is a continuing condition that paradoxically prevents immortality because lastness signals, as we will see, finitude, a way of thinking beyond high Romantic dreams of eternal transcendence. By thinking life as finite, Shelley continues to theorize what Percy began – how to live on in the Anthropocene. Mary Shelley thinks no immortality is possible and that the future roundabouts us into the present permanently, a permanent present that halts conceptions of the future predicated on lastness, on extinctualism, the paradoxical belief that we are both doomed to extinction and immortal. This temporal paradox, like the paradox of last-man-ness, is what allows us, in a contretemps of perverse irony, to think and envision the future for the first time at the time of the last man, who is also the man who is not even there, not even last because he is neither extinct nor immortal.

In perhaps the most compelling instance of Romantic temporal irony, Shelley draws on classical and foundational Enlightenment discourses to rewrite the state of nature, theorized most prominently by Hobbes and Rousseau, as the very basis of the social contract, that which creates political order out of anarchic chaos. Because Hobbes and Rousseau depict humans roaming around in nature after all socio-political institutions have fallen, post-apocalyptic narratives like Shelley's novel refamiliarize us with ideas about the state of nature because they return us – and this is the temporal irony – to a state of nature we have never really left. We are not in the realm of allegory, a referential symbology keyed to the past (as Paul de Man has it), but in the landscape of irony, a temporal scramble of past, present, and future that can only speak in the present.[12] In other words, post-apocalyptic Romantic politics, with its display of ongoing libertarian and social-contract choices, have always been what we talk about when we talk about politics. In the hands of Shelley, the post-apocalyptic sublime crosshatches the grim reality in which we now live with a temporally ironic hope of a better tomorrow – but only, she says, if we establish a politics of unconditional hospitality with nonhuman life today.[13]

Picking up from the idea that extinction, as Percy Shelley's work shows us, is the very limit of life's "living on" in the here and now, post-apocalyptic Romanticism, as I have been arguing, is not allegorical, not a "what-if?" bit of science fiction taking place in the future, but a reality we always already inhabit.[14] This presentness coming from the future manifests in different ways, though. Byron's poem "Darkness" and Shelley's *The Last Man* both anticipate modern climatic fears about a post-apocalyptic, posthuman future, with varying outcomes: Byron's poem struggles to and ultimately cannot break free from the anthropocentric politics of Hobbes and Rousseau while Shelley, as I've said, envisions a politics anchored in the nonhuman. Byron hypothesizes a post-apocalyptic world in which "the rivers, lakes, and ocean all stood still / And nothing stirred within their silent depths" ("Darkness," lines 73–4), and institutes a climactic battle of political philosophies. It depicts what happens when libertarianism wins out over social collectivity: "War, which for a moment was no more / Did glut himself again: a meal was bought / With blood, and each sate sullenly apart / Gorging himself in gloom: no love was left" (74, lines 38–41). In Byron's poem we retain a belief in anthropocentrism that trumps any social, affective relations and that leads to war in a return to the state of nature as formulated by Hobbes and Rousseau. For Hobbes, life in the state of nature was "poor, solitary, nasty, brutish, and short," leading to a *bellum omnium contra omnes*, "a war of all against all."[15] Contra Hobbes, Rousseau posits a social-contract society that prevents any such war by constraining individual liberty to the collective constraints of the "general will."[16] That War "for a moment was no more" indicates a brief collectivity, an attempt to live together after the disaster of the sun's expiration, before Hobbesian state-of-nature anarchy raises its ravenous head again.

Byron's "Darkness," written in the torrential downpours of this year without a summer, has often been identified as the first last-man text (though this is not entirely accurate), the originator of both this genre and the post-apocalyptic genre more generally.[17] Yet, in keeping with the theorization of last-man-ness I outlined above, the poem does not feature a last man, but rather dwells in extinctualism, offering on the one hand survival and on the other hand an affirmation of its impossibility. For instead of a last man, "two / Of an enormous city did survive / And they were enemies: they met beside / The dying embers of an altar-place / Where had been heap'd a mass of holy things / For an unholy usage" (lines 55–60). Enemies, they enact a two-person dramatization of post-apocalyptic Romantic politics: humans must either make common cause or engage in bloody individualistic one-on-one decimation that leads, a death at a time, finally, to species death. The enormity of the city finds itself metonymically reduced to a two-person state – the pair are not just representative of but actually become survival itself, since at this point all other humans and creatures have died during civilization's decline and fall in the poem. This highly specific localization of the remnants of human survival, however, reveals the constitutive blind spot of last-man poems: the omniscient narrator who informs us of their survival signals that neither of the men is omniscient – therefore they cannot know they are last men. Rather than being a last-man poem, the text resolves here into a no-man extinctualism poem as "even of their mutual hideousness they died":

> The feeble ashes, and their feeble breath
> Blew for a little life, and made a flame
> Which was a mockery; then they lifted up
> Their eyes as it grew lighter, and beheld
> Each other's aspects – saw, and shriek'd, and died –
> Even of their mutual hideousness they died,
> Unknowing who he was upon whose brow
> Famine had written Fiend. ("Darkness," lines 62–9)

There is never a last man, only two men who cannot, perforce, be last. While their mutuality, though centred on their ragged, starved hideousness, might clue them in to the fact that a commonality exists that should be blown into life like the embers of the dying fire, they instead die of this mutual effacement. Symbolically their mutual death by look signals that the gluttonous War who emerges once institutional safeguards have crumbled continues his rampage; humans are unable to break free of their enmity as enemies, even if only to become frenemies, to save themselves. The poem presents a human species plunging itself into War after the post-apocalyptic world in which the species finds itself living initially holds out the olive branch of peace ("War which was for a moment was no more"). In some versions of the myth Byron draws on, when Prometheus, clutching fire, descends from the heavens to aid humans in maintaining their life, it became humans' choice how to use this fire. Fire can nurture or annihilate, in either its respiration or its aspiration, burn or burn out. In "Darkness," humans choose to let the fire extinguish itself (in McCarthy's *The Road*, the novel-sized version of this poem, humans continually ask others if they "are carrying the fire," a metaphor, in that book, for life itself). The "feeble fire" and their "feeble breath" adjectivally equate while the life-giving flame turns to ashes, the ashes of the planet itself as it burns out, fading away in flickers, as a result of humans' inability to covenant themselves into a mutual, conspiratorial circle ("conspiracy" means "to breath with"), those who use fire to give life rather than to take it. Byron's vision is Hobbesian in the extreme. But it is not just humans who must or can make common cause – the poem, like Shelley's *The Last Man*, seeks to move beyond anthropocentrism, but it can only do so via killing off everyone and everything, a vision that models neither survival nor living on nor even complete extinction since the speaker remains. It manifests extinctualism: we will die but cannot die because there are no last humans, only humans perpetually dying without ever becoming extinct. We will survive, it seems to claim, even while dying, while going extinct.

Whereas the "last" two men ironically are enemies who die of fire-lit faces full of inhospitable reciprocal loathing, a pale glimmer of how life might continue appears with a dog who holds to his covenant with his master:

> The meagre by the meagre were devour'd,
> Even dogs assail'd their masters, all save one,
> And he was faithful to a corse, and kept
> The birds and beasts and famish'd men at bay,
> Till hunger clung them, or the dropping dead
> Lur'd their lank jaws; himself sought out no food,
> But with a piteous and perpetual moan,
> And a quick desolate cry, licking the hand
> Which answer'd not with a caress – he died. ("Darkness," lines 46–54)

Except for the faithful-to-a-corpse dog, the other "dogs assail'd their masters," an indication of the broken social scene and the animal liberationist ideology that power both this poem and Shelley's *The Last Man*.

The dogs, free at last from domestic confinement, signal the overthrow of human sovereignty even more so than do the fall of religious institutions as seen above ("Where had been heap'd a mass of holy things / For an unholy usage") and the fall of governmental institutions that occurs early in the poem as "the thrones" and "the palaces of crowned kings ... were burnt for beacons" (lines 10–11). With the fall of nations and governments, War recurs in a Hobbesian fashion, with individuals, couched in their own solitude, running wild in anarchist fashion because they are unrestrained in this remix of the state-of-nature theorization. In direct opposition to War, who bellies up to the table at humans' invitation to gluttonize himself on their famished flesh and brittle bones, the dog "sought out no food," and this starvation diet, unlike the humans' cannibalistic carnality, separates him from War who heartily fills his ever-hungry stomach. Instead, the faithful dog models a new form of social contract that can bind living beings together in this kingdom of darkness: humans, rather than take the lead, should follow the lead of animals and form contracts without an anthropocentric axis chartering mutual commitments (a form of passivity without passivity). Yet despite this shredding of the anthropocentric contract, Byron's poem climaxes with climate change dealing a death blow to the whole world; the dead dog who refuses to carnalize the world and its inhabitants as flesh is just one more version of how darkness's nihilism steamrolls any hope glimpsed by the fiduciary social contraction the dog has invoked.

For Byron, looking out at the raging storm tamping on the window of the Villa Diodati in 1816 and penning "Darkness," human survival appeared unlikely, and extinction was perhaps preferable, if the poem's conclusion wherein darkness "she was the universe" is any indication of his thinking. Writing during the dread light that beat against the scaffold in this year, Byron, himself a faithful mourner of dead dogs (requiescat in pace, Boatswain), had not yet discovered how to combat the anthropocentric chains that put humans on a collision course to kill off the animals he viewed as so much more faithful than humans. As we will see in chapter 3, it is only in 1821, with his sly animal-rights agitator *Cain*, that Byron argues that only by giving up the sacrifice of animals can humans thwart their own intertwined extinctualism of self-cannibalism and self-sacrifice geared towards no purpose other than a circular self-regard.

While human extinction is certainly one (not terribly optimistic or useful) way to break anthropocentrism's dominant spell, Shelley surpasses the nihilism of Byron's poem and proffers a different solution for how to live in the ashes of a post-apocalyptic world, by showing us the philosophical outlines of a workable posthuman contract. As I have been theorizing it, post-apocalyptic Romanticism forces us to re-envision what human and nonhuman life will be in the face of potential human extinction. Shelley's *The Last Man* is fully aware, as Byron's "Darkness" is not, that anthropocentrism underwrites Romantic apocalyptic narratives and continues to bedevil us. In contrast, the novel embraces living in a post-apocalyptic world, a world its sees as a staging ground for thinking the future this world purports to represent, *because this world is actually our present*. *The Last Man* unmasks anthropocentrism, exposing it as a kind of confidence man who hoodwinks us into misunderstanding the finitude of human life, mistaking the present for the future (and sometimes vice versa), writing us into a bad science-fiction novel that is neither scientific nor fictional. Shelley's novel journals the ruins of human history in order to think hope from the paradox of the fact that we are always already extinct because of our lastness, the inescapable finitude of human life that we cannot face, its penumbral futures constantly outdistancing us, even as we must inevitably, as Shelley insists, come face to face with lastness in the present in order to live.

By setting its initial orienting sun on the hills of Cumberland, the novel mounts a full-scale assault on apocalyptic Romanticism, the symbolic and literal manifestation of a paradise, as in Wordsworth's "Prospectus" to *The Excursion*. As Shelley and her readers would have, we immediately associate Cumberland with an invocation of the Lake school poets Wordsworth and Coleridge, the former of whom explicitly sets his project up as apocalyptic, an attempt to marry the human mind to the natural world and achieve transcendence beyond this too sullied flesh. Shelley takes us far elsewhere, to shadowed skies and sickening human bodies, the human species' death rattle, its final expiration of oxygenated breath taken from the world it thinks it possesses. Almost. Lionel Verney remains alive, last-manning it supposedly to the novel's conclusion, though his ostensible survival is vastly complicated, as we will discover.

In these opening chapters Shelley drives her point home by making Lionel a shepherd roaming the Cumberland hills in what is a comically obvious jab at the Lake schoolers. Lionel, unlike the civilized Adrian, spends his days tripping the stereotypical Romantic fantastic, a savage character completely free from the constraints of society and, as it turns out, of humanity. "Before dawn," he recounts, "I led my flock to the sheep-walks, and guarded them through the day," even as, later in the evening, he left the sheep to the guardianship of his dog so that he could "rendezvous" with his "comrades … to the accomplishment of our schemes" (and it is worth noting that in this pastoral setting the dog can form a community with the sheep) (*The Last Man*, 17).[18] This lifestyle he characterizes as one that increases his "fresh love of freedom, and contempt for all that was not as wild and rude as myself" (18). The pastoral scenes depicted here herald Lionel as the very image of a Rousseauvian pre-socialized, pre-governed creature (not entirely dissimilar to the creature in *Frankenstein*) who is not yet human, per his own description that borrows the Enlightenment trope of "the brute": "my life was like that of an animal, and my mind was in danger of degenerating into that which informs brute nature" (18).[19] He is not just a Rousseauian depiction of the state of nature, however; he is also Hobbesian: "I continued my war with civilization" (19). Lionel represents both forms of state-of-nature political potentiality. It is only meeting Adrian, the representative of all that is good, kind, noble, and virtuous in the novel, that leads Lionel "to discover how brutish, savage, and worthless [he] had hitherto been" (28–9). This meeting seals the fate of apocalyptic Romanticism at one level in the novel's eyes, and Lionel leaves behind his "silly sheep" for "a nobler flock" revealed to him by Adrian, "a flock of new-born ideas," the imagination in its quintessential Wordsworthian Romantic incarnation (36). His exit from the lush and green hills and entrance into Adrian's wainscoted library, as we will see below, shifts the setting from the Romanticism of pastoral lyricism to the Romanticism of high imagination, which the novel will also decree a fool's paradise.[20]

In essence, the novel wipes out with one hand the pastoral fantasies of paradise that define so much of the Lake school poetry (as well as the Frye-Abrams-Bloom lineage of criticism that has forwarded and disseminated this way of understanding the Lake school), even while it simultaneously repurposes Lionel's apocalypticism as exclusively anthropocentric, a vague transcendental, imaginative potentiality shot through with utopian political power. Lionel tersely captures what his tutelage under Adrian's teaching instils in him: "I now began to be human" (29). It is at this point that Lionel, newly become human, confirms Aristotle's dictum that man is a political animal, and enters into politics as an ambassador before returning to play the role of aide-de-camp to Raymond and Adrian when the two enter the public arena. Lionel's transformation from a Rousseauvian savage to a Percy Shelleyan human will eventually come under fire in the novel as well, when Lionel finds himself exterminated by what I will call the novel's "black pastoral politics" that emerge once the plague strikes. Lionel's is a transition, ultimately, from one type of apocalyptic pastoral Romanticism to a political Romanticism that is no less anthropocentric.

The Last Man's parliamentary sections demonstrate how the politics of Shelley's time are anthropocentric and reinforce the accordant belief in human sovereignty over the Earth. While it might be easy for readers to dismiss or overlook this part of the book as merely an obvious roman à clef that serves primarily to set up the novel's real interest and captivating action – the plague, read either literally or allegorically, a social scourge or prefiguration of twenty-first-century biopolitics – the political debates and depositions in this section are vital to understanding how Shelley, in the later sections of the novel, targets and takes down humans' notions of their own sovereignty over the world and its inhabitants.[21]

Two political discourses dominate the debate in the first part of the novel: republicanism (which for convenience I will refer to as democracy) and monarchism, each position represented alternately by Adrian versus Raymond and then Ryland versus Raymond, even though Shelley, as I've said, critiques them as disguised forms of the same anthropocentric sovereignty. Shelley draws the contrast between Adrian and Raymond immediately once this latter Byron figure enters the novel under the banner of his celebrated valour and victory on the fields of battle in Greece (a momentary reversal of the real-life Byron's failure and fate). Meanwhile, Adrian, who is himself from an aristocratic family, just like Percy Shelley, whom he personifies as a kind of living cenotaph, has come to a different conclusion about the proper form of governance and seeks, contra his mother's wishes, "to introduce a perfect system of republican government into England" (44). In a judgment that is – we will see – superbly misleading hyperbole regarding Raymond and Adrian, we are told, "no two persons could be more opposite than Adrian and he" (44). However, both Raymond and Adrian are described in versions of anthropocentric points of view about the world. Raymond, on the one hand, was "emphatically a man of the world" who "could not always square his conduct to the obvious line of self-interest," and believes that society and nature are harnessed to his will: "he looked at the structure of society as but a part of the machinery which supported the web on which his life was traced. The earth was spread out as an highway for him; the heavens built up as a canopy for him" (44). Adrian, on the other hand, "felt that he made a part of a great whole" and "owned affinity not only with mankind, but all nature was akin to him; the mountains and sky were his friends; the winds of heaven and the offspring of earth his playmates; while he the focus only of this mighty mirror, felt his life mingle with the universe of existence" (45). Even though Raymond "held in supreme contempt the benevolent visions of the philanthropist" the keynotes sound the same in each description (45).

Raymond believes that the world exists only for him, without regard for anyone or anything else around him, a stance remarkably similar to the speculative-realist critiques of Kantian correlationism, which sees the subject's thoughts as the only real conduit to secure understanding of the world. Meanwhile Adrian appears to deviate from this correlationist circle but nonetheless narcissistically sees himself reflected back from the mirror of nature as well. Adrian finds "nature akin to him," rather than understanding it as a differentiated, multiplicity of diverse entities, what are otherwise termed "his playmates." More problematically still, for Shelley, Adrian fails to recognize his own finitude and thinks instead that "his life mingle[s] with the universe of existence." Whereas Raymond suggests that the world was created as an instrument for him to wield – the "heavens built for him" – Adrian's philosophy is actually much of a muchness with Raymond's; the philosophies are just developed from opposite ends of the cosmic spectrum. Raymond takes the universe as infinite, as a "highway" searing out into the vast unknown, an unknown that inflates human life (in this case his own) with the same infinite cosmic-highway lifespan. Life, for him, is a highway, and he wants to ride it all night long. Adrian, meanwhile, reverses in the other direction: he reduces the "universe of existence" to his own existence, making finite what is infinite (or potentially so), a life that, when ended, will take the whole world with it (this, it should be noted, is what Mary felt once Percy died). While it may seem that this detour into political wheel-spinning takes us far afield of the Romantic pastoral fields with which the novel opens, these abstract philosophies actually provide us crucial insights into discerning how their apparently duelling political beliefs intersect.

By showing us how the two competing philosophical views dovetail with and indeed engender the monarchist and democratic politics each man adheres to, Shelley reveals, later in the novel, that these politics amount in the end, the end of the human species, to the same irrelevant and insufficient creeds irrespective of their respective claims to differ. Both philosophies and political positions derive from and finally rely on the same axiological anthropocentrism as raison d'être. Raymond, who is seen by society, and conceives of himself, as a god-like figure throughout the book, encapsulates the very notion of anthropocentrism in his regal ambitions. But he also mistakenly views himself as exceeding the common herd of humanity. At the end of his speech in Parliament that clinches his monarchical desire, his "face was lit up to superhuman brilliancy" (61). He wants to be king because the king, like humanity of which he is the apotheosis, is the figure around which the nation and (hence from the nation's perspective) the universe turn. It is yet another versioning of Kantian correlationism, only this iteration hands humanity a sceptre and a crown and sits it down on a throne, fully investing it with the power of state to decree what is what and off whose shoulders a head should come. While on the surface Adrian's progressive reformist view of politics – to transform England into a democracy – rejects any monarch, it manages a feat less straightforward but no less pernicious in its correlationist contours. Adrian's proposed democratic reforms benevolently crown all humans monarchs, elevating each individual to be the sovereign around whom the world turns. Each individual is the world, a universe unto itself that, while subsisting in and inhabiting a larger world, nevertheless boomerangs around in a circular form of logic to equate humanity with the supreme being of the universe. When its campaign rhetoric is peeled away, such politics, while seemingly marquee billing itself in the novel as a kind of democratic utopianism, stands unveiled as a form of Hobbesian libertarianism, each individual become God, completely free from social constraints to indulge her selfish impulses.[22] Adrian will confirm this disguised Hobbesian libertarianism after the plague hits when he declares that he must "rule England in anarchy," which we must read as libertarianism par excellence, as the warring factions of the novel are motivated and deceived by selfishness despite Adrian's efforts to draw them back into socialized groupings that prevent warfare (255). Both versions of politics promote the same anthropocentrism that Shelley condemns.

Such is the tale of anthropocentric sovereign politics told by idiots in the novel (at one point Raymond, in a moment of perspicacity, refers to society as a collective of "madmen and fools"), a tale compounded by its ideologically delusive, paradisiacal Romanticism. Adrian specifically links his revolutionary approach to an environmental paradise to come, a kind of new Eden recast from the earth's ecology by the unbridled, awful power of humans. After he recovers from his near-death lovesickness inflamed by his broken heart for Evadne (who loves Raymond and will eventually die from that lovesickness), Adrian's paradisiacal plotting returns with a vengeance. "O happy earth," he exclaims, "and happy inhabitants of earth! A stately palace has God built for you, O man! and worthy are you of your dwelling!" (74). Adrian's words espouse the nitty-gritty paradox of lastness philosophy, although he does not realize the doomed portent of his yearned-for apocalyptic perfectionism. To him, "the will of man is omnipotent." By reading humanity as omnipotent, he metamorphoses humanity into a last man – and this is the real last man of the novel's title – again endowing humankind with God-like omni-qualities capable of sculpting the earth's raw material to humanity's ends (76). This will to power leads, in his mind, directly to paradise: "the choice is with us; let us will it, and our habitation becomes a paradise" (76). Raymond, when he finally does affix the crown on his head, instead of diverging from Adrian's Edenistic society as his opposite-day politics would seem to dictate he should, unexpectedly follows in Adrian's footsteps, trekking back into this imaginary garden. We are told that under Raymond's rule "the state of poverty was to be abolished" along with sickness, starvation, and inequality – the very things that Adrian wishes to remove from the world so that humanity may flourish everlastingly (106).

Post-implementation of Raymond's reforms, before they are aware of the airborne phantom menace heading to a theatre near them, Adrian declares, referring to these reforms, "Let this last but twelve months … and earth will become a Paradise. The energies of man were before directed to the destruction of his species: they now aim at its liberation and preservation. Man cannot repose, and his restless aspirations will now bring forth good instead of evil" (219). Unlike Rousseau, who thought that a return to a state of nature would (but never really could) result in a Nietzschean life beyond good and evil, Adrian's ambitions are more straightforwardly in keeping with goodness flourishing on earth once humanity's liberation from its own individualistic imperatives is achieved. But by liberating humans from these imperatives, Adrian's plan *actually* dissolves civil society, since society exists precisely to restrain individualist motivations like greed for the sake of the greater good. There is now no need for the democratic governance that he predicts with his liberationist theology, which means that, unexpectedly and paradoxically, Adrian's democratic reformist plan will return people to the very libertarianism that it wishes to transcend: the individual's freedom to make whatever choice they like, which is, again, one version of anthropocentrism writ large. Or, to put it differently, everyone becomes Raymond as he is during the period before he agrees to undertake Adrian's ostensibly utopian plans: a singular god, a human god, who rules the universe. The novel, in other words, finds both libertarianism and democratic social contractualism reducibly the same, for both politics simply replay anthropocentrism as the song of the earth, trumpeting the arrival of an everlasting human species forever piping on in a New Jerusalem. But this anthropocentric sovereignty over the earth is, the novel argues, ultimately a mirage, a human illusion, one that philosophically and materially collapses humanity from dust into dust, into not even an ash.

Lionel, as it turns out, is in many ways the very model of modernity's obtuseness produced by the correlationist model of mind and world. His narrative's thesis is to retreat imaginatively from the horror around him to which he bears witness. Opening his tale, he writes that it is his "imagination" that clothes the "fictitious" horrors of this tale of lastness in "ideality" to take "the mortal sting from pain" (7). Later, after the deluge of the plague, Lionel glimpses the deceptiveness inherent to apocalyptic Romanticism. It abandons dreamers in an ur-reality that cannot last more than a moment, cannot outlast humans' lastness: "for a moment I could yield to the creative power of the imagination, and for a moment was soothed by the sublime fictions it presented to me. The beatings of my human heart drew me back to blank reality" (200). Although drawn into the paradisiacal fictions of Adrian earlier in the novel, here, sitting at the crossroads of apocalyptic and post-apocalyptic Romanticism, Lionel begins to get his head out of the clouds, to show us how to use your illusion to question the reality that Adrian spins. In these passages he links "sublime fictions" with the "imagination," merging Burkean Enlightenment aesthetics with Adrian's high Romanticism, a combinatory dispelling of the latter with a reworking of the former. What Lionel invokes here, in other words, is the post-apocalyptic sublime that Percy Shelley so powerfully limns in "Mont Blanc" – and it is this form of the sublime that can dispel anthropocentric delusions. The post-apocalyptic sublime is the horror arising from the clash of the imagination with a world that is indifferent to, even unaware of, its presence, a horror that forces us to acknowledge our finitude and, correspondingly, that the world is not *for us* but *without us*. As I showed in my reading of Shelley's "Mont Blanc" in the last chapter, the classic Romantic division of subject and object, in which the object is correlated to the subject's mind, finds itself exposed as a fiction of the imagination. Aestheticizing the world is one vehicle for how the correlation between the mind and the nonhuman object occurs: the mind claims the object as phenomenologically and epistemologically constructed by it, since such constructions are, by their very nature, aesthetic in that they impart meaning to an object via their subjective experiences of it. As such, by turning around the illusion of paradise to question its own genesis in the crucible of its own creative mental fictions, Lionel torpedoes the principles of Adrian's aesthetic philosophy that underpin his pretentions to realist politics. The imagination in the novel, when confronted by the horrors of the plague, clothes the mind in an idealization of this sublime encounter that remakes it as a "sublime fiction."

Only Lionel's affect, the "beatings of [his] human heart," can about-face him away from the anthropocentric machinery of Burke's aesthetic terror and Wordsworth's autobiographical epics that obscure the world and return him to "blank reality," an ability to see the world as it is rather than how it is for us aesthetically (rather like the phenomenal way in which the world was obscured for Percy Shelley in the last chapter). Affect, as Joel Faflak and Richard C. Sha point out, has long been ignored and denigrated as a "low" form of Romanticism papered over by the "philosophical robustness" of high Romanticism fostered in the period by critics like Frye, Bloom, and McFarland.[23] Whereas Faflak and Sha find affect and aesthetics as "intimately, irrevocably, unassimilably imbricated," *The Last Man* resists such intimations of the affective and the aesthetic, differently depicting the imagination as a by-product of delusive human faith and arguing for the consequent abjuration of aesthetic Romanticism (6). The novel embraces instead the frightening reality of, simply put, reality. And this is the post-apocalyptic sublime, a realization that reality might be blank *for us* because all of our efforts to colour it trample over what ontologically exists outside of our phenomenal perceptions of a world that we claim our very perceptions create. Lionel exemplifies how affect works in the novel in the "sublime fictions" passage above. His "realization" occurs, not in the mind, which is a cruel deceiver, but at the level of his affect. In the novel the post-apocalyptic sublime converts (and this may seem obvious, but that is part of the whole point) the affect of horror and fear that lies outside of us into a human emotion, to make us feel it, rather than aestheticize it as Burke does.

But for all of post-apocalyptic sublimity's efforts to poke holes in utopian, apocalyptic, Romantic fictions that predict a future-to-come paradise, the disquieting irony of post-apocalyptic sublimity is not simply in its undoing of high Romantic themes but also in its insistent decoupling, as I have claimed above, of anthropocentrism (the idea that humans rule the earth) from sovereignty (the political structures that arise from human theorization of earthly rule). To this end, *The Last Man* engages in the broader political contest between Enlightenment legacies – conservative libertarian anarchism on the one hand and progressive social contractualism on the other – but it does so not to nominate one or the other as its champion but to show how human sovereignty becomes denuded of its paradisiacal clothing by the indifferent materiality of the world. The novel rejects both of these anthropo-politics because of the fundamental interchangeability of libertarianism and progressivism, as seen with Raymond's and Adrian's versions of these ostensibly contradistinctive politics. Like her mother, Mary Wollstonecraft, Shelley sketches a political vision more radical and interesting than those of Burke, Hobbes, Rousseau, or even Paine, whose theories are, after all, underwritten by exclusionary premises, the patriarchal and mansplaining templates of, variously (and with a great deal of crosshatching), classical conservativism and liberal humanism. Much like Steven Goldsmith, who explicates Shelley's deconstruction of patriarchal order in the novel, I track her deconstruction of it from the compatible, but opposite, direction of the nonhuman.[24] Uncovering this interchangeable nature of conservative and progressive politics that eventuate in a singular anthropocentric social contract, Shelley drafts in their place the philosophical tenets for a genuine posthuman contract, one that will recognize both human and nonhuman life as subjects of, and subject to, political calculation on a world already without us.

Once the novel kicks into plague-gear in book 2, *The Last Man* seemingly swerves its topical focus from Romantic, political, parliamentary theatre to the extinction of mankind brought about by an unstoppable and most-unwelcome plague while Adrian attempts to ensure humanity's survival even as Raymond, in appropriate Byron-like fashion, succumbs to the dissipations of excessive capitalism. But this section of the novel contains an even sadder commentary on how and why life in the Anthropocene must be reconceived: it is a life of moral bankruptcy and ethical indifference. The novel's twin theses illustrate this refusal of that typified life. Lionel captures one thesis in a subjunctive exordium:

> Who that knows what "life" is, would pine for this feverish species of existence? I have lived. I have spent days and nights of festivity; I have joined in ambitious hopes, and exulted in victory: now, – shut the door on the world, and build high the wall that is to separate me from the troubled scene enacted within its precincts. Let us live for each other and for happiness; let us seek peace in our dear home, near the inland murmur of streams, and the gracious waving of trees, the beauteous vesture of earth, and sublime pageantry of the skies. Let us leave "life," that we may live. (*The Last Man*, 218)

Lionel, still governed by Adrian's pastoral politics, continues to yearn for a Brexit from capitalism and a permanent staycation in paradise. His yearnings are signalled in the language of festivity, drawn by Mary no doubt from the carnivalesque tomfoolery and promiscuous sexscapades the Shelleys observed Byron engaging in when they visited him in Venice.[25] We might also hear, in "the world," the Wordsworthian echo of "The World Is Too Much with Us," of "getting and spending."[26] Theorizing life, Lionel bisects it, placing a Rousseauvian state of nature on one side and the hurly-burly bustle of cities and commerce on the other, a classic Romantic division of the country and the city.[27] His subjunctive, though, surpasses this simplistic Romanticism to capture one defining aspect of how to live in the end-times: we must abandon life as it now is in order to live because the life we have constructed sunders communities we have formed, similar to the duelling yet ultimately identical anthropocentric politics of Raymond and Adrian. We remain caught within a recapitulatory narcissism that not only kills us but prevents us from seeing the greater world in which we exist but are not alive. In reminding us of "the sublime pageantry" of the skies, Lionel frames the "life versus live" dilemma as more than just a return to paradise; it is, too, a confrontation with that which is real but separate from us. And yet, the novel will disagree with Lionel that "we must act," investing instead in a passivity without passivity (218).

The "life" that must be left behind, according to this first thesis then, is the choking life of pleasurable and convenient capitalism, the life of doing and action, suddenly manifest as the plague. Although we often read the plague's origins as mysterious, it is quite clearly sourced in the novel. It is said to originate in Constantinople, a city repurposed by Emperor Constantine as the capital of his Christian empire. The Emperor's rule was marked by his dissemination of his faith, transmogrifying the pagan excesses of the Romans into the hypocritical laity of European cosmopolitanism. The hedonism associated with paganism provides the plague's other source, neatly captured in Raymond's quotation from *Twelfth Night* in riposte to Adrian's expostulation against Raymond's dissolute drinking: "Dost thou think, because thou art virtuous, there shall be no more cakes and ale?"[28] Cakes-and-ale revelry is exactly what Raymond chooses when he abandons his protectorate after the plague strikes; he returns, in other words, to the very type of rampant carnal capitalism whose immorality seems to have invoked the plague in the first place. By linking the discourses of theism and hedonism, the novel squares the circle: moral rot and decay, from whichever direction, induces the plague, a kind of autoimmune deficiency in the social sphere brought about by ideological human delusion.

The novel's second thesis adds to Lionel's reminder of the post-apocalyptic division of the human and the world, by reorienting the novel in a posthuman, anti-anthropocentric, black-sun direction (indeed a black sun rises at one point in the novel). Lionel poses the happily apposite, posthuman question I make so much of in the introduction:

> Will the mountains remain unmoved, and streams still keep a downward course towards the vast abyss; will the tides rise and fall, and the winds

> fan universal nature; will beasts pasture, birds fly, and fishes swim, when man, the lord, possessor, perceiver, and recorder of all these things, has passed away, as though he had never been? (*The Last Man*, 412–13)

The novel answers this speculative-realist question with its black pastoral politics. Amidst the pristine, still-standing leftovers of human cities and rural dwellings, the humans who remain trudging along the roads are framed by their own irrelevance against the backdrop of these decisively now-useless exemplars of human handiwork. Those who remain have all essentially become Ramses II from Percy Shelley's "Ozymandias" (1818), only in this novel they are looking on their own works and despairing mightily. In answer to Lionel's question, the novel retorts that humans are not sovereign over the world, are not its shepherds and stewards, and that the world will, in fact, go on after humanity has been extinguished as a result of their choosing consumptive capitalism instead of a heedless hospitality of compassion for nonhuman life.

While its apparent character juxtapositions – Raymond as cakes-and-ale glutton and powermonger, and Adrian as empath and emperor of compassion – seem to reassert the differing governing styles possible in the plague time of book 2, the novel meanwhile begins to sketch out a carefully non-anthropocentric stance, further disavowing, in the process, the idea that humans are the masters of the world. In his "speculations," Lionel muses, "our minds embrace infinity." The novel disagrees with Lionel, though, because the speculations throughout have been more of the speculative-realist variety than the anti-realist ones of Raymond and Adrian, and these speculations materialize here concerning the issue of contingent time. The novel argues that mentally wrapping our arms around infinity proves hostile to human finitude since it stop-gaps our understanding of our true relation to the world with the fervour of religious fantasy and faith. Drawing infinity towards us correspondingly pushes finitude away and allows for the flourishing of a self-destructive ideology that requires a belief in the human species' eternality, our infinitude, on earth. As Adrian's unmerry group of plague survivors continues to dwindle and nowhere dwell, none of them can ever quite believe that their species is wandering its way to extinction. Even when the group is reduced to Adrian, Lionel, Clara, and a dog, they think about the planet and yearn to repopulate it. Lionel writes that "we call ourselves lords of the creation … masters of life and death, and we allege … that though the individual is destroyed, man continues for ever" (230). Elsewhere Lionel explicitly links this point to conservative ideology by quoting from Burke's *Reflections on a Revolution in France* (1790): "'the race of man assumed dignity and authority. It was then no longer the mere gardener of earth, or the shepherd of her flocks; 'it carried with it an imposing and majestic aspect; it had a pedigree and illustrious ancestors; it had its gallery of portraits, its monumental inscriptions, its records and titles'" (*The Last Man*, 230). This big-headed masters-of-the-universism has a further Burkean, anti-post-apocalyptic consequence: "we glory in the continuity of our species, and learn to regard death without terror" (230). Terrorless, the inhabitants of earth, who see themselves as monumentalized in regal portraiture and marble busts – art as immortality – cannot develop methods of living on, because being human goes hand in hand with the never-arrival of finitude. Thinking like and as the human species is an idea that the novel reveals as belied by its own premise: it is the human species conceptualizing itself as a human species that leads to human extinction. Thinking like a species, in other words, proves horrifyingly circular: both the cause and the solution (to borrow what Homer Simpson once said of beer) of all of life's problems. In this sense, Burkean politics refute and approve Burkean aesthetics and vice versa in the same circular firing squad logic.[29]

For the novel thinks that being terrorless, shielding ourselves from the horror of post-apocalyptic sublimity, represents a significant problem for the inhabitants of earth because it is ultimately correlationist. Refusing to face reality disallows developing methods of living on, of dealing with the present, as long as being human goes hand in hand with the never-arrival of an infinite future in which the human species thrives. A climate-change scenario in the novel illustrates how the characters' beliefs are at odds with the novel's thinking. Having been stuck in England, huddling against the freezing chill that confirms winter is always coming, Adrian and company decide that it is time to migrate to warmer, southern climes. Lionel, watching the children bound before him, "pursuing the deer, or rousing the pheasants and partridges from their coverts," suddenly imaginatively uncovers and announces what he calls "the secret" (312). When pressed about this secret, he describes "our gloomy winter-life, our sordid cares, our menial labours" before revealing this epiphanic secret, which is that the north, with its chill climate, imperils their ongoing survival prospects. Here the secret reveals itself as another instance of revelation (*apocalypsis*): "we must seek some natural Paradise, some garden of the earth, where our simple wants may be easily supplied, and the enjoyment of a delicious climate compensate for the social pleasures we have lost. If we survive this coming summer, I will not spend the ensuing winter in England; neither I nor any of us" (312). Lionel assumes that the southern climates (the direction in which he says they will head) will prove more amenable to their frost-benumbed, enfeebled human constitutions. Yet, and it will prove so in the novel, this is a stunning assumption because migration to the burning suns of the south merely exchanges one unsustainable climate for another that will eventually turn to winter even if that winter proves mild. Seasons change. By recurring to apocalyptic Romanticism, a quest for a paradise on earth, Lionel's reasoning rests on the same anthropocentric idée fixe that underlines Adrian's and Raymond's disguised mutuality of philosophical political thought. Lionel thinks that humans can either control or escape the seasons, ignoring that the earth's seasonal variation depends not on the orientation of humans on the planet but on a cyclic process divorced from human constitutions and dispositions altogether. Like the others, Lionel continues to be bound by correlationist thought processes.

Their pilgrimage to what they see as hospitable climates highlights how the post-apocalyptic sublime begins to rewrite hospitality, for in their haste to continue onward into hopefully elongating human life, believing still in the infinitude of the species, Adrian and company abandon nonhuman members in favour of their newly made, changing climate human covenant. Lionel catalogues a menagerie that only needs an Egyptian crane to do the real-life Byron proud:

> There were many dear friends whom we must not leave behind, humble though they were. There was the spirited and obedient steed which Lord Raymond had given his daughter; there was Alfred's dog and a pet eagle, whose sight was dimmed through age. But this catalogue of favourites to be taken with us, could not be made without grief to think of our heavy losses, and a deep sigh for the many things we must leave behind. The tears rushed into the eyes of Idris, while Alfred and Evelyn brought now a favourite rose tree, now a marble vase beautifully carved, insisting that these must go, and exclaiming on the pity that we could not take the castle and the forest, the deer and the birds, and all accustomed and cherished objects along with us. "Fond and foolish ones," I said, "we have lost for ever treasures far more precious than these; and we desert them, to preserve treasures to which in comparison they are nothing. Let us not for a moment forget our object and our hope; and they will form a resistless mound to stop the overflowing of our regret for trifles. (*The Last Man*, 327–8)

Whereas earlier, in a rebuke to apocalyptic poetics, Lionel's affect drives away fictional constructs written by the mind, at this point in the novel nonhuman affect confronts Lionel. Their animal companions with whom they live in this embowered Eden are reduced, on the one hand, to "trifles" and, on the other, to "nothing." The former is at least something; the latter not. While the children well up with tears, Lionel shines in the high apocalyptic Romantic line, asserting an ontological privilege inherent to humans in opposition to their friends, the animals. Lionel's heartlessness pointedly contrasts to the out-of-the-mouths-of-babes vocalization of the children. They are not giving voice to accidental wisdom, as the bromide usually goes, but rather to intentional feeling of a compassion that will become the driver of the novel's final arc: how to feel for what is nonhuman, how to move beyond the limits of anthropocentric speciesism and recognize an egalitarian community of creatures.

To dispel these anthropocentric speciesist myths about human sovereignty, the novel depicts the earth continuing placidly on as humans perish, while animals now peacefully populate the empty city streets and magnificent monuments of human hubris. When Adrian, Lionel, and the remaining children visit St Paul's Cathedral, they find that "birds, and tame animals, now homeless, had built nests, and made their lairs in consecrated spots" (332). But animals contradict Lionel's assessment; they are not homeless; quite the contrary, they have found homes free from the yoke, the whip, and the oven. Sovereignty's deconstruction intermittently continues:

> Troops of dogs, deserted of their masters, passed us; and now and then a horse, unbridled and unsaddled, trotted towards us, and tried to attract the attention of those which we rode, as if to allure them to seek like liberty. An unwieldy ox, who had fed in an abandoned granary, suddenly lowed, and shewed his shapeless form in a narrow door-way; every thing was desert; but nothing was in ruin. And this medley of undamaged buildings, and luxurious accommodation, in trim and fresh youth, was contrasted with the lonely silence of the unpeopled streets. (*The Last Man*, 332)

One can almost see Nietzsche, another thinker of last-man powerlessness, running forth in sacrificial solidarity with the liberated horses.[30] Liberty's lesson, taught here by the horse, is one of unbridling and unsaddling, of getting down off the animal's back, literally and ontologically, of following the horse's lead in a gesture of radical democratization on "the unpeopled streets." *Demos* of course means "people," like the Demogorgon of Percy Shelley's *Prometheus Unbound* in the previous chapter, and yet here we can begin to feel the impact of post-apocalyptic sublime irony. Sovereignty has become delocalized, spreading out to the now unenslaved animals who "people" the clear streets and reheat capitalist leftovers as a hearty meal – entirely unlike War in Byron's

"Darkness," which masticates incessantly on humans and nonhumans alike. The animals roaming the ruins of society represent the telos of capitalism's natural timeline, culminating in humankind's eschaton.

Rewinding in the novel to the now-dead Raymond and his treatment of horses and dogs further presses home the novel's promotion of radical democracy by means of a *via negativa* on the road to Constantinople. Upon Raymond's approach to the empty city, "his very horse seemed to back from the fatal entrance; his dog, his faithful dog, lay moaning and supplicating in his path – in a moment more, he had plunged the rowels into the sides of the stung animal, who bounded forward, and he, the gateway passed, was galloping up the broad and desart street" (198). Exhibiting a witch-like sixth sense, the horse and dog seek to prevent Raymond from his oncoming fate. The horse literally wants him to hold his horses and not enter the city. Raymond, unfaithful to his dog (who recalls the dog of Byron's "Darkness") and unreflectively accustomed to animals' unthinking supplication, does not heed his horse and instead wounds him with the cutting rowels on his spurs, forcing the horse to action. Animals are faithful and true; humanity, faithless and false. This fiduciary animal rule holds shortly thereafter when Lionel searches the city for the never-returned Raymond and discovers, just like the dog in "Darkness," "the dying dog of Raymond crouched beside the mutilated form of its lord," the language of lordship a pointed irony in the usual sense since it is Raymond's claim to sovereignty that has led to his death. Contrastingly, the dog's fidelity deconstructs such an undemocratic "demos"-inflected notion of human mastery (206).

Early in the novel Lionel asks, "Could England indeed doff her lordly trappings, and be content with the democratic style of America?" (222). It can, Shelley's novel answers, but only by flensing the best parts of social-contract egalitarian democracy while simultaneously evacuating it of its mind-world correlationist anthropocentrism. Shelley thus contrasts an ethics of social-contract care – represented, at first, by Adrian's group – to the war-obsessed libertarianism of the novel's late-appearing, unnamed false prophet – whom we could call "Trump" – and his anarchist acolytes whose Hobbesian *bellum omnium contra omnes* mission statement foregrounds an individualistic nihilism that grinds out all life. Lionel describes the imposter prophet as a "selfish" man who "refuses not to adopt any means, nor awaken any passion, nor diffuse any falsehood, for the advancement of his cause," a cause that we learn is … himself (386). Like the "metaphysical disquisitions" and "utopian fictions" that Lionel and Adrian will shortly condemn as divorced from reality, conservatism or libertarianism appears here as dissociated from reality, an upside-down dystopian version of utopia mobilized to garner individual power (431). In this ideological contest, Hobbesian anarchy is felled at the hands of Adrian's Rousseauvian principles: for Rousseau, a social contract means alienating individual rights by vocal assent in favour of gaining rights conferred by electing wise and savvy leadership – in this case Adrian – that reflects individual self-sacrifice for the greater good (this is the "greater will").[31] Within the forged links of such a covenant, war becomes impossible since individual passion is given over; indeed, Adrian prevents, again and again, war. In articulating Adrian's ethos, Lionel defines the core of Romantic, post-apocalyptic, democratic politics: it is "kind, compassionate, soft," horizontal rather than vertical, veridical and affective rather than its antonym, imaginative, a continued rejection of Lake school poetics and politics (29). Indeed, we see early in the novel that Adrian must be drawn away from Windsor, where he spent his time caring for wounded partridges.

But even the apparent valorization of Adrian proves illusory. Adrian denies liberty to his horses, which he keeps riding to death despite bearing witness to the liberated horses in the cities, and thereby he differentially replays the selfishness of the prophet's faction that exists only for its own internecine, self-defeating investment in human dominance. It is another instance of the irreducibility of libertarianism and social-contract care. Adrian's final condemnation in the novel arrives when the sea takes his life in a raging tempest. His rule is "kind, compassionate, soft," but not kind, compassionate, and soft enough, as it turns out, since it fails to relinquish the speciesist correlationism that undergirds sovereign theories of democratic rights-based politics. Instead, Adrian's death marks the novel's plea for decoupling sovereignty from anthropocentrism, which will consequently allow for alternative modes not only of thinking but also of living, of contracting to live on with the creatures whose own living on humans severely curtail in their biopolitical efforts to elongate their species' life every day – which incidentally is the main driver of climate change. In contrast, Lionel, so often read as a hapless, uninteresting droid more than eclipsed by the giant personalities of the novel's Byron and Shelley avatars, emphasizes just how compassionate compassion must be. Late in the novel, when a male goat tries to gore him, Lionel has a chance to crush the goat but abstains even if the consequence might be his own death. Lionel's actions reflect a new kind compassion, which tracks with Derrida's concept of hospitality – a radical, unconditional opening to the other.

For Derrida hospitality is at the heart of the law, of justice, of rights, of politics, because it paradoxically breaches and transcends law, justice, rights, and politics in its fundamental deconstruction of these concepts.

Derrida reads the etymological ambiguity of hostis, which means both "host" and "hostage" in Greek, as shorthand to show how hospitality conceptually and practically maintains the irreducibility of hospitality when the stranger (xenos) or foreigner arrives on the threshold (limen) of the host's door. The stranger becomes both host and hostage because she is, at first, the hostage of the host, but, in being hostage, also hosts the host as hostage, a classic Derridean deconstructive double bind. Arriving on the threshold and asking, implicitly or explicitly, for hospitality, the stranger has built-in expectations, and the host is in turn expected to give hospitality and is held hostage by the laws of hospitality. How, then, Derrida asks, can one think hospitality in this ceaseless whirligig of hostage-taking and host-taking? How, moreover, does one offer hospitality – that is giving freely, even giving oneself – when hospitality is always already caught in an economy of the gift and reciprocity which, as Derrida notes, is not then a freely given gift of hospitality but only meeting a demand? In answer, Derrida writes that,

> The law of hospitality, the express law that governs the general concept of hospitality, appears as a paradoxical law, pervertible or perverting. It seems to dictate that absolute hospitality should break with the law of hospitality as right or duty, with the "pact" of hospitality. To put it in different terms, absolute hospitality requires that I open up my home and that I give not only to the foreigner … but to the absolute, unknown, anonymous other, and that I give place to them, that I let them come, that I let them arrive, and take place in the place I offer them, without asking of them either reciprocity or even their names.[32]

To be hospitable in the absolute sense – and so what hospitality claims to mean – would require the giving of oneself to the stranger entirely, without question, without regard, without condition, without even a name, remaining oneself an absolute stranger. To be hospitable, in the sense that hospitality itself means, would break with hospitality, would break the reciprocity inherent in the economy of host and hostage.[33] One cannot even ask a name, for that too would be a give and take and not therefore an unconditional gift; it would unmask the stranger's anonymity, her very strangeness on which hospitality depends in order to be hospitable. In its paradoxicality, its auto-deconstruction, as Derrida says, "the law of absolute hospitality commands a break with hospitality by right, with law or justice as rights" since hospitality serves as the basis for law and rights and for doing justice to the other.[34] But the only way to do justice to the other is through this unconditionality of hospitality, which, as Derrida points out, is not yet possible, because we have yet to think and enact hospitality in the interstices of the paradox of a hospitality that can only exist where it does not yet exist. Hence, justice does not yet exist, and nor does any government of laws supposedly predicated on justice, on doing justice to the other.

Kate Singer brilliantly argues that affect in the novel is a type of a figural materiality that shape-shifts bodies from human to plant to animal to object in new iterations of posthuman configurations, and that affect intervenes to shift hospitality to the unconditional as well.[35] Lionel, now believing himself alone on earth beside(s) the animals, solemnly declares to them, "I will discipline my sorrowing heart to sympathy in your joys; I will be happy, because ye are so" (459). Affectively speaking, Lionel's heart can become happy because of the bounding affect of the animals that perforates his body with a feeling he does not possess. "I am not much unlike to you," he says, "nerves, pulse, brain, joint, and flesh, of such am I composed, and ye are organized by the same laws" (459). The word "laws" refers to Lionel's belief in the natural law of the anatomical and biological composition of human and animal bodies, but it also signals the juncture that affective materiality shares with the social law of hospitality, and so with justice.

When Lionel stumbles upon the family of goats, it moves him into a zone of hospitable enactment that finalizes the novel's transition into thinking posthuman justice freed from anthropocentric sovereignty. Once the billy goat, protecting his family from the perceived threat of this stranger, charges him, Lionel suffers a nasty fit of self-pity that provokes a feeling of rage before he "snatched up a huge fragment of rock" with which he "would have crushed [his] rash foe" (459). While from Lionel's perspective the goat appears as a stranger invading and seeking to damage his bodily space, he also realizes the violence of his action and hurls the rock away, prepared to be gored and maimed and possibly to die. The goats, "aghast," gallop "back into the covert of the wood," and Lionel, his "heart bleeding and torn" from "the violence of bodily exertion," runs away too in order "to escape from [his] miserable self" (459). Peter Melville draws our attention to this passage as a scene invested in hospitality. Following Anne Mellor, who finds the novel a staging ground for Mary Shelley's complex thoughts about the domestic family, Melville claims that it is "the domestic metaphor [Lionel identifies the goats as mother, father, and kid] and its humanizing effects that guarantee the tragic results of the encounter" (147). For Melville these tragic results are a return to the human self: "if this scene begins with Lionel's benevolent desire to be hospitable to animal others, then it ends with the goats generously bestowing upon Lionel a great lesson for living in a world without other subjects: others rendered as objects (including goats and mirrors) are but reflectors of the subject's other selves, its humanity, its inescapable consciousness."[36] This reading, while astute, sees the scene in anthropocentric terms that do not fully capture the larger implications of how hospitality functions in this scene. If the goats reflect back, like mirrors, no more than Lionel's humanity, then this reflection is not hospitality – which, after all, others the host and the guest – but a return to the narcissism that lies at the origin of the human subject's irrepressible identification of self with self and the self's differentiation from the other. As Lionel says, "I ... sought to escape from my miserable self," not to find recuperative repair within narcissism's bubble (459).

If we track the movement of Lionel's action (and inactions) in the passage, we can see how it parallels the economy of hospitality before, indeed, inhospitably deviating from hospitality's classical structure, as explicated by Derrida, into "pure hospitality" (or, in Melville's marvellous rephrasing, a "hospitality-to-come"). Once Lionel spots the goats, his first move is to proffer a gift: "I gathered a handful of fresh grass, and held it out" (459). It is only at this moment, when the mother shields the kid that "timidly withdrew," that the male goat braces to charge and wound or kill Lionel (459). As we saw above when the host becomes hostage, hospitality always contains within its economy hostility or violence since the host, to be truly hospitable, must be able to be hospitable, to offer gifts, to those who would do him harm. Indeed, for Derrida, hostility is inescapable and necessary for hospitality to be. But at the same time, it is hostility that, for Derrida, makes hospitality impossible since any gift-giving is impelled by necessity and expectation, and in this fashion the host and guest become hostages of each other – another form of violence.[37] Lionel, as we have seen, finally picks up a rock, intending to meet the goat's charging violence with his own aggression, becoming the hostage in this turnaround to the goat's host even as the goat is the guest become enemy intending to invade, literally, Lionel's personal space, his body, with his horns. In dropping the rock, in giving himself over to potential death, Lionel sidesteps this violent exchange that makes hospitability so inhospitable.

With his quick mental footwork, Lionel gives a Derridean gift without a gift, the incalculable gift that evades the circle of gift and debt that hospitality itself has previously been unable to think. That the goat stops his charge in the scene – for reasons unknown to us – stages how radical inhospitable hospitality works. Face to face with the stranger, with the absolute other who, it turns out, is not like him, Lionel gives himself over with no hope of return payment – if he dies, no reciprocity is possible, nor is it possible for him to receive any beneficial exchange with the goat, from his perspective. The unconditional hospitality by which humans are unable to live – as seen in the various political machinations up to this point in the novel – only emerges as visible in a post-apocalyptic context that ironically reveals (*apocalypsis*) what hospitality cannot reveal: the posthuman. Hence, Lionel says that he "will not live among the wild scenes of nature, as "the enemy of all that lives," because he realizes that nature belongs to the strange beings unlike him for whom humans must be willing to sacrifice themselves in order to give up their anthropocentric notion of what "lives" and to enter a posthuman sphere of "living on." Rather than re-scripting him in the primal scene of narcissistic self-satisfaction in the self's self-enclosure, Lionel's hospitable inaction in action evacuates human sovereignty of human power and prescribes a passivity without passivity that accepts human finitude, a world in which humans turn to not only care but gift their lives for the finitude of others that are nonhuman and totally alien. In this scene, ethics, responsibility, and justice arise from an encounter with the other, the other that is nonhuman.

As part of this new theorization of hospitality, the novel reminds us that contingency, as Meillassoux argues, structures all life, a reminder that helps us to think outside of our finitude to what comes, to invoke Meillassoux's title, "after finitude." In an earlier passage in the novel Shelley sketches a version of an aleatory life that shares much with what Meillassoux terms "the necessity of contingency." As I laid it out in my introduction, according to Meillassoux, since scientific law obeys what he calls "factiality," the principle that all things are facts but that there is no reason why things should be one way or another (we can think, as we did in the introduction, of Newton's theory of gravity being overridden by Einstein's relativity, itself disputed by quantum physics), he concludes that the only truly fundamental necessity to the world is contingency, the dictum that anything can happen at any time, however unlikely or wild, since things are only factial rather than true, and this must, perforce, allow for the radically unexpected to occur. Scientific laws even are subject to contingency; they can change at any time, just as any law can. Furthermore, given that contingency governs the world, then it follows, he writes, that even contingency can become contingent, replaced suddenly with the arrival of an ultimate other who is, in his example, a god-to-come who does not yet exist.[38]

Similar sentiments are at play when Lionel reflects on the vanishing state of humankind: "Sudden an internal voice, articulate and clear, seemed to say; – Thus from eternity, it was decreed: the steeds that bear Time onwards had this hour and this fulfilment enchained to them, since the void brought forth its burthen. Would you read backwards the unchangeable laws of Necessity?" (*The Last Man*, 399). Lionel, in accordance with the notion of contingency, acts as if there is a deity who rules over the world, even if said deity is only now manifesting itself in his head despite his question immediately prior to this ("Did God create man, merely in the end to become dead earth in the midst of healthful vegetating nature?" [398]). Although he seems to believe in God, he still feels the necessity of imagining one in the form of the nameless voice in his head who he knows to be imaginary. In fact, he next names this voice as "unchangeable … Necessity," which is surely ironic given that he means that, as a result of this unchangeable Necessity, humankind proves contingent to the plant, and the planet to "vegetating nature," to "earth." Calling Necessity "Omnipotent," Lionel acknowledges the paradox of his lastness. He is not himself omnipotent but contingent so he can never know his last-man status (though he has not yet come to view himself as the last man in the novel) because of the infinitude of this Necessity that is "eternal" and "changeless" and with "busy fingers sittest ever weaving the indissoluble chain of events" (399). Necessity, pricking out events on the universe's tapestry with grand indifference to human life, underlines human contingency. To use Lionel's pronoun, it also underlines her own absolute contingency because anything can happen, including unexpected extinctions due to the decisions of humans to capitalize on the earth's resources and their own Raymondistic hedonism to induce plagues and climate change – unintended consequences that disprove anthropocentric absolutism. Because necessity and unchangeable laws are contingent, Lionel achieves an epiphany that will bear out in the novel's closing pages: "yet since what is, must be, I will sit amidst the ruins and smile. Truly we were not born to enjoy, but to submit, and to hope" (399). Although he evokes a belief in the absolute of "what is" here that appears to contradict the novel's belief in contingency, Lionel gestures to humankind's insignificance in the face of a world that has reduced society to "ruins." This contradiction is yet one more example of the novel's paradoxical irony – it undercuts Lionel's belief even while his thoughts are being expressed. Hopeless, he sits and smiles amidst the evidence of his own contingency. He thus gives voice to the thesis of *Romantic Revelations*: hope arises only from its ruin, from hopelessness.

Accepting reality for what it is allows Lionel to relinquish anthropocentrism and discover and nurture hope, fanning its ember to roaring life, as the last two enemies in "Darkness" could not. Twice he realizes the mind-world split and steps outside of correlationism: once when Adrian is still alive and once when Lionel is in his lonely thereafter. On the former occasion, though, Lionel cannot fully internalize this knowledge. While he and Adrian talk of "metaphysical disquisition," "fiction," utopian worlds, and "the workings of one particular mind," Lionel comes to see these as "wandering from all reality … in self-created errors" (431). This recognition fittingly encapsulates Shelley's dismissal of high Romanticism's human imagination that veils reality from our sight, much as we witnessed it do in the previous chapter as Percy Shelley stood gazing agog at Mont Blanc. In its place Lionel discovers that human eschatological end times are near while "time held on its accustomed course": "still and for ever did the earth roll on, enthroned in her atmospheric car, speeded by the force of the invisible coursers of never-erring necessity" (431). Yet this acceptance does him little good until he chooses a new form of hospitality in his encounters with animals. On the second occasion that Lionel gives up on anthropocentrism, he observes "a herd of cattle" "untended" and learns the final lesson that the post-apocalyptic sublime has to teach him, that "this is the earth; there is no change – no ruin – no rent made in her verdurous expanse; she continues to wheel round and round, with alternate night and day, through the sky, though man is not her adorner or inhabitant" (459). In answer to Lionel's earlier question, the earth does not need humanity to survive, and neither do the persecuted animals whose covenants remain intact and who retain "each their mate – their cherished young, their home." Lionel can only watch in misery and dismay and wish he were like them, not the last man but simply one creature among the earth's community of many. Amidst the hopeless ruins, here is hope.

The full irony of last-man-ness emerges from this hope: only bereft of other humans can Lionel appreciate modes of living not centred on anthropocentrism and sovereignty. Lionel's ontological belief in his last-man-ness allows this decentring. What Shelley reminds us of is that, in Romanticism and modernity, social-contract politics remain circumscribed within modes of discourse, of knowing, of being, of social norms, that frame such politics as an exchange between two or more people. Or of a give and take as an emancipatory politics driving towards equality. But, as Romantic post-apocalypticism shows, for social-contract ethics to exceed the traditional limitations imposed on them by heteronormative, anthropocentric, Western social power relations and biopolitical imperatives, these ethics must think through the complexities of hospitality, of duty, of gender, of the gift, of sexuality, of power, of even equality, of, in short, any type of economy that inscribes them in a reciprocal circle that endlessly circles itself. The type of social contract that Shelley models does not require reciprocity but is instead purely gifted, purely given without sense of preservation, like Lionel offering up his life. In effect, undoing the economies of social-contract exchange, learning to become hospitable, requires eschewing a social contract based on what some environmentalists call biocentricism – a position in which all species are considered equal – in favour of a focus on the other without expectation of benefit. It would mean allowing for difference, respecting difference, without wishing for difference to be different, what it would be if it were different, the same – what Lionel can finally not do by joining the gamboling families of animals whose home is the earth.[39] Consequently, he sails off alone, with only a dog who was unable to enjoy his newfound liberty and instead remained steadily fulfilling his shepherding role for his dead master.

In this sense, contra Andrea Haslanger, who does not think that Shelley's "cosmopolitanism is one in which nonhuman animals inherit the earth" but rather "that the novel's investment lies on the side of human survival," the novel is clear that human survival is only possible if humans give up on any notion of it, if they give over their lives in this passive non-act that respects and accepts difference.[40] Accepting difference, between human and animal, human and world, human and human, human and vegetable, is not a reciprocal act, then, but a deconstruction of the social contract as interchange, of what Rousseau calls self-love. But as Shelley sees it, to overcome this egocentricism we must relinquish self-love, accept an indifference to self, become hospitable, as a way of paradoxically learning how to die in order to learn how to live, with ourselves and with others, in the Anthropocene. This is why the novel opens with the scene of humans finding Lionel's story written on the Sibylline Leaves: Lionel was, indeed, not the last man, and humans have lived on once they, like Lionel, accept difference, accept their role as agents of a passivity without any passivity.

Shelley's stance limns a posthuman account of life in the Anthropocene that evades correlationist thought that tracks with and significantly and definitively exceeds Derrida's "democracy-to-come." The temporal irony evidenced by Mary Shelley's novel offers an alternative to correlationism when considered alongside Derrida's notion of *l'avenir*, or "living on," that I discussed in the introduction and the opening pages of the previous chapter. As Derrida thinks it, living on consists of the impossible future that can and does at each moment always unexpectedly arrive because it must happen at the moment after it happens, after it arrives. Owing to this contingency, living on structures the present, *is* the present. This temporal concept is also indicative of the temporal succession of the trace structure wherein each moment, so to speak, lives on in the next since each is always passing away into a future already passed. Derrida's trace, an absence that is not an absence, or a space that is not a space, is what subsists or occurs between these moments. Temporal succession is thus living on. Derrida sees life, specifically in the *différance* of contingent temporality, much akin to Meillassoux's own working out of the arche-fossil. These paradoxes of Romantic irony open onto Derrida's democracy-to-come, a hoped-for, still-to-be-defined democracy of the impossible future, something always to come, unexpected and impossible, the ultimate other or stranger arriving on the threshold of hospitality, leading to justice in and as democracy. In Shelley's Romantic post-apocalyptic articulation, however, this democracy-to-come does not necessarily mandate human sovereignty and rights, and thus she advances this concept beyond Derrida's own, which remains locked within a kind of Levinasian blind spot of anthropocentrism where animals are concerned despite Derrida's own attempts to traduce Levinas. Shelley develops living on as what it means to live, not as survival, a biopolitical bare life (remaining alive after disaster), but as living in the presentist time that follows from what cannot and does not follow: the future, alongside nonhuman life, without regard for self.

Nor is this a foreclosure on the future and an evacuation of meaning from hope as in Lee Edelman's no-futurism of queerness's nihilism, still less an embrace of the nihilism of Ray Brassier's anti-speculative philosophy.[41] Edelman wants to fight the future by replicating the present. On Shelley's account of temporality that is not possible. Either such promulgation depends on a future stabilized by its linearity on Chronos's wristwatch, whereas, here, for Shelley, no future is possible because there is no future because it is already here, in each moment, its very possibility an impossibility-to-come already present.

By thinking within the temporal vertices of futurist impossibility, Mary Shelley refuses to allegorize her deconstruction of sovereignty, instead marking it out, via the post-apocalyptic-sublime severance of subject and object, as here, now, before right now, yesterday, today, an irony of our own political assumptions and eschatological blindness that can no longer be ignored. Shelley's deconstruction of anthropocentrism's fictionality does not place us outside of "the human," or of politics as a strictly human affair, but rather reorients us to the world we live in, a world of objects and beings, things and language, ourselves and others. Similarly, Shelley's fabulistic post-apocalyptic state of nature establishes the nonhuman as central to a posthuman social contract but does so by taking account of not only the discursive formation of the polis but also the material existences that intrude, whether we like it or not, into the social, just like Lionel discovers on his walkabout through Europe, meeting with its new denizens, cows, sheep, horses, goats, birds, and dogs, not to mention creeping ivy and bounteous greenery. The final irony of Shelley's post-apocalyptic critique of the social contract, then, is that Lionel is not the last man, since we are all already, from this future-to-come that is the present, last men and women owing to the contingency of our own shortlivedness in the face of an indifferent world.

Mary knows, as Percy did, that extinction is bound within our very being, the condition that makes human life possible. But unlike Percy, for whom extinction also actualized the imagination, Mary turns against this classically high (and now we can see its hallucinogenic properties) Romanticism to feel, or rather, more, to give over to the nonhuman other. Seeing the writing on the wall of the underlying anti-correlationist principles of a posthuman social contract, giving up on a sense of human mastery over the world, giving ourselves up to the other unconditionally, may at last make us truly last men and women because no longer anthropocentric, no longer strait-jacketed by our own fear of finitude, of lastness, and hence last men and women in the sense of the transition as the last of the last of us before we enter into a posthuman existence. From this non-anthropocentric rather than anti-anthropocentric standpoint, post-apocalyptic Romanticism allows us, finally, to begin to think a new politics, one capable of staving off human and nonhuman extinction, what we might call a democracy without the "demos," without a human hinge diplomatically folding the contract. Beyond sovereignty's human limits, an impossible futural, presentist democracy begins to be seen. Accepting powerlessness, or a passivity without passivity, amounts to "living on" in the present or, what it means in Lionel's terms, to leave this thing we call "life" that we might live.

3 Byron's Speculative Turn: The Biopolitics of Paradise

Cain is apocalyptic – a revelation not before communicated to man.

Percy Bysshe Shelley

In this chapter I build on the paradoxically presentist prophecies of the Shelleys developed in my first two chapters to show how Byron thinks through the concept of justice for humans and nonhumans alike. Byron (like the Shelleys) imagines a world without us, but he does so (unlike Percy in "Mont Blanc" and Mary in *The Last Man*) by setting his closet drama *Cain* (1821) in the original post-apocalyptic scene: the unformed, burgeoning society developing in the wake of an exit from the first apocalyptic paradise, the Garden of Eden. Within this society that is almost still presocial, humans tarry interstitially between the two poles of our political spectrum: the Hobbesian libertarian anarchism of war and the Rousseauian social contracts that demand individual liberty be given up for society's all-in-this-together fable of stable life. Byron, in other words, thinks beyond both of these anthropocentric politics, fulfilling the promise of crafting a better world that the Raymond character based on him could not in *The Last Man*. But whereas Percy offers the theoretical framework that Mary works through in *The Last Man* to sketch out an initial version and vision of a posthuman social contract for the Anthropocene, Byron, in *Cain*, gives us a radical understanding of the justice underlying Mary's new contract as well as providing the ethical imperative for accepting that contract. Justice, for Byron, we will see, does not mean, as it is put in contemporary philosophy, "to do justice to the other" but instead to allow the other to-come, to allow the other to bring justice to the human. In a surprising twist, what Byron shows us is that humans, by mass murdering millions of animals, are actually murdering themselves, eating themselves as a species into extinction by eating the other.

Working through this twist, which is the work of this chapter, brings us to a place on the hither side of climate-change thinking: figuring out how to put a full stop to the spread of human despoliation of the planet as overpopulation continues in direct proportion to the amount of food animal slaughter produces. Byron's justice allows for the reproduction of the human species long into the future if and only if we choose the non-act of eschewing the criminal putting to death of ourselves via our non-criminal putting to death of the other. Justice, on this conception, arrives from outside the law, outside of legality, outside of justice itself.

Byron, writing to his friend and confidante Francis Hodgson in September 1811, echoes one of his familiar epistolary themes, a refusal to imagine human beings living on beyond the terrestrial plain: "I will have nothing to do with your immortality; we are miserable enough in this life, without the absurdity of speculating upon another. If men are to live, why die at all?"[1] While the secular humanism of the Enlightenment has come to be understood traditionally as the triumph of rational empiricism over faith-based cosmographies, Byron, in refusing to speculate about immortality, not only denies the foundational logics of religious hegemony, he also questions, in a subsequent letter to Hodgson, the very desirability of heavenly paradise. He writes:

> As to immortality, if people are to live, why die? And our carcasses, which are to rise again, are they worth raising? I hope, if mine is, that I shall have a better pair of legs, than I have moved on these two-and-twenty years, or I shall be sadly behind in the squeeze into Paradise. Did you ever read "Malthus on Population"? If he be right, war and pestilence are our best friend, to save us from being eaten alive, in this "best of all possible worlds."[2]

Although Byron doubts the likelihood of immortality, if it is to occur, he does hope that life after death will reconstitute his malformed bodily frame in addition to transmigrating his soul into the kingdom of heaven. But the references to Malthus and cannibalism reframe Byron's thoughts on life and death in biopolitical terms, as a war for bodily sustenance and corporeal survival on earth. Overpopulation increases the demand for food that maintains physical life, but it also contrarily leads to war and human extinction (the Malthusian apocalypse), events that prevent cannibalism and so paradoxically reaffirm the humanity of humanity. However, as Byron's wry tone indicates, in linking corporeal and earthly finitude to paradise in Voltaire's phrase (adopted from Leibniz) – "this best of all possible worlds" – Byron also casts doubt on what E.D. Hirsch claims is his defining belief system, that is, the immanence of "terrestrial paradise."[3] Instead, he embraces finitude over infinitude, the life *The Last Man* envisions.

Indeed, the doubts Byron expresses in these letters concerning eschatological matters continue unabated and become inextricably bound up with a Lucretian atomism.[4] "Why I came here, I know not," he writes to his future wife, Anna Milbanke, and "where I shall go it is useless to inquire – in the midst of myriads of the living & the dead worlds – stars – systems – infinity – why should I be anxious about an atom [a clear paronomasia on Adam as metonym for *man*]?"[5] In this later letter – which elsewhere contains the same allusion to Voltaire – in a classic example of gleefully resigned Byronic irony, humans become mere atoms, infinitesimal matter in a universe of infinite matter. In this atomistic reflection Byron suggests that an obsession with mortality and immortality is futile; humans should reconcile themselves to their own transience, as but one form of matter briefly existing in an indifferent cosmos of many worlds, some dead, some alive. For Byron, humans therefore should adopt the universe's indifferent attitude regarding their own immortality and importance in the cosmos, a stance that paradoxically reorients life as earthly rather than divine, quotidian rather than empyrean – even if, ironically (both in its typical sense and in the temporal one that I have developed throughout), humans, as no more than atoms, prove irrelevant as motors, or even factors, in the earth's continued revolutions. Perhaps no earthly Elysium is eventual, warranted, or desirable. Byron seeks finitude rather than infinitude – and therefore life.

It is these concerns that Byron takes up in *Cain*, a work that Percy Bysshe Shelley called "apocalyptic – a revelation not before seen by man."[6] Within the frame I have developed, however, Shelley is rather mistaken; *Cain* is a work of post-apocalyptic Romanticism. Similar to "Darkness," which harnesses historical calamity to end-times disaster narratives, *Cain* yokes the historical geological discovery of the fossil record with end-times theology.[7] This coupling allows Byron, as his intentionally disingenuous preface to the poem makes clear, to counter orthodox theodicy with heterodox, what he calls, "speculation."[8] The poem mobilizes Georges Cuvier's early paleontological theory of extinction in opposition to classical humanist theory, dramatizing these competing theories as a battle of sceptical philosophies between Cain and Lucifer in a post-lapsarian biblical world.[9] But more than simply dramatizing, as Byron states in the preface, "that the world had been destroyed several times before the creation of man," Byron uses Cain's and Lucifer's discussions to explore ontological doubts about the future of the human species.[10] Byron's depiction of Edenic exile, in fact, finally exceeds Cuvier's catastrophism in that Byron connects extinction to a nascent, and surprising, catastrophic evolutionism that argues that the world's current human inhabitants will gradually destroy the whole of their own species and be replaced with newer, updated life forms of an entirely different, unknown sort. But, as I show in this chapter, an unaccounted-for aspect of the play – Cain's moral outrage over the slaughter of animals – offers a possible intervention in this cataclysmic cycle. For Byron, it seems, ontological replacement will only occur if humans refuse to stop killing nonhumans as represented by the animal sacrifices that induce Cain's fratricide, actions that humans nonetheless seem ironically (again understood as both romantic literary trope and the temporal presentist paradox I laid out in the last chapter) incapable of ending.[11]

At the poem's outset, Cain – married to his sister, Adah, and neighbour to his parents, Adam and Eve, and to the eventual victim of his fratricide, Abel – is differentiated from his family through his scepticism of the Almighty and the laws of the natural world attributed to Him. This Humean scepticism attracts Lucifer, who visits Cain early in the poem and, like the provocative Satan of the Gospels, tantalizes Cain into journeying to his realm, Hades. Lucifer here reveals to Cain an essential truth about human beings: despite their current appearance, they are simply a configuration of atomistic particles, given creaturely form but with no earthly permanence. Indeed, Lucifer's nomination of Cain as "dust" – "I know the thoughts / of dust and feel for it and with you" (*Cain*, act 1, scene 1, lines 100–1) – denies to humans any materiality beyond their terminal sojourn on an earth that is not made for them but from which they spring, as if dust is briefly hylomorphically transfigured. Lucifer later helpfully explains: "thou / shalt soon return to earth and all its dust / 'tis part of thy eternity and mine" (2.1.148–50). The cyclical recurrence of dust to corporeal form and back to dust is, Lucifer suggests, the fundamental architectonic feature of human and creaturely life on earth. Hence, when he shows Cain "the history of past, and present, and of future worlds," originary precursors to human beings inhabit the afterlife, but human beings do not; their spatio-temporality remains in flux, mutable lives of the present that will nonetheless inevitably pass away as did the lives of the mammoths and leviathans (2.1.23–5). Cain, already harbouring doubts that he is no more than dust – "were I quiet earth / that were no evil. Would I ne'er had been / aught else but dust" (1.1.290) – grasps that the anthropomorphism of dust confirms his gloomy suspicions that God "after flattering dust with glimpses of / Eden and immortality resolves / it back to dust again" (3.1.72–4). "For what?" Cain asks. In effect, God's rematerializing of dust as corporeal flesh confirms Cain's earlier suspicions that life itself is simultaneously full of contradictory structural matter, short in its duration but of uncertain length, vast in its potential but blunt in its finality. Cain says: "But I live to die and, living, see no thing / To make death hateful, save an innate clinging, / a loathsome and yet all-invincible / instinct of life, which I abhor, as I / despise myself, yet cannot overcome / And so I live" (1.1.110–19).

Cain's stance recalls Byron's letter to Hodgson. If we are to die, Byron asks, what, then, is the purpose of life beyond the inescapable instinctual drive to continue living that "cannot be overcome"? Intuitively Cain grasps that death, more than a spectral futurity, is a constantly present presence, built into the very fabric of ontological necessity and teleology ("I live to die"). Yet it is precisely this idea of death as part of life that the play will question when Cain murders Abel. Prior to Cain's murder of Abel, death as a physical event lacks the tangible evidence of a corpse: "*Lucifer*. Dar'st thou to look on Death? *Cain*. He has not yet been seen" (1.1.249–51). Up until Abel expires at his brother's hand, death remains an elusive, existential, conceptual threat that confuses ontological and epistemological certainty.

Confluent with this confusion, the play's atomistic depiction of humans as unhappy, transitory dust has disastrous ecological implications. Atomism equates humans with biomass – the sum total of living matter in a given area – because humans will return to the ground as material fertilizer for the earth's future survival even as, prior to that eventual reality, humans are invested with powers of mass ecological destruction. The "earth," here meaning "dust," or the outer covering of human form, will perish, and Cain, returning to dust (which he is already), will, as Lucifer cheekily puts it, "live for ever" as both a part of terra firma and possibly as a spirit like Lucifer – "It may be thou shalt be as we" (1.1.120). Lucifer helpfully explains a form of this logic to Cain: "Thou livest and must live for ever. Think not / the earth, which is thine outward cov'ring, is / Existence; it will cease and thou will be / no less than thou art now" (1.1.116–19).

The temporal present, in the cataclysmic process Lucifer explicates, contains – indeed is – its own eternal end. Therefore, as Cain realizes, happiness, like life, is temporally fleeting, and, rather than living only to die – "I live / but live to die" (1.1.109–10) – not to have existed at all is preferable because the afterlife will contain within it inextinguishable resonances of present-day life: "*Cain*. Are ye happy? *Lucifer*. No" (1.1.120–1). In any event, Cain does not believe that he will ever become immortal like Lucifer. As he puts it later in the play: "For what must I be grateful? / For being dust, and grovelling in the dust / till I return to dust?" (3.1.114–16). Having heard Lucifer's affirmation of his own thoughts, Cain draws the surprising yet logical conclusion that begins his narrative progression from ethical quandary to moral outrage: "to give birth to those / who can suffer many years and die / is merely propagating death / and multiplying murder" (2.1.68–71). A mouthpiece of Enlightenment secularism, Lucifer pushes the bellicose logics of the murder-as-life concept into Hobbesian territory, claiming that ecological destruction and death are the consequence of human life after the Fall: "war with all things / and death to all things and disease to most things / and pangs and bitterness" (2.2.149–51).[12] Whereas Cain thinks the inevitability of human death exponentially increases murder – a criminal act the world has yet to witness – Lucifer's logic is even more grandiloquently expansive as he reveals death to be the transitive property of "all things," a phrase of such universal undefined vagueness as to suggest living and non-living, animate and inanimate, human and nonhuman actors.

Indeed, Lucifer's explanation of the logic of life in Edenic exile triggers a question from Cain that, for reasons that remain opaque at this point in the play, appears at odds with his relatives' moral cosmography. Hearing Lucifer's Hobbesian schematic, and having seen the mammoths in Hades, Cain turns his thoughts to animals' fate in this new world:

CAIN: Animals –
  Did they, too, eat of it, that they must die?
LUCIFER: Your Maker told ye, *they* were made for you,
  As you for him. – You would not have their doom
  Superior to your own? Had Adam not
  Fallen, all had stood.
CAIN: The hopeless wretches!
  They too must share my sire's fate, like his sons;
  Like them, too, without having shared the apple;
  Like them, too, without the so dear-bought *knowledge*! (*Cain*, 2.2.153–60)

Not only does Cain's question and apparent sympathy for animal life counterpoint the position of his relatives – who, after all, routinely sacrifice animals – but the "things" of Lucifer's Hobbesian, ecological exordium undergo a specific verbal and material conversion into affective beings who can experience agonized suffering and, just as significantly, death. But Cain, his psychological distress heightened, of course, by his hyper-awareness of his own telluric finitude, links the suffering animals with his own anguished mortal dilemma, an implication that, as it turns out, will guide and indeed is a key to the whole play.

He offers Lucifer an anecdote that forges suffering and finitude as part of a co-terminal continuum between humans and animals:

> CAIN: Why do I exist?
> Why art *thou* wretched? why are all things so?
> Ev'n he who made us must be, as the maker
> Of things unhappy! To produce destruction
> Can surely never be the task of joy,
> And yet my sire says he's omnipotent:
> Then why is Evil – he being Good? I asked
> This question of my father; and he said,
> Because this Evil only was the path
> To Good. Strange Good, that must arise from out
> Its deadly opposite. I lately saw
> A lamb stung by a reptile: the poor suckling
> Lay foaming on the earth, beneath the vain
> And piteous bleating of its restless dam;
> My father plucked some herbs, and laid them to
> The wound; and by degrees the helpless wretch
> Resumed its careless life, and rose to drain
> The mother's milk, who o'er it tremulous
> Stood licking its reviving limbs with joy.
> Behold, my son, said Adam, how from evil
> Springs good. (*Cain*, 2.2.279–97)

Cain draws the anti-theodicean lesson from this anecdotal, revisionist "morality play" that animals, like humans, suffer arbitrary harm and violence in the world, an unjustifiable facet of life precisely because of the futility of existence, which itself owes its meaninglessness to death's incipience. Morally speaking, the anecdote expresses, via comparison of humans to animals, Cain's most deep-seated belief that the nature of life should not be morally random: "'twere / a better portion for the animal / never to have been *stung at all* than to / purchase renewal of its little life / with agonies unutterable" (2.2.300–4). Life is inscribed within a moral and physical economy dictating that it can only be "purchased" by paying in pain, a particularized re-inscription of Christ's crucifixion as structural human and animal telos. Good arises out of evil, as Adam says, no doubt in reference to Satan's temptatious seduction of Eve vis-à-vis the Tree of Knowledge of Good and Evil, just as Christ's passion bequeaths salvation to the human beings who commit Christ to the cross if they believe faith will save them. Cain's use of the lamb and the stinging creature obviously draws on, respectively, the traditional allegorical substitution of Christ as shepherd for the human flock he tends, and Satan's representation in the Garden. But he does so in order to negate faith in God as justification for this suffering. He wants to talk about real animals, not allegorical representations; the scene he describes is, after all, not meant by him as allegorical at all but rather is a witnessed event that has real-world consequences for suffering animals independent of faith in God, even as he uses the scene to critique that very faith.

Suffering, as Cain sees it, is an empirical rather than a metaphysical matter, hence his own heresiarchical doubts, which do not indicate a loss of faith (at least at this point) so much as a loss of faith in faith's justificatory power. Therefore, for Cain, if life functions via the dialectical mechanics of good and evil, then not only is it better for animals and humans not to suffer even if occasional relief temporarily appears to alleviate that suffering, but morality also becomes problematically relativistic. Critiquing earthly life as governed by religious transcendental law in this fashion thus neatly inverts orthodox ecclesiastical principles: according to Cain, divine law is empty precisely because it is contingent rather than universal and concrete. Syllogistically, Cain potently argues that divine law, if it is to exist at all, *should* not be relativistic but ironclad, a reified promissory note that guarantees that humans, and the little lives of the poignantly helpless lambs, will be spared senseless, unnecessary "agonies unutterable." Instead, divine law offers an exchange of wracked bodies emitting inarticulate screams: capital punishment as capital payment for a life that guarantees only imminent death.

Cain's solitary espousal of moral repugnance at the economic logics of the unbearable and fruitless suffering inherent in religiously orthodox tenets, and his tender feelings for animal life, are the key to interpreting the ethical demands raised by act 3. In this act, Byron employs Lucifer's vision of mortal strife and creaturely finitude to reframe the traditional story found in Genesis that distinguishes humans as rulers of an earthly kingdom.[13] Upon witnessing the primal scene of Abel's lambs slaughtered on the altar and offered as a sacrifice to the Lord, Cain experiences an anagnorisis that helps to account for Byron's choice to write about the story of Cain and Abel: humans' violent and chaotic slaughter of animals appears to be part of the built-in texture of the natural cosmic order, but it is in reality an act that, if subverted, will alter the destructive, culturally woven fabric of society and end the reign of war on earth between all things that Lucifer describes. Therefore, Byron stages Cain's and Abel's competing sacrifices to God as a duel between those who are proper environmental stewards and those who are agents of carnal consumption and destruction. Cain reaps his sacrifice from the ground, "the fruit of the earth, the early, beautiful / blossom and bud, and bloom of flowers / and fruits these are a goodly offering to the Lord" (3.1.105–7). But God, in his one ephemeral appearance as a whirling wind, rejects this sacrifice and endorses Abel's instead. Abel's offering, composed of "the blood and lambs and kids … fed on milk, to be destroyed in blood," returns Cain to the knowledge of cataclysmic life he gained from Lucifer. Contrasting himself to Abel, Cain refers to his own vegetable sacrifice as "a shrine without a victim, an altar without gore" (3.1.266–7).

Within this oppositional sacrificial logic Cain recasts Abel's sacrifice: his is a shrine with a victim and an altar with gore. In doing so, Cain revises what Giorgio Agamben, following Foucault's revisionary historicizing of the biopolitical, calls "bare life," human beings who are excluded from both divine and human law.[14] According to Agamben, because "bare life" exists outside any ecclesiastical or juridical frame, it is literally "before the law" (to borrow Derrida's phrase) and therefore can be "killed but not sacrificed."[15] In Agamben's conception of sovereign power, this exclusion of bare life is also paradoxically foundational to sovereign power since sovereignty "first constitutes itself through an exclusion (which is simultaneously an inclusion) of bare life."[16] The killing of bare life justifies itself by this violent double exclusion: "this violence – the unsanctionable killing that, in his [the human designated as 'bare life'] case, anyone may commit – is classifiable neither as sacrifice nor as homicide, neither as the execution of a condemnation to death nor as sacrilege."[17] Cain conceives of sacrifice and murder differently – at least when it comes to animal life. In this primal sacrificial staging between Cain and Abel, animals, like bare life, can be killed but not sacrificed or murdered, even though these pious killings are termed sacrifices to God. But whereas for Agamben, biopolitics as he analyses its emergence encompasses only human beings, while the exclusion of bare human life is the originary founding moment of a juridical society under sovereign power, Cain differs in that, for him, animals are bare life, too, and it is their status as such that constitutes God's sovereignty. Cain, in other words, identifies a contradiction at the heart of Agamben's articulation of biopolitics. Although Agamben's project seeks to show how modern biopolitics emerges by means of an inclusion and exclusion of *zoë* – "the simple fact of living common to all living beings (animals, men, or gods)" – in society, his actual discussion of the paradoxes at the heart of modern biopolitics nevertheless fails to take the full meaning of the term into account to include nonhuman life.[18] That is, if biopolitics is a function of the paradoxical inclusion and exclusion of *zoë* in the polis, then any analysis of biopolitics must account for not only humanity but also the other terms of Agamben's cited definition: animals and gods. Therefore Agamben remains thoroughly in an anthropocentric mode that, given Cain's concern for animals and the nonhuman world, is, for Cain, limited and finally unhelpful in negotiating the full compass of life.

And, pivotally, Cain thinks others should conceptualize life like he does. Although, in the post-lapsarian state of society in which he lives, animals are subjects excluded from the consequences of being sacrificed or murdered and are therefore *not*, strictly speaking, sacrificed or murdered, they are, for Cain, "victims" and not mere material for abased supplication in the form of this non-sacrificial sacrifice (or non-murder murder). For Cain, then, like Nicole Shukin, this creates a zoopolitical (*zoë* means "all living beings") framework for understanding life wherein all living creatures are recognized as subject to biopolitics (and hence subject to sacrifice and murder) and in which animals stand "before the law" but do so on equal footing with human beings in this post-lapsarian state.[19]

Abel, of course, refers to the sacrificed animals as "victims" too, but, as is absolutely crucial, in pushing the biopolitical into the zoopolitical, Cain's questioning of sacrificial logic also puts into question the inherent sovereign violence of God and life itself (*Cain*, 3.1.297). To Abel, violence can only occur between human beings; what he does to animals at God's behest is, contra Cain, not an act of violence, since his exhortation to Cain implies that his altar has been untouched by violence:

ABEL: Brother, give back! thou shalt not touch my altar
With violence: if that thou wilt adopt it,
To try another sacrifice, 'tis thine.
CAIN: Another sacrifice! Give way, or else
That sacrifice may be – –
ABEL: What mean'st thou?
CAIN: Give –
Give way! – thy God loves blood! – then look to it: –
Give way, ere he hath *more*! (*Cain*, 3.1.305–11)

Cain's point, which will soon take physical form in his slaying of Abel, is that Abel's sacrifice is an act of violence even if it only concerns animals. Because of God, who "loves blood," violence – and this hearkens back to Cain's scepticism in his conversation with Lucifer – structures life for all living beings (a "war of all things," as Lucifer says). Therefore, Abel can also be sacrificed (or murdered) just as Cain indeed threatens to do to him in his ironic, violent rage concerning the violent structural basis God has used to frame the world. Though blind to the irony of his own violence, Cain clearly sees the irony of God's position. Abel says, "I love God far more / Than life" (3.1.315–16). Cain responds by ironically exploiting God's irony: "Then take thy life unto thy God / Since he loves lives" (3.1.317–18). In Cain's usage, God does not want "lives" after death, the soul that moves on, but rather wants the *lives of the living*, an assertion that at this point in human history Cain derives from the only evidence available: God's wanting to take one sort of lives, the lives of animals. Thus, by killing his brother and showing (to his eventual great woe) that humans can be sacrificed – which in this case, at the moment it happens, immediately becomes not just a sacrificial act but a true act of murder such that the two become interchangeable – Cain, again, places animals and humans on a creaturely continuum, a genuine zoopolitics of bare life that seeks to account fully for how all living creatures are subject to sovereign control. In terms of contemporary biopolitical debates, Cain, for now, sides with Roberto Esposito, who concludes that "every life is a form of life and every form refers to life."[20]

It is at this crucial point in the play post-murder that life on earth becomes inextricably tied to physical death for the first time. Abel's wife, and Cain's and Abel's sister, Zillah, cries out, "Death is in the world," marking the transformation of life from its personified mythicality in the earlier social order of the play to a physically real, temporally finite event; its limit becomes manifest with Abel's corporeal form made incorporeal. But previous to this appearance of physical death, animals, the only beings that were killed on earth at this time, were not associated with either the mythical or physical concept of death. Only Cain thinks that animals can die. Death as literal and not mysteriously immanent enters the world only once Cain introduces murder into the world. As Cain tells Lucifer earlier in act 2,

> Spirit! I
> Know nought of death, save as a dreadful thing
> Of which I have heard my parents speak, as of
> A hideous heritage I owe to them
> No less than life – a heritage not happy,
> If I may judge, till now. But, Spirit! if
> It be as thou hast said (and I within

> Feel the prophetic torture of its truth),
> Here let me die: for to give birth to those
> Who can but suffer many years, and die –
> Methinks is merely propagating Death,
> And multiplying murder. (*Cain*, 2.1.60–70)

As discussed, Cain initially thought that human existence was a form of multiplying murder because existence leads only to death despite that death has never been seen. However, his sympathy for the sacrificed animals, expressed as outrage at the savagely bloodthirsty God – "what was his pleasure in / the fumes of scorching flesh and smoking blood / to the pain of the bleating mothers, which / still yearn for their dead offspring?" – forces the realization that, in the world as it currently exists, animals cannot be murdered although they can be senselessly sacrificed (3.2.298–301). Conversely, in the post-lapsarian world, Cain's murder of Abel demonstrates that a human being is only alive if he or she can be murdered because, prior to Abel's death, neither death nor murder existed in the world except in Cain's eyes, which saw animal sacrifice as murder. Cain's murder of Abel – that is, the death of a human life – and Cain's witness of Abel's sacrifice – that is, the death of animal life – makes legible the structural limit of death that Cain has been seeking throughout the play.

Therefore, in the poem, murder moves Cain and his family out of the pre-socialized, pre-juridical, pre-modern state of nature that they inhabit and into the sphere of culture governed by the biopolitical act of murder. Once murder is introduced into the world, it charges life with a new valence. Life's priority becomes the continued existence of the human body, the postponement, for as long as possible, of the tyranny of death, of a return to dust. The introduction of murder into the world in the place of sacrifice revises the concept of life so that it means earthly survival, a condition to which Adam's family did not heretofore aspire. At the same time, in opposing Abel's ovine slaughter to Cain's proto-environmentalism – "From earth they came / to earth let them return," Cain says of his vegetables – and by juxtaposing this with Cain's murder of Abel, the play, for now, flattens the concept of life by flattening the crime of murder and its attendant concept of death (3.1.283). In other words, the play dissolves the technical, legal, and social distinctions between human life and animal life. As Byron explains in a letter to his publisher, John Murray, on 3 November 1821, Cain's "rage and fury against the inadequacy of his state to his conceptions … discharges itself rather against Life, and the Author of Life, than the mere living."[21] What Cain seeks is not, paradoxically, the murder of Abel – "the mere living" – but the murder of a "Life" that entails death for humans and animals alike: he wishes to murder this "Life" and by extension, to borrow Jacques Derrida's phrasing, "to sacrifice sacrifice" since animals are "the mere living" too.[22] As Cary Wolfe explains it, sacrifice seems inescapably inscribed within life because "the violence of sacrifice for which the distinction between human and animal has historically been bedrock" provides "for the law the 'foundations' for its exclusions that the law cannot provide for itself." Hence, Wolfe continues, "as Derrida, Agamben, and others have reminded us, those who fall outside the frame ... are always threatened with a 'non-criminal putting to death.'"[23] Wolfe's point is that animals fall outside of this frame and are thus subject to sacrifice and death, but it is precisely these excluded animals that allow for sacrifice's existence in the first place. Cain seeks to end this sacrificial framework of life – what he thinks of as the multiplication of murder – with the actual murder of the one, Abel, who represents this framework.

Hence, he murders Abel, not, as Byron himself says, "in a fit of dissatisfaction ... with the politics of Paradise," but in a fit of dissatisfaction with the biopolitics of paradise.[24] Or, in the play's terms, he wants to halt the sacrifice of animals, to thereby sacrifice sacrifice, to eradicate the human sacrifice of animals and end all killing that inheres in life's sacrificial and murderous economy. Cain is not murdering Abel so much as he is attacking "Life" and, by extension, as it is God who approves the animal sacrifice over the vegetable sacrifice, "the Author of Life" (and this recalls his anger over God's moral relativism). Cain reasons that if it is wrong to commit fratricide, then it is equally wrong to sacrifice animals, as committing either act is a method of extinguishing "the merely living" in life's post-murder contours. But even as Cain wishes to abolish the sacrificial economy of mortal life and death altogether, the play itself circumvents this unheralded possibility as murder and sacrifice crucially mediate and define life and death; that is, they provide, as Wolfe recalls from Derrida, the "exclusions that the law cannot provide for itself."[25] These exclusions are at the heart of one of the play's final great ironies: Cain himself receives immunity from death for introducing human death to the world:

ANGEL: To mark upon thy brow
  Exemption from such deeds as thou hast done.
CAIN: No, let me die!
ANGEL: It must not be. (*Cain*, 3.1.500–3)

Cain's immunity also delivers the surprising ironic twist that challenges, even as it seems resigned to accept, the anthropocentrism of Abel, Adam, Eve, and God. Once Cain has been cast out and exempted from death, his point that animals are also subject to death is lost on both humanity and the divinity. Cain's exemption functions (though more on this below) as the exclusion that reinforces the rules of life's anthropocentric sacrificial logic – death remains in the world because it now has a human dimension; that is, those other human beings who are not Cain can die. Thus, ironically, sacrificial animal rites continue despite Cain's protestations even as, by virtue of his introduction of death into the world, something like modern human life begins in the desire to survive (to put off death interminably) at the expense of animals, which will culminate in Byron's own time with the beginning of industrialized animals-as-food production. The premodern "gentleness" (as the Angel of the Lord will put it) of Abel's sacrificial violence gives way to Cain's abolitionist, lost-cause, modern violence wherein the mass slaughter of animals is guaranteed to be justified.[26]

But for all that this reading of the play explains the fury Cain feels towards a vital sacrificial economy, his indignation nonetheless suggests an ethical stance more in line with Percy Bysshe Shelley than with Byron. Indeed, Byron's own ambivalence about eating animals seems to challenge the very possibility of achieving the utopian non-violent society that *Cain* both advances and disputes. Long ago, G. Wilson Knight sketched Byron's personal love for animals and his belief that he shared more affective affinities with them than with other humans.[27] His love for his dog Boatswain, for instance, is well known, commemorated in his poem "Inscription on a Newfoundland Dog" in which Byron describes Boatswain as the only friend he ever knew. The dog was later buried, at Byron's express command, in the family vault at Newstead, where Byron himself wished to be buried. An incredulous Percy Bysshe Shelley famously completes this picture of Byron's love of animals, detailing the astonishing community Byron had gathered at his villa in Ravenna. Shelley counted "two monkeys, five cats, eight dogs, and ten horses" and later amended this recital with greater astonishment upon meeting "on the grand staircase five peacocks, two guinea hens, and an Egyptian crane."[28] Years after this staircase encounter, and after Shelley's tragic death, Byron's relationship to his menagerie is complicated still further during his move from Pisa to Genoa in 1822, as he takes particular care to bring three caged geese that he planned to eat on Michaelmas Day; later he refuses to order their slaughter, "to test the theory of their longevity."[29] In light of Shelley's ethical vegetarianism and his obvious sympathy for animals, Byron's diet puzzles as it appears to owe more to his fear of corpulence and hatred of food in general: "I wish I could leave off eating altogether," he writes with his typical sense of melancholic self-pity and amused detachment.[30] In a letter to his friend Hobhouse, following his tour of Europe in 1811, Byron reveals that he has "left off animal food," and on the boat home he orders a vegetarian larder be prepared for him by his mother at Newstead. He later conflates his loathing of society with his diet in several letters to Lady Milbanke, his closest confidant.[31] To his mother he writes on 11 June of that year: "I must inform you that for a long time I have been restricted to an entire vegetable diet neither fish or flesh coming within my regime, so I expect a powerful stock of potatoes, greens, & biscuit, I drink no wine."[32] Eventually, though, Byron returned to eating animals, intermittently going back to a vegetable diet apparently to lose weight. On 9 February 1820, when Byron was living at Ravenna and had just completed Cantos IV and V of *Don Juan*, he writes in a letter to William Barnes, "Ay! And you will find us eating flesh too, like yourself or any other cannibal, except it be upon Fridays."[33]

The vexed nature of his own complex relationship with animals, and eating them, is indicative of more than a hypocritical cast to Byron's thinking. Like *Cain* and its final ironies, this relationship provides a snapshot of the historical juncture of post-Enlightenment, post-industrial ideals embedded in Regency-era society, a juncture now identified as the genesis of the Anthropocene era, the time of human-made climate change, and the beginning of the slaughter of animals for food on a massive, mechanized scale.[34] *Cain,* in questioning the "non-criminal putting to death" of animals, historically reflects the period that saw the intersection of duelling imperatives: the technological and industrialized means to produce animals as affordable food and the genesis of modern animal welfare and rights programs.[35] Both Byron's relationship with animals and *Cain*'s disavowal of animal sacrifice posit that, in a world with no promise of an afterlife (recalling Byron's own doubts expressed in his letters), the moment of ethical decision on an imperfect terrestrial plane turns on demanding, difficult questions about "the non-criminal putting to death" of animals.[36] Hence Byron's own discomfited registration of his complaints about eating. If in his actual life Byron vacillated regularly on matters pertaining to animals, *Cain* offers a concrete ethics of human-animal interaction while retaining a hard-nosed realism about the unlikelihood, and perhaps impossibility, of abolishing this "non-criminal putting to death" of animals, of sacrificing sacrifice, of doing away with the sacrificial structure that governs modern society (animals are now supposedly killed or sacrificed for human survival).

This probable impossibility appears to be why humans are not wise enough to survive in the cosmic scheme of the play's overall plot; so they are replaced by more senescent beings, beings who, in any event, if what Cain sees in the primordial afterlife of Hades is any indication, might share more biologically with animals than with humans. Therefore the play's final, ironic judgment on the silence of the lambs, and the silence of Abel, appears to be that humans are the problem and the solution, as they will eventually wipe themselves out, as Cain does to Abel and as humans will continue to do to animals. At issue then is what Lucifer, and more recently Derrida, termed humans' "war" against animals in their endless quest to survive, a war that, ironically, threatens to create a literal world without us because the mass putting to death of animals is destroying the planetary parameters that make human life on earth possible.[37] By not questioning how animals fit within biopolitical paradigms, we have reached a true catastrophe, a turning or tipping point whose solution requires moving beyond human concerns just as the play suggests we must. Moreover, as *Cain* instructs us, there are matters of justice here that exceed our current perceptions that we must attend to regarding nonhuman life in the Anthropocene. We must halt the Hobbesian war against all animals in exchange for a social contract centred on nonhumans.

This futuristic, post-apocalyptic, speculative turn in Byron's paleontological poem is connected to the problem of contemporary climate change as it relates to potential human extinction. Byron, of course, referred to *Cain* as "speculation," but the play takes on added resonance in relation to this word when seen in the light of speculative realism. As I discussed in my introduction, Meillassoux argues that correlationism has long been the dominant post-Kantian means by which humans understand their place in the world, "the idea according to which we only ever have access to the correlation between thinking and being, and never to either term considered apart from the other."[38] According to Meillassoux, correlationism is problematic because "an ancestral reality anterior to terrestrial life" such as "an isotope whose rate of radioactive decay we know" presents evidence of a world before us and after us that is at once documentable and incomprehensible to the human mind.[39] This problem of "ancestrality" discloses "a temporal discrepancy between thinking and being – thus, not only statements about events occurring prior to the emergence of humans, but also statements about possible events that are ulterior to the extinction of the human species."[40] That elements like uranium exist before and potentially *already* after humanity problematizes humanistic conceptual understandings and imaginings of our place and purpose in the world.

In other words, Meillassoux's identification of this divergence between thinking and being suggests that a robust posthuman conception of life is needed in response to the Copernican questions expressed by Mary Shelley's Lionel Verney and Byron's Cain about whether humanity orients the earth.

In fact, the climate concerns about the likelihood of human extinction and the correlation of thinking and being Meillassoux discerns as fundamental to scientific and philosophic modernity would seem to render strangely naive the human beliefs in their centrality to life on earth. As Eugene Thacker details, when confronted with this ontological dilemma, humans' knee-jerk reaction is to engage in a reflexive recuperative humanism that repositions the decentred humanity reality disorients: "when the non-human world manifests itself to us in these ambivalent ways, more often than not our response is to recuperate that non-human world into whatever the dominant, human-centric worldview is at the time. After all, being human, how else would we make sense of the world? However, one of the greater lessons of the ongoing discussion on global climate change is that these approaches are no longer adequate."[41]

As but one example of this recuperative operational schema, in light of the findings of the Intergovernmental Panel on Climate Change and the UN that controlled animal feeding operations are the largest contributor to climate change, many environmental activists claim that humans must stop the slaughter of animals not because it would save animals' lives but in order to save the human species.[42] As Slavoj Žižek points out, climate change is not just an environmental problem but also a problem of "the particular deadlock of the capitalist mode of production," which is, in part, the industrialized slaughter of animals.[43] Byron's speculative turn in *Cain* intervenes in this re-inscription of pre-scripted humanism as it offers a posthuman engagement with the issue of animal slaughter: on the one hand, the play posits that humans killing animals leads directly to a literal posthuman world in line with post-apocalyptic thinking; on the other hand, the play argues that humans must disavow their supposed sovereign dominion over animals that authorizes this killing. In other words, *Cain* adds an ethical dimension to this debate: humans must think beyond humanity, must stop killing nonhumans, not because this will save them (though it might) but because nonhumans can be murdered too, and murder is simply unjustifiable – hence Cain's punishment at the play's end despite his being its ethical agent. Given this unjustifiable slaughter, the way of life as conceived in these schemas must, to put it in *Cain's* metaphoric terms, be murdered – and that is just. In the world of *Cain*, humans must learn to imagine, even prioritize, life, and worlds, ulterior to human history – to give up anxieties about their own mortality, as Byron says in his letters – in order properly to contextualize life in its present state and re-examine their own everyday, casual, accepted destructiveness. This will allow humans to be alive for the first time.

Byron's more famous discussion of paradise in canto X of his masterpiece *Don Juan*, written a year after *Cain*, completes his speculative posthuman vision of life as it relates to the revelation of earthly paradise. As in *Cain*, the Fall of humankind is not an event of moral degeneration but rather the impetus for potential scientific and technological progress. In the opening of the canto, Byron enfolds the biblical Fall within Newtonian mechanics:

> When Newton saw an apple fall, he found
> In that slight startle from his contemplation –
> 'Tis said (for I'll not answer above ground
> For any sage's creed or calculation) –
> A mode of proving that the earth turn'd round
> In a most natural whirl, called "gravitation;"
> And this is the sole mortal who could grapple,
> Since Adam, with a fall or with an apple.
>
> Man fell with apples, and with apples rose,
> If this be true; for we must deem the mode
> In which Sir Isaac Newton could disclose
> Through the then unpaved stars the turnpike road,
> A thing to counterbalance human woes:
> For ever since immortal man hath glow'd
> With all kinds of mechanics, and full soon
> Steam-engines will conduct him to the moon. (X, 1–16)[44]

As James Chandler argues, in this passage Byron "creates and erases" any distinction between eighteenth-century natural philosophy and moral philosophy.[45] But Byron also rejects, at once, the idea of earthly paradise as a fundamental condition of life undone by humans' entrance into the wilderness of sin. In other words, rather than simply creating and erasing this distinction, Byron, like Milton before him, posits the Fall into sin as the moment that places humans on a moral track. The Fall is not a moral crisis for humanity but its salvation by way of humankind's ascendance out of the unchanging stability of prelapsarian bliss.[46] Progress, as defined by Enlightenment tenets like Newtonian mechanics, is, by the very static nature of paradise, not possible. For Byron, the Fall thus comes to represent the first step on the path to scientific and technological modernity because it introduces knowledge into the world, and with knowledge comes ethical decision, the ability to make decisions about what counts as progress. He thus reshapes the Fall as necessary to Enlightenment prerogatives tied to rational decision-making. Hence, the Fall does not divide the world into prelapsarian and post-lapsarian states based on original sin; rather, the Fall distinguishes between a false paradise of scientific naïveté and ignorance and a world of creative plentitude and analytical possibility, even if, as the wryly jesting reference to the "steam engine" suggests, technological progress entails wondrous inventions "to counterbalance human woes" with off-planetary potential.

On the surface, then, this passage seems to read like a standard Enlightenment narrative of secular triumphalism over unsubstantiated religious mythology. But under the surface, Byron's intertwinement of the two narratives does not actually privilege one over the other so much as forge the competing moral mythologies of the day into a unified "what if" predicated on sinful transgression as moral and scientific exemplarity. Whereas Milton's felix culpa vacillates indecisively between understanding the Fall as fortunate or unfortunate, Byron never hesitates in linking ethics' entrance into the world as a passage through the gates of sin. As the proposed trip to the moon referenced at the end of stanza 2 hints, earthly paradise necessarily entails that humans be able to screw up the world and leave it behind once technical modernity of the industrialized sort humans have created either allows for a leisurely lunar tour or an escape from the destruction they have wrought upon the earth. In fact, Byron's conclusion in this later canto of *Don Juan* mirrors Cain's conclusion in Hades concerning the Tree of Knowledge: although the tree does grant knowledge, that knowledge is "deadly." And, connectedly, Cain's observation of his prehuman ancestors and the biblical knowledge it reveals – that the fates of humans and animals are assured – impels him to launch his attack on "Life" and the "Author of Life." Byron, in other words, sees quite clearly that Enlightenment and religious narratives about the human mind propelling social progress amount to the same thing in that both are conversely and perversely contrary to the reality of life on earth. Sacrificial religiosity and secular humanism coolly contradict their own belief in earthly paradise – hence, in the final couplet, the speculative necessity of the *Star Trek* trip off the planet to new worlds and new civilizations, which recalls the "myriads of living and dead worlds" and "the stars" of his letters.

Byron's "speculative turn" – that is, his embrace of a post-Cuvierian picture of human extinction that thinks life ulterior to human thought – pits itself against the classical Keatsian identification of a Wordsworthian egotistical sublime and its perceptual connection to the world, recalling what I have been calling throughout this book the post-apocalyptic sublime. As Lucifer puts it in reply to Cain's question about the possible ways humans can resist God's plan, "by being yourselves … Nothing can quench the mind, if the mind will be itself / and centre of surrounding things – tis made to sway" (II, lines 215–19). But it is precisely this solution that Cain as *dramatis persona* and *Cain* as poem disavow. By the poem's end (as in canto X of *Don Juan*), Cain's newfound knowledge of idealized Enlightenment principles paralyses him in an attitude of scepticism that vacillates between hope for the future and the grim suspicion that, for there to be a future, "the tree of knowledge" (here a synecdoche for the human mind) must be relinquished as part of the bargain that the world makes for its own survival. Simultaneously, Byron's post-apocalyptic forecast reclaims the earth from human disaster, as humans return to the earth, ashes to ashes, dust to dust, a literal posthuman world, or what Byron might call "this best of all possible worlds." Ultimately, *Cain* solves the crisis of extinctualism by literally ejecting from the earth the humanist tenets of Genesis – that humans "have dominion over the fish of the sea, and over the fowl of the air, and over the cattle, and over all the earth, and over every creeping thing that creepeth upon the earth" – just as *Don Juan*'s Newtonian mechanics symbolically eject humans from the planet altogether.[47] A Romantic post-apocalyptic sublime thus makes the speculative-realist "discrepancy between thinking and being" a legible problem that demands a posthuman revision of "life." If we are to survive the Anthropocene era, we must, to appropriate the words of Mary Shelley's Lionel Verney that ended the last chapter, "leave 'life,' that we may live" (*The Last Man*, 218). *Cain* exemplifies how, in the Anthropocene, we have not yet been alive.

Moreover, *Cain* offers just such a speculative exodus from "life" to life, to living on. To return to Cain's immunity from death at the play's end, a plot and a thematic twist occur that reverse much of what we thought we knew about Cain. His exceptional condition opens on to something more than the flattening of life that Cain himself believes he has enacted with Abel's murder and the attendant, for him, symbolic murder of life's sacrificial, operational system encoded by God. He is forced to straggle across the earth without ever dying. Cain's singular exemption demonstrates a new and wholly unanticipated form of life (what, indeed, at first looks like what Lucifer tells him will occur) – that which cannot die, that which exceeds the bounds of life on the earthly plane and in any potential afterlife. Cain's life is totally defined by its finitude in the sense that he will never transcend earthly life. Cain is, in every way, singular, a lone figure with no living correlative *in life*. As such, Cain's immunity from death, and his consequent status as new life, deepens and expands life's definition beyond Esposito's notion of an affirmative biopolitics that recognizes all forms of life as equal. While Cain's exemption from death might at first seem, within the contrasting terms and competing visions of contemporary biopolitics – between, on the one hand, a negative thanatopolitics and, on the other, an affirmative zoopolitics – to fall within the parameters of the former (for one, Cain's life might be said to be a life worse than death), it actually exposes, if not expresses, the radical juncture between these two apparently differing ends of life's spectrum.[48] For Cain's singularity, wholly unanticipated by the conditions of life on earth, suggests that life can never truly be flattened in the way Cain yearns for but rather is always perpetually open to a return to the violence that is the target of hoped-for eradication. Condemned by his mother and indemnified from death by the Lord's angel, Cain is not redeemed or welcomed as part of the human or animal community; rather, he becomes an outcast from both, a new ontological kind altogether, though not the kind revealed by Lucifer in the underworld. Instead, Cain's banishment crosshatches Lucifer's point in Hades: the sweep of the universe makes human violence towards other humans look irrelevant, whereas human violence to animals and the nonhuman world may ultimately destroy much more than human life. Moreover, human life, in any event, according to the play, is supposed to end at a certain point rather than destroy everything – and that destruction, finally, is what the play seems to find unforgivable. Cain's violent murder of his brother is thus but another part of this destruction of everything, of what Lucifer described as the war of humans against all (including themselves), since the human community immunizes itself from Cain's critique of its structural fundamentals by exiling him and thus protecting its own murderous Hobbesian heart.

Esposito and Derrida describe this type of immunity as biopolitical society's autoimmunity effect that both protects and destroys that society.[49] A community will expel threats but in the process will self-destruct, just like the human community in *Cain* does when it refuses to question, let alone end, its own wholesale non-criminal putting to death of animals. But, ironically, humans are also putting themselves to death, a means of perpetual, autoimmune, endless war. Cain's punishment is thus double: he is condemned to live on as an outcast for the murder of his brother, and his actions perpetuate rather than halt the non-criminal putting to death of animals that will eventually take on a mechanized life-threatening scale in the modern world. The play seems to place Cain in this final position: a posthuman ethical crossroads after his tour through Hades affords him knowledge of human life's short duration coupled with the damage humans do during that time to the animals and world around them. And although the play poses these difficult posthuman, speculative, non-anthropocentric, ethical paradoxes, it does not provide any answers, because the questions are just as important as any longed-for answers since they reveal our own blind spots about our thoughts, about the world, and about our place in it.

It is within these blind spots that *Cain* articulates a theory of justice that comprehends more than the human and thinks beyond the legal and illegal disjunctions that structure the law that justice underwrites. Cain's expulsion from the post-apocalyptic society of his family places him outside apocalyptic living as well; he resides neither in the paradise of the Garden nor in the world post-paradise. In this sense, Cain exists in a nebulous undetermined region that evades the structures of state-of-nature thinking represented by Hobbes and Rousseau: beyond the law, residing within justice. This places him in a unique position to view the institutional norms of paradise and society and render judgment on them, a judgment that acts as both critique and its own theory of justice.

Cain is a free agent, living outside of apocalyptic paradise and in a post-apocalyptic space that stands outside of conservative and progressive politics, outside of life and death, and outside of the desire for infinitude and immortality. Cain has therefore achieved what other humans have not – and, according to the biblical tradition, no other ever will – and become alive in a posthuman sense, the first human of a new species that is both human and nonhuman. This posthuman levelling-up occurs directly as a result of his giving up sacrifice, giving up the putting to death of the other – and therefore the putting to death of humanity as well. He has transitioned to obeisance before the law's tribunal to being outside the law altogether – a last man as well as a first. As Derrida argues, "justice will never be … reducible to laws and rights."[50] What Cain is, then, is justice, but he is justice precisely because he exists beyond the bounds of the law and justice. His actions thus speak to the fact that justice arrives from the other, from those excluded as nonhuman. This exclusion is the fundamental tenet of justice because it not only foregrounds but demands that difference – in this case Cain's radical new ontology – be heeded rather than papered over in a rush to construct the law that applies equally to everyone.

Cain, in other words, demonstrates what is unjust about justice in its anthropocentric political guise: it elides difference in favour of homogeneity and thus assimilates the other as the same. In so doing, justice commits an unjust act – is, in fact, unjust – as justice claims to render what is deserved to the one under prosecution but cannot do so if it relies on the idea of a universal justice that applies to those who are inside the law and those who are outside of it. For the latter there can be no justice because there is no legal recognition or standing; animals may be killed but not murdered. Cain, post-exile, cannot be murdered but can be killed. Cain shows us that justice dwells outside the legal and the illegal. The law makes justice unjust. Justice, paradoxically, impossibly, means allowing the other, for whom no justice can ever be present, to judge what is just, allowing for the other to be justice. The only way to evade the injustice of legal justice is to be unjust by existing outside the law, like Cain, and thereby to critique the life structured around this law. Being legally unjust, a nonhuman, is the only space from whence justice can come. In the politics of this courtroom drama, justice holds open lines of difference and suggests ways to live differently with those who are different. More than simply a vision of extinction, with *Cain*, Byron mitigates apocalyptic euphoric finality with post-apocalyptic grim hope for the future end of "life" as we know it, a hope that emerges when there should be no possibility of it: the end of not being alive and the beginning of life as posthuman.

4 Birds Do It, Bees Do It: John Clare, Biopolitics, and the Nonhuman Origins of Love

Byron wanted animals to live; John Clare wants this, too, but he also wants to watch them live so he can glean how they love. Indeed, Clare is one of the great poets to chronicle the daily lives of animals, their sounds and shapes, their habits and habitats, their wonder and welfare. But for all of his keen attention to the pleasant and enchanting minutiae of animal life, Clare is also attentive to the sorrows and sufferings animals experience at the hands of human beings. During the years 1818–35, for instance, he wrote hundreds of idyllic poems about the birds and animals native to his Helpston parish, even while he charted, in poems of this period, how the national enclosure process in the English countryside instituted new forms of violence between humans and animals.[1] For Clare, enclosure was a very personal affair, one that disrupted the ecology of Helpston, the rocks, streams, trees, fields, and animals he loved. He encapsulates these disruptions in an early poem, "The Lamentations of Round-Oak Waters" (1818), that features the Round-Oak stream apostrophizing a swain seated on the riverbank detailing how enclosure – represented in the poem as "lawless foes / and Laws themselves they hold / which clipt-wing Justice can't oppose" (lines 181–3) – has destroyed his natural habitat: "look backward on the days of yore / upon my injur'd brook / in fancy con its Beauties o'er / how it had us'd to look / O then what trees my banks did crown / what willows flourished here / hard as the ax that Cut them down" (lines 157–64).[2] Clare's emphatic use of "Cut" drives home the harsh brutality of enclosure, characterizing it as a malevolent ax that severs the connection between the trees and the stream, thus ending their environmentally rich sympathetic interdependence.[3] In several other enclosure poems (what Johanne Clare calls Clare's "enclosure elegies"), Clare expands this focus on the barbarity of enclosure, and laments, for instance, "how enclosure came and trampled on the grave / of labour's rights and left the poor a slave," penning in "sheep and cows," which had been formerly "free to range" without "the bonds of men" (lines 19–24). Another poetic elegy, "The Fallen Elm" (1820), notes that enclosure drives animals out of their natural habitats, out of their normal modes of existence, and ultimately scrambles moral codes: "wrong was right and right was wrong" (line 63). But whereas these early enclosure elegies are fuelled by regret for a lost past, the poems Clare will write years later, once he moves from Helpston to Northborough (around 1835–7), are filled with a volatile anger that indicates a redirection of Clare's creative and critical energies. These poems stage violent encounters wherein humans view animals as creatures to be idly abused, punished, or killed rather than cared for, an obvious, if unexplained, feature of Clare's depiction of quotidian creaturely life.[4]

In this chapter I argue that, although human sport like badger baiting occurred long before enclosure, the startling shift in Clare's poetry from the peaceful bird's-nest poems of his mature adult years that describe animal *umwelt* – Jakob von Uexküll's term for the unique biological and semiotic world of each animal – to primal portraits of tortured animal bodies reflects his ethical anxieties about what will happen to animals post-enclosure.[5] As we know from his poems "The Fallen Elm" and "The Mores," Clare worries about the commons, a rural living space that, to him, symbolizes freedom for humans and animals. The enclosure of this common democratic space surfaces in reflections on the erasure of grazing pasture in "The Mores" and the predatory alteration of "the common heath" in "The Fallen Elm" (60). In both poems Clare carefully observes how the enclosed common encompasses specific animal lives. For example, in "The Fallen Elm," "Een nature's dwellings far away from men / The common heath, became the spoiler's prey / The rabbit had not where to make his den" (59–61).[6] In Clare's vision, enclosure's reach extends beyond public spaces, transforming the private lairs of animals into confrontational staging grounds between humans and animals.

Clare's shift in focus from the privacy of protected space (nests and dens) to predation and deprivation in public spaces – in other words, from poems on animal life to poems on animal death – also constitutes the main plot of "The Badger" (1835–7), where, like the rabbit who loses his den to "spoiler's prey," human predators lure the badger from his burrow to the common village thoroughfare. As in the case of the rabbit's den, enclosure repositions the badger's habitat – the physical and biotic parameters of an animal's home – and thereby repositions the location of the badger burrows, increasing badgers' contact with humans. All of this is, of course, not to say that the poem "The Badger" is a product of enclosure (though it may well be; obviously a great deal of Clare's poetry is inflected by it) but rather that enclosure helps to explain the aggression and disembodied voice of "The Badger," even as this poem, in turn, delineates new stakes of the human-animal relations Clare's birds-nest poetry adumbrates. In fact, "The Badger" is exemplary even among the distinctive sheaf of Clare's animal poems from this period because it experiments with poetic form in a way in which the other animal poems do not. Accentuating the new life-and-death stakes of these works, it is the only poem in which the featured animal, the badger, dies.[7] The poem conjoins form and theme, abruptly ending on line 12 of the final sonnet in the sequence as the badger "cackles groans & dies," as if the formal structure of the poem (a unique feature I will discuss in more detail below) mirrors the cessation of the creature's life. I also spotlight the exemplarity of "The Badger" because, as Johanne Clare points out, Clare's enclosure elegies employ prosopopoeia, whereas most of his poetry does not, allowing him to give "ironic emphasis to his belief that too few human voices were raised in defence of the rights and needs of labour."[8] Reappropriating Clare's observation, I argue that part of the innovation of "The Badger" lies in its simultaneous embrace of the fundamental paradox of prosopopoeia: the chiasmatic combinatory blur of the human and the nonhuman. Exploiting this paradox, the poem attempts to decouple human observation of the world from the human speaking voice of poetry even as the poem also lends human voice to a "defence of the rights and needs" of animals. Clare, in these later poems, links up with Byron and the Shelleys in his thinking on the nonhuman; he does not view animals as anthropomorphic grist for poetic mills but as sentient, autonomous creatures who hurt, who suffer, and who die painful deaths. His formal experimentation thereby presents a challenge for humans to observe, as he does, the real world of animal others to which he fears that the life-altering events of modernity will blind us.

Clare's larger oeuvre, which includes over one hundred poems devoted to birds and birds' nests, routinely depicts human-animal relations as consciously and conscientiously respectful and gentle, true idylls of rural country life. Clare was a devoted amateur naturalist and spent hours rambling in the fields around Helpston, observing birds and their nests. According to James Fisher, Clare's knowledge of birds was prodigious: "he knew from personal observation about 145 wild birds, of which 119 can be identified with reasonable certainty."[9] His approach in his bird poems, perhaps unsurprisingly, as an amateur naturalist, hews to the observational rather than the metaphorical.[10] The exhortation to the reader in "The Yellowhammer's Nest" (1825–6) evidences this inspective methodology: "Let us stoop / And seek its nest" (lines 3–4).[11] In this poem, Clare marvels at the idiosyncratic sticks and stones of the nest:

Aye, here it is! stuck close beside the bank,
Beneath the bunch of grass, that spindles rank
Its husk-seeds tall and high: – 'tis rudely planned
Of bleached stubbles, and the withered fare
That last year's harvest left upon the land, –
Lined thinly with the horse's sable hair.
Five eggs, pen-scribbled o'er with ink their shells,
Resembling writer-scrawls, which Fancy reads
As Nature's poesy, and pastoral spells –
They are the Yellowhammer's; and she dwells,
Most poet-like, where brooks and flower weeds
As sweet as Castaly her fancy deems;
And that old mole-hill is Parnassus' hill,
On which her partner haply sits, and dreams
O'er all his joys of song. Let's leave it still
A happy home of sunshine, flowers, and streams.
Yet is the sweetest place exposed to ill,
A noisome weed, that burthens every soil;
For snakes are known, with chill and deadly coil,
To watch such nests, and seize the helpless young;
And like as if the plague became a guest,
To leave a houseless home, a ruined nest:
Aye! mournful hath the little warbler sung
When such like woes have rent his gentle breast

("The Yellowhammer's Nest," lines 7–30)

As in his other bird poems, Clare is here attuned to the eccentricities of nests, the "horse's sable hair" that cross-stitches the thatch along with the leavings of "the withered fare" from last year's harvest. Because of details like these, the yellowhammer's nest is not simply one nest among others to Clare; it is instead a unique composition, expertly crafted by this individual bird within a particular ecology, "a happy home of sunshine, flowers, and streams."[12] On the whole, the poem presents a sweetly gentle picture, but Clare is nevertheless always aware that even "the sweetest place" is "exposed to ill," as the baleful, bad, Satanic predator preys on the eggs that the yellowhammer has so carefully and peacefully built a nest to protect, a shield to guard against external nonhuman threats. When an egg is destroyed, however, Clare views this as a matter not of ecological necessity but of wanton violence; for this reason it is also a moment of unqualified mourning for him and for the yellowhammer who warbles melancholically at the poem's end. This picture of the yellowhammer's peril therefore suggests an ethical awareness in Clare's poetry concerning animal mortality – that is, its fragility and tenuous temporality, even in what appears to be a natural cycle of predation. In other words, Clare recognizes animals as beings with their own ecosystems, life forms whose finitude, and the related capacity of humans to mourn animal death, signal affinities with human affection and mortality even as he respects their tremendous differences. Nonetheless, the fact of their finitude, like the finitude of humans, re-marks on humans' new "life" in the world, a life that allows for being with animals in societies of mutual living. It is a new form of conceptualizing life, similar to how the Shelleys and Byron think life as more than merely human.

Because of this affinity, in observing these sheltered nests Clare seeks to capture the animal *oikos* while also questioning the anthropocentrism of human sovereignty over animals. Hence, as many of the bird poems close, Clare tries to dissipate the authorial voice that he figures as co-implicated in human intrusion, a technique anticipating Clare's experimental form in "The Badger."[13] The speaker, accordingly, becomes more disembodied and reflects on his intrusive presence before a departure that restores an unseen, but hoped-for, natural peace. In "The Yellowhammer's Nest" he equates the bird's nest to Parnassus, home of Apollo and the Muses, the classical site of divine poetic inspiration: "and she dwells / Most poet-like, where brooks and flower weeds / As sweet as Castaly her fancy deems / And that old mole-hill is Parnassus' hill / On which her partner haply sits, and dreams / O'er all his joys of song" (lines 10–15). Such a comparison would seem to remap the bird's home as the wellspring of human figurative signification, distorting and displacing its apparent uniqueness as a nonhuman site existing cleanly in a natural world divorced from human culture, a true state of nature free from war. Yet, as if the invocation of the poetic muse mandates its own disavowal, if not rejection, the speaker incorporates his readers into the subjunctive "Let's," ordering them to preserve this sheltered nest from their own non-figurative presence ("Let's leave it still / A happy home of sunshine, flowers, and streams").

A similar divorce of a loco-descriptive animal scene and human voice occurs in "The Nightingale's Nest" (1832).[14] The poem begins with an exhortation by the speaker to the reader: "Up this green woodland-ride let's softly rove / And list the nightingale – she dwelleth just here" (lines 1–2). Like the earlier poem this one takes dwelling as its focus:

How curious is the nest no other bird
Uses such loose materials or weaves
Its dwelling in such spots – dead oaken leaves
Are placed without and velvet moss within
And little scraps of grass – and scant and spare
What scarcely seem materials, down and hair
For from mans haunts she nothing seems to win.

("The Nightingale's Nest," lines 76–82)

Although watching birds may seem to be a relatively passive activity compared to the predation Clare will write about in his poems on fox lairs and badger baiting, the speaker nonetheless characterizes it as hunting: "Laughing and creeping through the mossy rails / There have I hunted like a very boy / Creeping on hands and knees through matted thorn / To find her nest, and see her feed her young" (lines 11–14). The line "laughing and creeping" at once suggests the insouciant irreverence that humans hold for nonhuman life, even while it evokes the deadly earnestness with which they sneak into their habitats. Clare's use of the simile "like a very boy" references his own retrospective chagrin at snatching eggs out of birds' nests as a boy, a practice he discontinued as his ecological, and ethical, consciousness matured.[15] But, despite the growing disquiet shadowed in these later lines, the poem begins, like "The Yellowhammer's Nest," with the speaker face to face with the nightingale: "And where those crimping fern-leaves ramp among / The hazel's under boughs, I've nestled down / And watched her while she sung" (lines 18–19). In this observant posture, the speaker describes the nightingale anthropomorphically, granting to the bird alien qualities that pervert the nestedness of Uexküllian *umwelt*, the biological foundations that are particular to each life form and engender that life form's unique signifying capacity. Granting the bird sonic musicality metaphorizes avian vocality as human signification (obviously bird noises share rhythm, tone, and pitch with human songs, but this does not make them cognitively mutual); the description of the bird as a being who "would tremble in her ecstasy" and with "mouth wide open … release her heart / Of its out-sobbing songs" indicates not empirical observation, then, but metaphoric anthropocentric intrusion on the bird's abode and the bird itself (lines 23–5). The speaker, though, seems aware of this intrusiveness, as it is his "happy fancys" (a word that repeats from "The Yellowhammer's Nest": "Five eggs … which Fancy reads / As Nature's poesy" [13–14]) that "shapen her employ" ("The Nightingale's Nest," line 26). This signification is paradoxical as the human/bird confrontation on display in this poem leads the speaker suddenly to notice the disruptiveness of his presence: "But if I touched a bush, or scarcely stirred / All in a moment stopt I watched in vain / The timid bird had left the hazel bush / And at a distance hid to sing again" (lines 28–31). Clare's speaker watches "in vain," and this attitude indicates the ethical calculus involved in bird-watching since it mandates the nightingale flee its home. Observing birds in their nests leads to greater understanding of them but also equals another trespass on the natural world (that is why the nightingale escapes "to sing again"). Indeed, as John Goodridge and Kelsey Thornton note, trespassing troubles Clare in all of his work and is, perhaps, something of an idée fixe.[16] Robbing the defenseless birds of eggs and observing their nests poses the same dilemma that Clare's later animal poems present: human intrusion into *animal umwelt* converts private animal space into human public space, transforming the state of nature into society, a change that carries the burden of the destruction inhering in human communities.

The bird's nest poems, ultimately and unexpectedly, work to imagine an alternate vision of human-animal relationships that does not circumnavigate the ethical quandaries of anthropocentric assumptions concerning human invasion of private animal space. For instance, late in "The Nightingale's Nest," after the nightingale has flown away, the inclusive attitude of the opening lines returns, and "We will have another search today" (line 47). No sooner does the speaking voice become an expansive synecdoche for a collective *we* than "we" are kicked out of the bird's nest because "we" begin to sympathize with its "choking fear" when it notices our approach (line 60). Therefore, "even now / we'll leave it as we found it" because "our presence doth retard her joys" (lines 65–6). The poem ends on a scene of ecological understanding and peace that is reminiscent of Clare's other bird poems, and we are told, again, that we will not do the bird harm: "We will not plunder music of its dower / Nor turn this spot of happiness to thrall" (lines 69–70). Significantly, "thrall" is the same harsh word that Clare employs in "The Mores" to indicate the destruction of enclosure – "the rude philistine's thrall / Is laid upon them and destroyed them all" ("The Mores," lines 64–5). In leaving the nightingale and her eggs "still unknown to wrong," then, "we" enact the argument the poem puts forward, the paradoxical knowledge that such relational contact can both nurture and destroy. This presents the same dilemma as *The Last Man*: Hobbesian conservativism and Rousseauian liberalism culminate in the combinatory one-two punch of war and peace, which are ultimately irreducibly the same. Hence, the poem views the observation of animal Umwelt as both a profanation and the realization of that profanation, knowledge of a world space that should not be trespassed upon.[17] Otherwise humans run the risk of committing the atrocities of enclosure. Clare notes this at the end of "The Mores": "A board sticks up to notice 'no road here' / And on the tree with ivy overhung / The hated sign by vulgar taste is hung / As tho' the very birds should learn to know" (lines 69–71). This partitioning induces a prelapsarian exhortation: "And birds and trees and flowers without a name / all sighed when lawless law's enclosure came" (lines 77–80). Whereas the lack of names alludes to Adam's nomination of animals in the Garden and thus signals the unspoiled paradisiacal space of bird life pre-enclosure, the extrajudicial nature of enclosure tramples the natural order and rights guaranteed by this space. Hence, animal lives post-enclosure have no recognized Umwelt and become beings with no ecological safety from the encroachments of nationalized modernity. They have entered the post-apocalyptic wasteland that is society and are now caught up in the exclusionary mechanism of that society. Like Byron, who thirsts for but cannot find justice, Clare seeks a world where violence against animals becomes outlawed by the public covenant to protect and preserve life. But Clare wants that "life" to include animals, just as Byron did.

The experimental series of sonnets that surround "The Badger" in the Northborough manuscripts (written between 1832 and 1837) help to clarify how this singular poem addresses the practical and poetic problems of human-animal contact raised by the bird poems.[18] Of the series of animal sonnets in these manuscripts, "The Badger," alone, in its final section, abandons the typical fourteen-line sonnet structure, highlighting its exorbitant, radical importance for his deep-sleeved thinking about nonhuman life. It is also distinguished, as mentioned above, as the only poem in which the titular animal dies. "The Martin," a sonnet of fourteen lines that appears in the manuscript before "The Badger," describes the martin, in a fashion contrary to the fate of the badger in that eponymous poem, as "like a badger," a creature who escapes from his human tormentors, "left free from boys & dogs & noise & men" (line 14).[19] In the fourteen-line "Starnel" sonnet, the starnel, the blue cap, the willow biter, and the wagtail are depicted trying to build nests safe from human intrusion.[20] Conversely, in "Schoolboys in the morning," another fourteen-line sonnet, the bull hurries the boys who have snatched a bird's nest away from it, thereby saving the nest from desecration and dismemberment.[21] The sonnets that lead up to "The Badger" hinge on the familiar and continually reworked theme of human intrusion on animal life, but in all of these sonnets the animals defend themselves or drive off the human invaders. For instance, the sequence called "The Fox" (two fourteen-line sonnets) stages the fox as the pursuer, chasing off the shepherd, the ploughman, the old dog, and the woodman and eventually finding refuge in a "badger hole" (line 26).[22] "He lived to chase hounds another day," the poem concludes (line 28). Likewise, a sonnet sequence on turkeys that appears in the manuscript after "The Badger" allows the turkeys to defend their eggs from all intruders, whether they be boys or other animal predators. "The Tame Badger," the sonnet that immediately follows "The Badger," is, in juxtaposition, perhaps the most disturbing of all the sonnets as it envisions a "tamed" badger who interacts peacefully with humans, licking their hands and playing with them, part of their peaceful society.[23]

In fact, while sonnets like "The Hedgehog" narrate human pursuit of a hedgehog with a bleak closing line ("and still the strife goes on") that seems to emphasize the destructive impulses made manifest in "The Badger," the entire set of poems closes, unexpectedly, with sonnets that begin to resurrect the ecological harmony of Clare's early Helpston verse (14).[24] Indeed, in one of the late untitled sonnets in the series, humans and animals coexist in harmonious rural rituals, while the final line evokes the common pastureland of the village as constitutive of ecological intersubjective peace, a kind of messed-up snapshot that exemplifies Byron's rewriting of that law as fundamentally unjust because of its rejection of justice:

The barn door is open & ready to winnow
The woodman is resting & getting his dinner

& calls to the maiden with little to say
Who takes the hot dinner and hurrys away

The hens in the dust and the hogs in the dirt
The mower is busy and stript in his shirt

The wagon is empty and ready to start
The ploughman is merry and drinking his quart

The men are at work and the schoolboy [at play]
The maids in the meadow a making the hay

The ducks are a feeding and running about
The hogs are a noising and try to get out

The dogs at his bone and the ass at his tether
and cows in the pasture all feeding together. (Untitled, lines 1–14)

Given the languid, peaceful view of village life in this sonnet, with the villagers tending respectfully to the animals on the common and the animals acting on their own impulses ("feeding & running"; "noising & try to get out"), the violence of the villagers on display in "The Badger" is surprising. This violence returns us to a hospitality that is not the pure hospitality we see *The Last Man* develop precisely because it is mired in hospitality's reciprocal violence. Differentiating the poem further, its formal experimentation spotlights the badger's finitude. Instead of being a fourteen-line sonnet, the third stanza sonnet of "The Badger" is abruptly cut off at line twelve as the badger "cackles groans & dies," as if the poem's formal structure is inextricably linked to the badger's vitality, ending as the badger's life ends.[25] This dramatically different thematic and formal emphasis on finitude in "The Badger" seems indicative of poetry's potential culpability in exploiting animal death as a poetic vehicle.[26] It is for this reason, as I suggested at the outset of this chapter, that "The Badger" rethinks prosopopoeia and the lyric speaking voice; it is a poem that wants to think nonhuman finitude as non-correlationist finitude made animal flesh, the nonhuman just as finite as the human.

It is worth recalling, then, that Paul de Man theorizes prosopopoeia – to give voice and face to the dead or absent by personifying and reifying them in the present – as the master trope of not only autobiography but poetry itself.[27] For de Man, prosopopoeia is both restorative and privative in that it depends on a paradox: the constitutive effacement of the subject in the act of personifying it. Prosopopoeia, in other words, is the speaking voice of the lyric as it paradoxically instantiates an absent speaker as a present speaking voice. Because a speaking human voice cannot be fully present, prosopopoeia marks how the human speaking voice of poetry is also indubitably nonhuman since the actual human voice is, indeed, absent. Based on this essential othering function of the trope, Sara Guyer reads prosopopoeia as deconstructive in its implications since it decentres the human subject from its assured position as the lyric voice. Guyer, therefore, argues that Romantic literature is animated by a rhetoric that paradoxically affirms the voice and face of humanity in poetry even as it "reflects a radical displacement of the human subject," giving life to a poetic figure that is not alive.[28] Prosopopoeia in "The Badger" similarly disavows the human subject by effacing the very face to which it purports to give face. But more than simply a disavowal, in Clare's poem, the paradox of prosopopoeia replicates the intrusiveness of humans' sovereignty over animals and their habitats (which, historically, undergo a reorientation due to enclosure). "The Badger" demonstrates how the intrinsic function of prosopopoeia to both limn – make the human legible as the speaking voice – and attenuate this legibility effaces the human voice to contrast the animality of humans with how humanized the badger is. In other words, the poem, beyond viscerally illustrating the physical violence the badger suffers, also spotlights how prosopopoeia, as a poetic trope, critiques the literal violence of the figural humanization of animality. The poem's prosopopoeia links the literal violence of badger baiting with the figural violence of anthropomorphic poetics. To humanize the badger is, therefore, a form of intrusive human violence.

And so "The Badger" seeks to showcase a speaking voice that avoids the human viewpoint typical of Clare's bird's-nest poems and the animal poems surrounding it.[29] Stephanie Kuduk Weiner's thorough explication of Clare's management of narrative presence in his poetry helps us to see how weirdly different the speaking voice of "The Badger" is in Clare's oeuvre:

> The voice of his poems almost always belongs to Clare himself. His poems are usually spoken by a lyric "I," a "Clare," whose identity with Clare himself is relatively straightforward and unproblematic. But the way in which that "I" makes itself present in each poem is more complex. Some poems feature a highly present, meditating and feeling "I" while in others he withdraws almost entirely, registering his presence merely by organizing images around his own vantage point or by implying a subject to whom those images are intelligible or meaningfully.[30]

The identity of the speaker of "The Badger" is not disclosed; rather, the speaker appears, as per Weiner's formulation, as a withdrawn presence, ostensibly witnessing the scene but distanced from it. But the speaking voice is also different than the withdrawn presence Weiner notes; here the images are not merely being arranged, but a story is being told, implying a consciousness aware of witnessing a teleological progression of events. And yet – and this is key – despite apparent cognizance, no meaningfulness is assigned to the story the speaker narrates. Nor does the speaker mimic the voice of the badger, a technique Clare himself employed in his earlier poem "The Lament of Swordy Well," in which the dying tree of Swordy Well sad-face narrates its own post-enclosure decline.[31] The badger, though central to the poem, has no direct spoken expressions, or even any onomatopoetic ones, which, again, is not standard for a Clare poem featuring animals – he knows they don't speak so they don't "speak."[32] He wants to hear them speak from their non-speaking, a silence that speaks in its impossibility, a silence attuned to silence without assimilation to silence.

"The Badger" is also a demanding and distinctive poem in Clare's work from a lyrical point of view. While Weiner notes that parataxis is "Clare's central syntactic strategy during these years," in this poem Clare eschews parataxis for enjambed continuous narrative, thereby adding urgency to the baiting of the badger that is not present in the bird's-nest poems.[33] In the poem an unknown speaker recounts how the townspeople, at midnight, track a badger to his lair, apprehend him, and bring him to the main village thoroughfare for violent, meaninglessly cruel sport and amusement: "When midnight comes a host of dogs and men / Go out and track the badger to his den / And put a sack within the hole, and lie / Till the old grunting badger passes by" (lines 1–4). However, despite the grim picture the poem paints as the townspeople shout at, set their dogs on, and hurl rocks at the badger, the sympathies of the speaker are never revealed.[34] Humans do not, to Clare, care; that much is clear. Nor does "The Badger" cohere with M.H. Abrams's classic description of how the romantic lyric works:

> Some of the poems are called odes, while others approach the ode in having lyric magnitude and a serious subject, feelingly meditated. They present a determinate speaker in a particularized, and usually a localized, outdoor setting, whom we overhear as he carries on, in a fluent vernacular which rises easily to a formal speech, a sustained colloquy, sometimes with himself or with the outer scene, but more frequently with a silent human auditor, present or absent. The speaker begins with a description of the landscape; an aspect or change of aspect in the landscape evokes a varied but integral process of memory, thought, anticipation, and feeling which remains closely involved with the outer scene. In the course of this meditation the lyric speaker achieves an insight, faces up to a tragic loss, comes to a moral decision, or resolves an emotional problem.[35]

In Abrams's formulation of the lyric, the speaker assumes a self-consciousness about what is being described that culminates in a revelation that resolves some dilemma the speaker has been contemplating. "The Badger" refuses these strategic poetic leitmotivs, defying the traditional modes of the Romantic lyric. Rather, its sequential logic aspires to a kind of rigid observational narrative that denies the moral authority of the speaker to pronounce a judgment upon and about the scene being documented, and therefore evidences no resolution or insight. In contrast to, say, Coleridge's "To a Young Ass," an apostrophe to the ass that deplores the animal's condition, "The Badger" never addresses the animal (nor is it clear who is the addressee) and features a neutral tone, as if, perhaps, the moral (if there is one) ought to be obvious enough from mere empirical, observational description of badger baiting alone.[36]

So, despite its apparent moral apostasy, "The Badger," alongside the other poems in the manuscript, does share Clare's empirical eye, and, though less detail oriented than the microcosmic, quasi-taxonomical depictions of the birds' nests, the poem also ecologically locates the badger within the rhythms of his habitat. The poem's opening words – "the badger grunting along his woodland track" – immediately place the badger in the foreground of the poem as the subject, noting as well, with the gerund "grunting," that the badger has non-terminal agential qualities (though, again, not spoken ones). With sparse but no less informative details, the badger appears in action on this track: "with shaggy hide and sharp nose scrowed with black / roots in the bushes and the woods, and makes / a great high burrow in the breaks" (lines 3–5). Clare, having deployed a rather general descriptor with "shaggy," gets more specific with the Helpston-dialect verb "scrowed" to illustrate how the badger's nose is "marked or scratched with lines," a distinctive biological identification.[37] Careful attention is likewise paid to exactly what the badger is doing, and the poem acknowledges, with the verbs "roots" and "makes," that the badger acts according to his own designs. The badger's Umwelt, therefore, is on full display as he trundles along his "woodland track" and excavates a sheltered home for himself ("makes a great high burrow") in his natural habitat.

However, once humans appear on the scene, they receive a cursory, obfuscatory, and generalized grouping as a "host of dogs and men," with the dogs subjugated to their masters' purpose to chase the badger, another instance of reckless, feckless, unheeding human violence towards animals (lines 8 and 13). Once the badger is brought to the town and baited up and down the street, the humans are not brought into any sharper relief; they are simple, universally undistinguished and indistinguishable groups: "the crowd" and "all" (lines 39, 45; 25–34). Only in the final sonnet of the sequence does Clare provide any details about the humans (none of whom appear as particularly delineated specimens) as we are introduced to a "drunkard," "a frighted woman," and a "blackguard"; the drunkard "swears and reels" while the woman runs away with the children, and the blackguard "laughs and hurries on the fray" (lines 40–2).[38] Although we do not see fully fleshed out human beings, the poem creates a faceless community of human killers, what Eric Miller calls "a democracy of destruction," which recalls us to the juncture of Hobbesian war and Rousseauvian human democracy.[39] Therefore, when Clare refers to the humans being driven away as "rebels" (line 28), it pressures these generalized descriptions of humans as somehow rebelling against the natural order of things: the badger was trundling down his woodland track, burrowing hither and thither, minding his own business when the humans set on him in their leisure for cruel sport. In other words, the badger is forced out of his state-of-nature abode and into the social world of human beings. The implied etymological suggestion of "rebels" then seems to be that humans are upending the natural order by their intrusiveness, but even this is not made an explicit voiced concern of the poem. To borrow what Alan Vardy, writing on "The Vixen," says, "the poem does not make moral pronouncements."[40]

The poem's innovation lies then not only in its dispassionate depiction of human-on-animal violence; by refusing to moralize explicitly, it also evacuates the privileged human authority of the speaking voice and attempts to fulfil the tacit promise of prosopopoeia: to manifest a nonhuman voice decoupled from the human voice (again, the very nature of prosopopoeia is that it assumes the voice of the other). While the shadowy human characters remain thinly sketched, ephemeral, and largely inert, the badger claims nearly all of the strongest, present-tense, active verbs in the poem (indeed, he would be a great writing instructor): he "passes," "runs," "bites," "turns," "drives," "starts," and "grins." (Similar action occurs in "The Vixen": "If any stands she runs among the poles / And barks and snaps and drives them in the holes," lines 7–8.) Significantly, the badger continues to turn and drive throughout the poem:

He turns about to face the loud uproar
And drives the rebels to their very door
The frequent stone is hurled where'er they go
When badgers fight, then everyone's a foe
The dogs are clapped and urged to join the fray
The badger turns and drives them all away
Though scarcely half as big, demure and small
He fights with dogs for hours and beats them all
The heavy mastiff, savage in the fray
Lies down and licks his feet and turns away
The bulldog knows his match and waxes cold
The badger grins and never leaves his hold
He drives the crowd and follows at their heels
And bites them through the drunkard swears and reels

("The Badger," lines 42–56)

In turning to "face the loud uproar," the badger comes face to face with his attackers, or he would, except for the curious fact that none of them have faces. The obscuration of human presence suggests that, more than a pivot from a defensive position to an offensive stance on the badger's part, the volte to face and turn away from humanity is actually a revisionist turning of the trope of prosopopoeia. As the central motor driving the poem's action, the badger, in turning to face the attackers and poetically overpowering them with his overpowering verbs, turns to face outward from the poem, to manifest that nonhuman life can occupy the subject position of lyric poetry without being appropriated as expressive of human thought. The more he "turns," "grins," and "drives," establishing a space of survival, the more the humans retreat from the poem itself, as if the badger is also driving off the voice and face prosopopoeia would force on him.

Yet, he cannot, ultimately, drive off poiesis. Emphasizing the figural and literal chiasmatic crossroads of prosopopoeia, the poem employs words whose etymology implies both aspects of mortality, the contemporaneity of life and the eventuality of death. In the third stanza of the poem "the badger grins and never leaves his hold." According to the *OED*, "grin" as a verb can mean "to pull back the lips into a smile"; as a noun it can mean "a snare for catching birds or animals." Etymologically, then, the word signals the ineluctably entwined figural and literal violence of prosopopoeia. The word "hold," which can mean "a refuge, place of shelter, temporary abode, or a lurking place for animals," is intentionally ambiguous. After all, the badger has been forcefully taken from his "hold," where he lives, by the men at the beginning of the poem: "When midnight comes a host of dogs and men / Go out and track the badger to his den." And yet, torn and beaten on the village thoroughfare, the badger and his "hold" are linked to his "grin" as if to contradict the sense of safe harbour implied by "hold" with the ensnarement of "grin's" double meaning. That the badger's place of safety appears to be mobile – he is evidently "carrying," so to speak, his hold with him if he has it on the street – shifts the meaning of "hold," and the poem, from the ontological space of the badger's private life to, in the final couplet, the eschatological space of his public death. Hence, the closing line of this couplet – "he leaves his hold cackles groans & dies" – reveals the full spectrum of the semiotic confusion encoded in the poem: a "hold" can also mean a "dead body or corpse." Peacefully ensconced in his own hold at the beginning of the poem, the badger retains his habitat, his *umwelt*, his life, as an animate body. Leaving his hold at the end of the poem, the badger relinquishes his hold on not only habitat and *umwelt* but on his very life itself and becomes an inanimate corpse.

The anthropomorphism of the final lines is all the more paradoxical then as these lines turn towards an externality the poem defies while simultaneously embracing: the badger, in the moment of his death, becomes more human and hence more pathetic as he "cackles groans and dies" (line 52). By indexing the verb "dies" to cackling and groaning, emphatically human traits, the poem implies that death is recognizable only as a human experience. Rather than allow the badger the dignity of his own animal autonomy in his final moments, the poem humanizes the animal, which implies that human traits will always pervade, if not dominate, any portrayal of nonhuman life by virtue of the chiasmatic figurative force of prosopopoeia that humanizes animals and animalizes humans. Yet, the complex logic of prosopopoeia is such that even as it apparently undercuts animal autonomy, the chiasmatic effect of prosopopoeia yokes the human and the animal at a point of contact in which the easy divisions of "the human" and "the animal" give way to inexorable relationality. Prosopopoeia in "The Badger" blurs the human subject and the animal subject. Indeed, it marks the permeable boundary between both the human and the animal, the living and the dead. Given this paradox, that prosopopoeia, as a trope, works by its irreducible dialectic between the living and the non-living, the human and the nonhuman, this fluid permeability demonstrates how the unrepresentable – the animals that cannot have a poetic voice, the absent, the dead – are actually fundamental to poiesis. Anthropomorphizing the badger as he dies in the final lines is therefore a literal actualization of the figurality of prosopopoeia itself – the master trope of poetry – since prosopopoeia, which figures a voice from a non-voice, is anthropomorphic in its very heart.[41] In a sense, this duality of the human and the animal at the heart of prosopopoeia is the condition and uncondition of poetry's possibility.

What we might call Clare's exposé on how prosopopoeia works in terms of human and nonhuman relations has a corollary function of turning the poem into an ethical site of powerful import. "The Badger," by foregrounding the inherent problems of prosopopoeia, also discloses the ethical imperatives that arise from human violence towards animals. The poem's odd speaking voice, in its remove from itself and its subject, suggests that literal and figural violence are poetically indistinguishable. A violent virulence, this speaking voice gives the poem ethical force as it induces the reader to re-evaluate what reading about a tortured badger means. On the one hand, the poem appears to reinforce the static perception of human society as hapless, hopeless observers of human cruelty. The reader is, after all, not a witness to the baiting of the badger but is, as a reader of the poem, a witness to his or her own non-witnessing of the event. On the other hand, however, precisely because of the complex, distanced, and distancing nature of the speaking voice, the poem itself functions much like what Niklas Luhmann calls "a second-order observer," an observer who can see the systemic categorization that most observers are unable to see.[42] The poem observes and forces the reader to observe its own observance of what it does not see: the real badgers being abused by human beings in the actual world. The nexus of the reader and the poem thus creates a literal blind spot between reality and representation. This blind spot is not inert, though, and indeed its invisibility calls the eye to its presence. Exploiting the gap in its meta-poetic contours, between the bleeding badger of the poem dying alone on the street and the real badgers who suffered real baiting, the poem takes on urgent ethical purpose and clarity – it wants justice.

In failing to bridge the visceral gap between reality and representation, the poem turns the reader's attention to the problem of prosopopoeia – the need to observe, to become conscious of, failures of conscious observation. Although the visceral experience of reading the poem directs our attention elsewhere, at the words on the page and not on the badger bleeding to death on the street, the ethical charge of the poem's mimetic aperture redirects us to our misdirected focus: the real animal. What might seem like the poem's strange and extravagant refusal to foreground and background (discussed above) a moral in a human speaking voice, therefore, testifies to Clare's awareness that offering one enforces unexamined sociological attitudes instituted by post-enclosure practices. These are practices that Clare, apparently, fears may make animals' deaths seem not only justified but a matter of human indifference.

During one of the last years of his life Clare wrote, in a quavering hand, while alone in the asylum, a final poetic fragment that explores similar concerns about how, counter-intuitively, observational obfuscation can compel ethical elucidation. Called simply "Birds Nests" (1864), it totals seven lines:

> Tis Spring warm glows the South
> Chaffinchs carry the moss in his mouth
> To the filbert hedges all day long
> & charms the poet with his beautiful song
> The wind blows blea oer the sedgey fen
> But warm the sunshines by the little wood
> Where the old Cow at her leisure chews her cud.[43]

The chaffinch is in the act of carrying moss to the "filbert hedges," presumably to construct a nest, but either it takes the chaffinch all day to build its nest, or the poem keeps the nest perpetually suspended from completion to emphasize that the point is the ultimate impossibility of capturing a nest in poetic form. In this poem, Clare sees birds as being able only to "charm the poet," not to advance an understanding of avian life. Indeed, it is as if the poet literally became charmed, unable to focus on the purported subject of the poem – no birds' nests actually appear – and closes transfixed on an image of another animal, the cow, chewing her cud. Poetry, Clare seems to think, contains dangers of charming us, of making us less observant of the subject at hand (birds' nests) than we should be. What if the final overall aim of Clare's poetry, then, is a call to rethink how humans observe animals, how they use them as grist for their own poetic mills? And does not this intertwining of ethics and aesthetics, ultimately, pose that humans must rethink prosopopoeia, and poiesis itself, as paradoxically constitutive of an invocation of real-life ethical affect in the literal violence of its very figural heart?

The answer to this question, I think, lies in Clare's refusal to distinguish ethics from aesthetics. Like Vardy, I believe that "Clare insists that ethics and aesthetics are intertwined," but whereas for Vardy this helps to explain Clare's politics, I think that Clare's perspectival shift to ethics can also profitably be understood within the context of the emergence of biopolitics that Michel Foucault has identified as endemic to the eighteenth century and which I discuss in the last chapter.[44] If, for instance, we understand enclosure in the register of how Arthur Young, one of its leading proponents, described it, that is, as a means of population control and species extension, then we can also see enclosure in terms of how Foucault defines biopolitics, the power of, as he famously phrases it, "making live or letting die" in regard to human beings.[45] Enclosure, in other words, is a biopolitical process, an exercise of biopower, which Foucault defines as the deployment of diverse strategies "for achieving the subjugation of bodies and the control of populations" in the move from pastoral power to political governance.[46] As Timothy Campbell puts it, "biopower thus is that which guarantees the continuous living of the human species," a goal perfectly captured by John Howlett, friend of Arthur Young, who wrote that "the most valuable productions" of enclosure were "human creatures" because enclosure led to a national population surge.[47] To analyse the deployment of this epistemic shift in governmental control – roughly from monarchy to democracy – Foucault argues that we should study the "peripheral bodies" on which the application of biopower is legible.[48] As we have seen, intruding on a nightingale, robbing a yellowhammer's nest, torturing a badger are actions that are never peripheral to Clare. His poetry anticipates biopolitical blind spots – Foucault and Agamben focus on humans – even as it extends, as Byron's *Cain* does, what Cary Wolfe calls "the frame" of biopolitics, beyond humanity to the making live of animals.

Indeed, if Clare's literary resistance experiments to the enclosure of the commons (an instantiation of biopower) question what it means to make animals live or let them die, then Clare's work can be read as an intervention in current debates regarding whether biopolitics can be repurposed as positively progressive rather than as negatively thanatopolitical.[49] For, if it is equally true that "the enclosure elegies" are about the cultural, social, and political losses imposed on humans by enclosure and that the bird poems are Clare's retreat from, as Johanne Clare says, "society into nature" without an exploration of "social injustice," then "The Badger" represents a transition in his work to how social injustice relates to animal life as the human spectres of the poem watch the badger bleed to death on the street, just as we, the readers, watch the badger "bleed" to "death" on the page.[50] Considered from this frame, Clare's poetry reclaims the commons lost to enclosure by envisioning what I have called a democracy without the demos to-come of peaceful coexistence predicated on an awareness of the fragility and precariousness of all creatures, both human and animal.[51] The lives of the marginalized and "minor" creatures are, for Clare, crucial to the covenants of such communities.

In other words Clare, unlike Michael Hardt's and Antonio Negri's contemporary biopolitical, neo-Marxist critique, does not fail to account for the presence of the nonhuman in global economies.[52] While Hardt and Negri argue that workers are alienated from their own labour and life, they miss what Clare does not: nonhumans and their role in the decades-long reorganization of the global commons undertaken in the eighteenth century. Clare saw very clearly that, for capitalist biopolitics to work, it must alienate humans from nonhumans – the various animals, trees, rocks, springs, fields, and hills that signify across his poetic ethnology and anthology of the English countryside.[53] For Hardt and Negri, combating the forces of capitalism requires reconfiguring the people-populated commons as a multitude of singular beings able to be mobilized and bound by the affective affinities of love, a term that they define based on its human transactionality.[54] In contrast, Clare's work affords a crucial critique of this idea of a reconceptualized commons underwritten by an exclusively human love. Animals and other nonhumans, singular beings in their own right, Clare's poems show us, must be incorporated into any democratic multitude if it is to avoid unwittingly rebuilding a global biocapitalist common fuelled by excluding nonhuman life. In fact, love, for Clare, is a form of poiesis, a specific kind of ontological space-time, that is conditional not on knowing, or even feeling, but on being. Poetry, in Clare's theorization of it, because of its limnality, is the common area of trespass between the human and the nonhuman, the ontological space of love.

One of Clare's most recurrent openings – "I love to see," followed by an empirical observation of nonhuman life – indicates how nonhuman life occasions such a feeling even as it implicates the human subject as affectively movable only in relation to something other and alien. As with Byron, it is the nonhuman that actualizes the political. Clare's ecology has long been recognized as built on a human–nonhuman interinvolvement – as he writes in "Helpston Green," "as are the changes of the green / so is the life of man" (lines 62–3) – but under-explored is his insistence that the co-implicate of human–nonhuman offers us a different understanding of love.[55] In "I Am," Clare writes "even the dearest, that I love the best / are strange – nay, rather stranger than the rest" (lines 10–11).[56] What this poem on Clare's own non-identity exemplifies is how the estranging features of nonhuman life are what make love possible at all. After all, as we know from the above line that repeats again and again – "I love to see" – what Clare loves the best is nonhuman life.

As we have seen, John Clare the trespasser and John Clare and community are both well-known tropes of his poetry, prose, and life.[57] Clare presses his deconstruction of these tropes in the bird's-nest and animal poems above to think how trespassing into the nonhuman or sticking with the communal human commons in "I Am" and "Sonnet: I Am" works (the two poems that seemingly contemplate human ontology) evokes a sense of ontological homelessness.[58] In "I Am," Clare acknowledges and abjures his former trespass in the same breath: "I long for scenes where man hath never trod." His invocation of such scenes, of course, acknowledges and abjures the communal as well, removing Clare from any shared space impressed with the footprints of humans. It is easy to read this longing for solitude transcendentally, as, in fact, Clare himself seems to turn our ontological hopes and eyes upward to domestication with the divine: "to abide with my Creator God" ("I Am," line 15). This ascension actually shifts the poem to an ecological division; Clare's ecstatic vision rends heaven, earth, and human life, leaving Clare feeling "the grass below" while he stares up at "the vaulted sky" (line 18). The poem's paradoxes unravel at this meeting place of discrete humanness and nonhumanness, the earth below and the sky above, both greenly and bluely not Clare. Despite this distinction, Clare finally stakes out an ontological space that does not simply fall on one side or the other of the trespass-communal divide but rather exists in the common interstices between them. Finding peace as a being existing – simply existing, emotionlessly "untroubled and untroubling where I lie" – Clare nonetheless finds something different than solace: "the dearest that I loved the best are strange – nay, rather, stranger than the rest" (lines 17, 11–12). Although the "strange" "dearest" are often read as those who Clare thinks have forsaken him in the asylum, since what Clare loves the best is nonhuman life, the things and nonhumans, trees, rocks, skies, fields, and badgers that are stranger than humanity, we can now see the full force of the poem's rhetorical textures as it connects to his autobiographical loves. It is literally a poem about self-life-writing wherein the life overwrites the writing of the self, even though the self's love estranges the self from the very nonhumans who make love possible. To be or not to be is not Clare's question. Rather, this ontological estrangement of self and self, and self and other, in this poem sets the stage for love as a nonhuman act of poiesis.

While "I Am" traces the movement from Cartesian-style epistemological doubts to an ecological and ontological estrangement between humans and nonhumans, the under-read "Sonnet: I Am" makes the leap past the human social commons altogether:

> I feel I am, I only know I am
> and plod upon the earth as dull and void
> earth's prison chilled my body with its dram
> of dullness, and my soaring thoughts destroyed.
> I fled to solitudes from passions dream
> but strife pursued – I only know I am.
> I was a being created in the race
> of men disdaining bounds of place and time –
> a spirit that could travel o'er the space
> of earth and heaven – like a thought sublime,
> tracing creation, like my maker, free –
> a soul unshackled like eternity,
> spurning earth's vain and soul debasing thrall
> but now I only know I am – thats all. ("Sonnet: I Am," lines 1–14)

Immediately the poem jams together feeling with knowing, not so much conflating them – since the comma places a caesura between feeling and knowing – as making them conspirators. Just as a comma marks a breath taken between two words, so feeling and knowing conspire – which means, as we recall from *The Last Man* chapter, "breath with each other" – in the misery of Clare's existence. However, "being created in the race / of men" is, strikingly, a post-transcendental and post-sublime existence, "disdaining the bounds of place and time." Already then this poem takes us beyond Timothy Morton's reading of Clare's "dark ecology," which Morton defines as a melancholic awareness of our own very earthly being, stuck in the real mud of a real place, our mortality made uncannily immanent by the stark realness of the world swampily coagulating around our feet.[59] For the poem pointedly "spurn[s] earth's vain and soul debasing thrall," the last word of which, "thrall," as seen above, is Clare's recurrent word for human threats to the environment and to animals in poems like "The Nightingale's Nest" and "The Mores."[60] But, oddly, Clare also associates earthly life with the place and time of eternity before saying he now exists beyond earthly life. "I was" marooned on earth, he says in the octave, even though "now I only know I am." Clare's emphasis on epistemology in this poem is odd since scholars like John Barrell and Erica McAlpine have convincingly argued that Clare is not interested in knowing, that is, in acquiring knowledge, about the natural world around him, but rather in empirically perceiving it accurately.[61] Here he is not interested in feeling either. Merging the earthly and the eternal means that he exists beyond eternity; he is in a place and time that is totally beyond all human ken, a place and time that humans cannot know or feel.

Knowing and feeling, then, are foregrounded in order to enact their erasure by the ontological. Clare, in "Sonnet: I Am," has no time for earthly or immortal place and time, explicitly aligning himself with something nebulously nonhuman, a space and time with no epistemological certainty, only nonhuman ontological surety. In this sonnet Clare *is*, but is not actually plodding the earth or spinning in some otherworldly realm "unshackled" from "eternity." Trespassing beyond the confines of human community and eternity, Clare sketches an idea of nonhuman space and time, but rather than the other humans of "I Am" who neither care nor know what he is, here it is Clare who knows he is but does not care that he is. The poem dissimulates, stating its intentions to be about affect (caring) and epistemology (knowing) in order to ultimately be about neither, about the nonhuman ontology Clare can only conjure up instead of capture – because the nonhuman is something *is*-ing in a spacetime so different than the human that it, apparently, can only be limned through a not-knowing and not-caring.

This paradoxically affectless and anti-epistemological space of neither-nor-ness, of sheer isness, is the space – that is, also, neither the place nor the time of ecology – that allows Clare to figure what love consists of, what it is. Famously, Clare writes in "Sighing for Retirement":

"I found the poems in the fields and only wrote them down."[62] Previous to this most deflationary statement of Romantic sublimity, Clare claims that "the book I love is everywhere," said book being Nature, capitalized a few lines above: "O take me from the busy crowd / I cannot bear the noise! / For Nature's voice is never loud" (lines 14–15). Yet, Clare's claim to a poetics absolutely empirical is likewise deflated by his fletching together of the different materials of books, poetry, and nature. While the "book of nature" is a common eighteenth-century trope of which Clare was no doubt well aware, he, unlike other writers who dealt in the trope, does not read this book as *readable*; that is, he does not think we need to read it or interpret it. Clare, it is clear (again!), would fare poorly in introduction to poetry classes when asked to write explications. Nor is Clare's revision of the book-of-nature trope another example of what some have referred to as Clare's natural-history hobbies. Rather, this nonhuman field book of poetry interprets us and not us it. In so doing, the trope engenders a love absent the "I," even as it constitutes that "I" that loves. Faced with the many of the "crowd," the non-noisy murmuring of nature sounds out to Clare instead of him speaking or singing to it; he is now hearing the silence. It is as if nature's sounds imbue Clare with nonhuman sound that is "everywhere the same," and can be written down anywhere in the world that is untrespassed-on by humans. Poetry, a supposed human art form, in reality, as we saw with "The Badger," stems from the nonhuman. This is not another recourse to mimetic representation; Clare does not claim to be representing the world but rather that the world is unmediated poetry. It is possible, or should be at least, according to Clare, to transcribe poetry not as representation or mediation but exactly as it exists in the fields, the natural world that is itself poetry.

This unknowable nonhuman space-time is not a kind of ecology, dark or otherwise, but rather wrought only through poems and their unique ability to create human and nonhuman ontological space-time – exactly the problem that "The Badger" outlines as necessary to avoid anthropocentrism. It is in this strange being and space-time of poetry where Clare gleans what love consists of, what it is, which is paradoxically poetry itself – and this pays off Percy Shelley's theory of poetry as eternal.

"The Progress of Rhyme" anatomizes this difficult, non-anthropocentric poiesis.[63] This longish poem on poetics begins with Clare in an attitude familiar to us from the bird's-nest poetry – wandering about the fields and sticking his nose into the communities of animals that he encounters on his walkabout – yet the poem resolves with his reflections on the impossibility of love between humans. The poem ends with an invocation to Mary, the lost love of Clare's life, bemoaning his fate at that love's spiritual and physical non-consummation. This movement is important, for we would at first think that considerations of love between two humans would be anthropocentric; it needs no long ramble in the fields, examining nonhuman phenomena, to explicate, evoke, or understand it. However, Clare's progression here from the other direction suggests just the opposite: that the nonhuman world somehow has something to tell us about not just love among humans but about how love works and subsequently how to love as humans and to love beyond the human.

The poem opens with another meditation on strangers even as love is yoked to "poesy" as if they naturally coexist. It is only when poetry surrounds him that any type of feeling becomes possible: "It was an early joy to me / That joy was love and poesy … No hope to think of, fear or care / And even love a stranger there" ("The Progress of Rhyme," lines 39–40, 47–8). He continues: "Yet hardly turned my sheepish eye / I worshipped, yet could hardly dare / To show I knew the goddess there / Lest my presumptuous stare should gain / But frowns, ill humour and disdain" (lines 52–5). Poetry, in Clare's careful formulation, exists beyond affective realms of "fear or care" because poems themselves, in their nonhuman nature, are filled with an affect that is not human determined. Poetry, here, is associated with love that, because it lies beyond feelings like "fear or care," is not perforce human love but a different kind of affect altogether. Despite the possibility of love between strangers that the speaker mentions, this emotive union gets quashed by human inability to worship "the goddess," poetry. Paradoxically, poetry is a goddess that requires worship, even if this worship is never really possible. Poetry rebuffs Clare's "sheepish eye" because poetry estranges humans from her on the basis of her nonhuman nature, causing his "presumptuous stare" to reflexively turn Clare's smile upside down with "frowns, ill humour, and disdain." The other paradox, then, is that poetry is a form of love different from human feeling – one that proceeds from the nonhuman space-time of poetry.

In this fashion "The Progress of Rhyme" intimates a radically nonhuman orientation of love:

For everything I felt a love
The weeds below, the birds above
And weeds that bloomed in summer's hours
I thought they should be reckoned flowers
They made a garden free for all
And so I loved them green and small

And sung of some that pleased my eye
Nor could I pass the thistle by
But paused and thought it could not be
A weed in nature's poesy. ("The Progress of Rhyme," lines 83–92)

Here the weed, compared to beautiful flowers, symbolizes how even the meanest feature of the natural world creates the speaker's feelings. The weed, like the thistle, cannot be "a weed in nature's poesy." Often in Clare's poetry – the animal poems above, for instance – the emphasis on parataxis has a tendency to overwhelm thought or narrative as the individual images and objects pile steadily atop each other. While this formalist dimension disembodies, if not disappears, Clare from his own poems, "The Progress of Rhyme" sustains a complete thought about the speaker's feeling of love. At this point Clare delivers a poetic shock: the weed, in other words, is not a weed, because there are no weeds in the sense of bad verse or doggerel in "nature's poesy." Weeds, in nonhuman poetry, are the same as flowers. But weeds are also thistles. And these weeds rain down amidst "plenteous showers" that water the gardens of flowers as well as fall on "sheep and cows and oxen." A thistle, which is also a weed, growing among the garden of flowers, is also the rain that comes pouring down to water that garden. Crucially, despite the apparent comparisons, none of these weeds, flowers, and thistles are, in the end, metaphors of any kind. Clare means that there is a radical egalitarianism of feeling that equates every thing and being in the nonhuman world of poetry. But, the crucial turn happens at the end of this startling sequence: it is "nature's love," found "even there," and not his love, that is egalitarian and which instructs Clare how to correctly see, not observe but truly see the weed in nature's poesy – not the life of things but the love of things, the love between things. Nature, it turns out, does not love all things; nature is love, and, as this poem shows, this type of love becomes for Clare a model for a type of posthuman love that founds new communities of humans and nonhumans.

Clare reverses the trajectory of loco-descriptive poetry from the human gaze to the ontological space-time of the nonhuman: it is nature's love that informs the poet's love. Suddenly his "musing" becomes enough "to meet with praises" because his "heart had love for poesy." He recounts:

When I was in the fields alone
With none to help and none to hear
To bid me either hope or fear

The bird or bee its chords would sound
The air hummed melodies around
I caught with eager ear the strain
And sung the music o'er again
Or lover or instinct flowing strong
Fields were the essence of the song
And fields and woods are still as mine
Real teachers that are all divine. ("The Progress of Rhyme," lines 134–41)

Alone in the fields of poetry, Clare again finds himself without "hope or fear," beyond human feeling and space-time, at which point the "bird or bee its chords would sound," their humming poetic notes swarming in the air around him. Caught now by the buzzing and twilling music, Clare learns the birds and the bees of poetry. Kind of. For he is not really learning from the natural world, despite describing it as "real teachers," so much as he has found gainful employment as a music copyist. Any song of his own, he points out, may be "weak or tame," but this is due to his mistranscriptions of buzzes and twills. Poetry, real poetry, must be untamed, like the birds and bees freely roaming the fields. Clare puts this lesson into actuality later in the poem when he onomatopoetically tries to transcribe the bird's song: "wew-wew wew-wew chur-chur chur-chur" (line 247). As Kuduk Weiner points out, Clare "integrates ontomatopoetic words into the poem's rhymed iambic pentameter couplets," and this "transforms the bird's song into his own lyric."[64] Writing bird burbles or bee buzz into poetic measure immediately alters it into something partially human-made. To repeat what Clare writes in "Sighing for Retirement": "I found the poems in the field and only wrote them down." Ironically, then, taking the poetry out of the field and transcribing it with human hands into a "poem" transforms it from nature's poetry into what quantum theorist Karen Barad would call an "intra-action," the instantiation of a new medium, a human and nonhuman poiesis that entangles and blurs subjectivity and objectivity as this new phenomena, this new poetry, comes into being.[65]

This is why we discover in the poem's last line – "And hope, love, joy, are poesy" – that poetry is love, which means consequently that love, like poetry, is impossible for humans to experience as merely a human phenomenon divorced from the natural world (lines 347–8).[66] Clare describes his obsessive focus on Mary and his mistaken reading of her face: "I saw thy blush and thought it love" (line 328). But, as we know, it was not love.[67] Instead, the blossoms of human passion grow on apathetically while the blossoms of poetry carry all that is hope, joy, and love in the world. He writes:

I saw thy beauty grow with days
And tried song-pictures in thy praise
And though I dare not look to thee
Of love – to them I talked aloud
And grew ambitious from the crowd
With hopes that I should one day be
Beloved with the praise of thee.
Yet that same cheer in after toils
Was poesy – and still she smiles
As sweet as blossoms to the tree
And hope, love, joy, are poesy. ("The Progress of Rhyme," lines 331–48)

While his blossoms "grow," he feels an ambition to step forward from the many of the "crowd" to become her beloved, only to end up becoming a faceless member of that crowd because his poetic blossoms are human only, not real poetry, weeds brought to his beloved rather than flowers. His "song-pictures" fail because they are not the poetic songs of birds and bees but rather only marks on paper, abstract picture art, not poetry – and certainly not love, because love, as we have seen, exists in the ontological space-time of human and nonhuman poiesis that Clare claims he has not quite achieved.

Clare's poem, it turns out, is something of a modern fable of the bees: poetry, with each new iteration, brings into being a common space-time that can serve as the political medium for forging communities of humans and nonhumans bound by this radical, expansive, non-speciesist love. We will never, according to Clare, be able to love until we not only hear the birds and the bees but also trespass without trespassing on, occupy without assimilating, live life in common in the ontological space-time of the birds and bees. How such an event is supposed to transpire Clare does not tell us because it is not a matter of knowing. We might say, instead, that it is a question of to bee or not to bee. While Hardt and Negri, and other theorists of global biopolitics like Agamben and Žižek, may continue to give love a bad name, if we instead heed Clare's ontological poetics, both humans and nonhumans will no longer live unloved. Rather, we may finally learn to love in common with those with whom we have nothing in common.

5 The Best of All Possible End of the Worlds: Jane Austen's *Frankenstein*, or Love in the Ruins

The work is rather too light, and bright, and sparkling; it wants shade; it wants to be stretched out here and there with a long chapter of sense, if it could be had; if not, of solemn specious nonsense, about something unconnected with the story; an essay on writing, a critique of Walter Scott, or the history of Buonaparté, or anything that would form a contrast, and bring the reader with increased delight to the playfulness and epigrammatism of the general style.

Jane Austen, *Letters*[1]

It must have seemed like some twisted drawing-room comedy, the kind of thing Jane Austen might have written if the lightness, brightness, and sparkle of her country houses had suddenly been nightmarishly distorted by the entrance of *Frankenstein*'s creature – which is exactly what happened. Holed up in the drawing room of their Genevan chateau, Mary and Percy Shelley, Lord Byron, and John Polidori sheltered in the perverse safety of a story contest about ghosts, monsters, and corpses from the unbecoming, funereal blackness that palled the days during 1816, the year without a summer. It is this summer scene, as we famously know, that lends inspiration to Shelley's novel even though at the same time such scenes could not seem further from the idyllic pacificity of Austen's world.[2] But while the idea of the creature's intrusion into Austen's ordered, polite, proper estate manors might seem counterfactual, if not plainly absurd, it is worth examining the crossroads of heteronormativity and monstrous otherness that tarry together in this strange moment in literary history that intersects the climate-change realities of the Anthropocene.[3]

For of all the definitively modern contradictions issued forth in the Romantic era, one of the more conspicuously odd is the simultaneous realization of the country-house romance in the hands of Austen and the emergence of post-apocalyptic poetry and prose that appear almost designed to disrupt such neat heteronormative narratives.[4] While Austen's novels focus on the courtship rituals and mating habits of the rural gentry, it is also the novels' and the real-life gentry who are plotting the continuance of the species through heteronormative reproductive practices enacted by strategic marriage alliances. The world without us that I have been exploring in this book thus resonates with Austen's fears about the extinction of life and love when marriage matches fail, since this potentially curtails the human species. In its visions of human extinction the Anthropocene questions whether these reproductive practices will, should, or even can continue. At this point in the book we can see that this state of contradiction, between love's and life's continuance and love's and life's extinction, lies at the heart of the Anthropocene: biological human reproduction can both create and destroy because human reproduction exacerbates the climate change that holds forth the promise of one meaning of the phrase this book has been exploring – a *literal* world without us.

Given their historical situation, then, Austen's neighbourhoods function as a synecdoche for human societies that stare extinctualism in the eye while they obliviously commit to it, dancing away to doom in their drawing rooms, allegorizing humanity's own paradoxical credulity and confidence in its ability to reproduce its way out of dying out. Her world order, in other words, is thoroughly post-apocalyptic. Of course, as I said at the outset of this book, *Pride and Prejudice* is not considered a post-apocalyptic text – Elizabeth and Darcy achieve the happy ending that *Frankenstein* prevents its characters from experiencing. But, taken together, both novels depict the same central paradox of the more obviously post-apocalyptic texts that are the subject of previous chapters. We can see this in the odd doubling of the courtship rituals in Shelley's *Frankenstein* and Austen's *Pride and Prejudice*: the creature threatens to extinguish humanity if he is not provided a mate to continue his genealogy; while Mr Darcy is accused by Elizabeth of "despising his fellow creatures ... of descending to ... inhumanity," an accusation that derails, for a time, their final love match and any possibility of continuing their own two-person lineage.[5] Darcy, Elizabeth memorably tells him, is "the last man she would ever consent to marry" (*Pride and Prejudice*, p. 134), marking him out as potentially the last of his line, the last man – just as we all always already are as seen in Mary Shelley's *The Last Man*. But while this singular Darcy extinction does not rise to the level of mass species death, it does, however, remind us of the ways social relations make humans into nonhumans by expropriating their identity as a member of a species and thereby situating them as the last remainder of that species. They therefore become of no species because a species requires collectivity to exist; becoming the last man of the human species means that that species is extinct, while, simultaneously, it means that the still living last man is also *not* human. The last man is not, cannot be, the last man. Because extinction is the condition of human existence, even as it leads us to believe in our own immortality – what I have been calling extinctualism – humans, in effect, are not yet alive. We are always already last men and women and hence are not last men and women, not human at all. As Cary Wolfe puts it, "the 'human,' we now know, is not now, and never was, itself."[6] If post-apocalyptic texts, as I have argued throughout this book, envision new forms of life after this not-aliveness that is lastness, then so does Austen's novel, the characters scrambling to find an appropriate other with whom to mate. They resemble the creature's ambitions even though those ambitions ultimately lie torn and frustrate on the floor of Victor's second laboratory when he rends the female creature to pieces, an action meant, he tells us, to preserve the human species, the biopolitical, apocalyptic purpose par excellence.

In this chapter I argue that we can understand both the species extension of Austen's heteronormative protocols and Victor's fears about human extinction in the context of Foucauldian "biopolitics" that I explored in the verse of Byron and John Clare. To briefly rehearse, Foucault describes biopower as a "set of mechanisms through which the basic biological features of the human species became the object of a political strategy, of a general strategy of power."[7] Prior to the eighteenth century, Foucault says, political power had been defined in terms of negation, a right to take life. Hence, the monarch can demand that a subject's head be delivered to him forthwith, and someone will do it with dispatch. But rather than being a monarchist head-chopping affair, biopolitics, as developed in the eighteenth century, transitions to a form of modern democratic social authority that intends to regulate and support the generation of human life. Biopolitics, in other words, wants to ensure that humans live on for all the days of their lives through socially engineered processes that protect them.

It is worth, however, considering the cautionary note Foucault sounds about progressive narratives of human advancement that seems to unwittingly invoke *Frankenstein*. Biopolitics can always exceed human control because "it becomes possible … to create living matter, to build the monster, and, ultimately, to build viruses that cannot be controlled and that are universally destructive."[8] Shelley's creature in *Frankenstein* presents, literally, the monster's construction and the subsequent manner in which biopolitical creativity can boomerang on its creators and destroy them – as the creature does to Victor and his lineage, making Victor a last nonhuman, too, just as the creature is a last nonhuman. This biopolitical building of the monster shares much with what Derrida calls society's "autoimmune structure": that is, how the pursuit of life's advancement leads to its destruction. Like an autoimmune disease that creates antibodies that flip backwards and blitz the body that created them, society, in the age of biopolitics, by trying to maintain human life, inevitably produces nonhuman monstrous life that simultaneously closes the possibility of life it paradoxically discloses. This phenomenon is extinctualism in that it advances the prospect of infinite human life in the same moment it spawns forms of life that annul that very possibility. The creature, let us remember, represents humanity's extinction either in terms of its obsolescence – since, for one thing, humans cannot survive the harsh, cold climate like the creature – or through the creature's intentional extirpation of the species, making him an avatar of climate change itself. However, the creature's mutated human genetic code that gifts him super strength, speed, and endurance of the Arctic climate heralds the spectre of human endurance in some new form.[9] So, while Shelley's creature – termed "an abhorred monster" by those who encounter him – augurs the disruption of English life's apparently ordered stability guaranteed in the marriage plots of Austen, *Frankenstein* ultimately insists on that same ordered social paradigm of extinctualism.[10] The creature, whose non-identity as a pre-socialized being initially opens up a space for the possibility of radical, nonhuman impossibility, comes to be regarded as a social pariah and imperils the norms of human reproduction. In response, the novel forecloses the norm-defying, end-of-humanity threat that the creature poses when Victor prevents the creature from attaining connubial bliss and procreating a new species.

Pride and Prejudice, with its insistence on species preservation via marriage plotting, shares similar thematic concerns with the post-apocalyptic imperatives of *Frankenstein*. Like that text, which does not allow the creature to sire his own species, the world of Austen's novel mobilizes the exclusionary mechanisms of species preservation; in the process, however, it unknowingly introduces the unlooked-for presence of the nonhuman other into that world's gene pool. Species distinctions, on my reading, lie at the heart of the discourses of gendered and sexual identity in these novels (published within half a decade of each other) because both gender and sex distinctions invoke species difference as common exclusionary ground.[11] Harnessing species difference, the marriage plots of *Pride and Prejudice* serve as exemplary attempts to conserve traditionalist and heteronormative social orders even as they nevertheless disrupt the biological frameworks of these foundations. The exclusions of species difference work by means of what Niklas Luhmann calls a "closed social system," which, in the context of these novels, is a social system that accesses the nonhuman to maintain control over conditions of identity and personhood.[12] It is precisely through its referential contact with these nonhuman species systems external to it that such a closed system can constantly recuperate its own internal order.

However, these novels depart from Luhmann's account of how Romantic love works within a social system. For Luhmann, Romanticism's desire to love the natural world – to merge, as I said in this book's beginning, the subject and the object – causes a shift in the semantics of love, and love in the Romantic period came to concern, he argues, self-referentiality. This self-referentiality, according to Luhmann, occurred by means of Romantic irony, an undercutting of the individual in the very affirmation of that individuality. He writes, unconsciously referencing *Pride and Prejudice*'s famous opening sentence, that "their greatest faculty, for example, was no longer assumed to be the ability to recognize *universal truths*, but instead the capacity to form a self-referentially constituted relationship to the world. This faculty individualized people as subjects different from the world – and no longer as members of the exceptional human species as distinguished from the species Animal."[13] While Luhmann is right that the Romantics, in their resistance to biopolitics, as we saw in the last chapters, do not seek to reify humans as a distinct ruling species, he is wrong in that they do not seek to love the natural world but rather to think a version of love that stems from the nonhuman towards the human. And as we will see in *Pride and Prejudice*, love is not self-referential in this way; instead, it is a process of co-creation. Love is a process of writing the other into existence – which Darcy and Elizabeth do in reading the face of the other (in which reading is also a process of writing) and by sending textual and verbal letters whose characters create their characters. This is why, of all the characters in the novel, Elizabeth and Darcy are the dynamic ones; the rest are static. But they are not so much changing as *coming into being, into life, for the first time through their love*. It is in this way that the novel radically revises human heterosexuality by showing that likeness can only be found in difference, acceptance in rejection; indeed, acceptance must retain difference's rejection in order for two people to love, and it is in this way that they become, like Elizabeth and Darcy, co-creations of the other even while they remain other.

Despite surface appearances to the contrary, on my reading, *Frankenstein* turns out to be a novel about protecting normative institutions, whereas *Pride and Prejudice* turns out to disclose the nonhuman conceptual origins of human social networks that threaten to, and do, up-end the normative social order.[14] *Pride and Prejudice,* then, unlike *Frankenstein,* preserves the nonhuman in the human, rewriting a post-apocalyptic future that does not simply make humans extinct or abjectly exile nonhumans from the human world but instead fashions a new entanglement of both, a future-to-come. Such a future beckons in Elizabeth's and Darcy's theorization and enactment of love as unconditional, a radical praxis that shows how life and love can remain, in the face of potential post-apocalyptic extinction, surprisingly, if radically, possible. By envisioning love as unconditional for the other, whether human or nonhuman, Austen's novel counters the death drive of post-apocalyptic biopolitics, which is tied, again, to human sexual reproduction.[15] Decidedly not incorporative, a subsuming of the other in an egalitarian human democracy, Elizabeth's and Darcy's unconditional love is instead non-exclusionary in its exclusions because it recognizes that humans are not wholly human. In this sense, the novel's heterosexuality gets decidedly queered. Their non-exclusion erects barriers in order to open them to the constant arrival of difference between the human and the nonhuman that inheres inside the human. It lets the nonhuman in from the inside, and not just the outside, which limns a powerful model for "living on" in the Anthropocene.

In *Frankenstein,* biopolitical concerns about the reproduction of the human species are also tied to Enlightenment accounts of imaginative sympathy, a key word in *Frankenstein* (and as David Marshall convincingly argues, perhaps *the* key word) and a conceptual driver of the marriage plot in *Pride and Prejudice.*[16] Adam Smith, the most influential writer on sympathy of the time, theorizes sympathy as a context-based act that reproduces normative humanness, a type of narcissism of reflection and replication. "By the imagination we place ourselves in his situation," Smith says of the sympathizing self and the sufferer.[17] Seeing emotions expressed on another person's face and in body language gives rise to imaginative associations and substitutions in the mind of the observer, creating a mechanism for the subject to sympathize with the other (sympathy is both the emotion and the mechanism that engenders it). Such mental processes are not, properly speaking, cognitive, though. Instead, as Thomas Pfau reminds us, they operate through automaticity since "neither sight nor behavior involved any sustained cognitive effort" given that they "can only signify on the basis of an already established ... matrix of socio-cultural values."[18] Because these matrices are set, seeing the other automatically induces this thing called sympathy without rational thought. Valuable as Pfau's reminder is, however, it tends to elide that Smith's sympathy requires both socio-cultural *and* bodily processes to activate and substantiate the emotion. For sympathy, as Maureen McLane notes, depends on the specular economy of the body, the *self-evident* nature of the human form; the sufferer must look human, a necessary predicate in David Hume's equally influential concept of sympathy, although his model retains cognition that can allow thought to negate sympathetic automaticity – but only, as we will see, if the other humans do not look like you.[19] Smith and Hume both precede Levinas, whose philosophical project articulates the ethical imperatives of the human "face" to think in non-Heideggerian terms about ontology ("otherwise than being," as Levinas puts it), because sympathy requires the mediation of face-to-face interaction, a process premised on the identification of another whose face and figure are recognizably human; it is worth recalling too that, for Levinas, the face is not circumscribed to the face on the face of the human head but encompasses addressability, the voice spoken to the other.[20] According to Smith, communities are formed on this model, and moral action undertaken, based upon empirical observations converted to affective affinities by this imaginative transference. Hence, in Smith's example of seeing a body on a rack being tortured, "we enter as it were into his body, and become in some measure the same person with him,"[21] precisely because we can identify with that body as like ours. More than a simile, since sympathy works without conscious thought, our volitional prerogatives are mentally overwritten, literally, by species identification.

But if sympathy enacts social incorporation, it also, at the level of species identity, stages social differentiation. "Were it possible that a human creature could grow up," Smith writes, "without any communication with his own species," he would be "provided with no mirror" to view "the beauty or deformity of his own face," a problem fortunately mitigated, according to Smith, "in the countenance and behaviour" presented by the bodies of humans sharing social networks.[22] Smithian sympathy works explicitly to exclude the deformed and the nonhuman – forms that do not fit a normative standard; as the reference to a homogenous species implies, this social mirror indicates the a priori assumption of a universally recognizable human form, one that distinguishes faces as beautiful or deformed without thought. Therefore, for Smith, limning human form produces social solidarity, just as, equally, the self-evident otherness of nonhuman form excludes them from social inclusion. In effect, to sympathize with another is to recognize his or her personhood, a form of identification crucial in structuring the economic, legal, and ethical institutions that lend themselves, in

Smith's words, to the "multiplication of the species."[23] Levinas's thinking, too, demurs over whether nonhumans can have a face, a problem unsatisfactorily re-litigated by Derrida in his own animal study.[24]

Austen and Shelley face these issues in their turn to face the face of the nonhuman, whom they both recognize may not have a face on Levinas's terms, but whose very existence, very being, with or without a human face, makes it possible to love the nonhuman. These two Regency-era texts, then, both effectively showcase sympathy's restrictive limits when faced with the outcast forms of life it helps birth, and theorize post-apocalyptic Romanticism's love. Employing sympathy's species discourse, Austen and Shelley discover within its aporia a posthuman conception of face-to-face relationships that situates the face of the nonhuman other (even when, especially then, that nonhuman face is conceived of as human) as foundational and necessary for life and love in the Anthropocene.

Animated by these species concerns, *Frankenstein*, in its frame narrative, defines "romantic" as a quest for sympathy with someone like you, someone of the same species.[25] The would-be polar discoverer Captain Walton unwittingly proffers a definition of Romanticism with a specifically homosocial, homogenous valence, eliding difference in favour of what Luce Irigaray names "the Same."[26] "You may deem me romantic," Walton writes to his sister, but "I desire the company of a man who could sympathize with me."[27] The frame narration, indeed, frames the novel with this thesis about sympathy and sets the stage for what Scott Juengel calls the novel's "ocular wish-fulfillment" that considers how ethics are grounded in face-to-face relations.[28] For David Marshall, in his influential reading on Rousseauvian sympathy in the novel, Shelley's tale is "a parable about the failure of sympathy" in which the creature "does not understand that it is his sameness that is most threatening," because his sameness derives from his likeness to his creator.[29] Yet, such a reading would seem to elide Shelley's insistence on the creature's absolute alterity, his unlikeness from all humankind, the difference society in the novel must, and does, shut down. It is about, I think, the success, not the failure, of sympathy.

In this sense the novel's production of the duelling speciesist insistence on homogeneity and heterogeneity discovers sympathy's limits in dissimilarity, the deformed physicality of the creature's form, his disfigured visage and ill-proportioned frame. On that "dreary night in November" when the creature first opens his yellow eyes, Victor finds himself "unable to endure the aspect of the being I had created" and he "rushed out of the room" (36). Later in the novel Victor will describe "the deformity of its aspect" as "more hideous than belongs to humanity" (50). "Aspect" can mean both face and body, so in this passage, more than his face, it is the creature's entire physical form that marks him as excluded from the face-to-face economy of imaginative sympathy. During Victor and the creature's talk on Mont Blanc, Victor says, "I compassionated him, and sometimes felt a wish to console him; but when I looked upon him, when I saw the filthy mass that moved and talked … I could not sympathise with him" (103). Much like the contextual apparatus of putting oneself in the other's shoes that operates Smithian sympathy, Victor would have to exit his own spatial area and inhabit the creature's; only, due to the "filthy" materiality of that physicality, he cannot step outside of his shoes and strap on the creature's. He remains shod in his own human-fitting shoes, stabled safely away from the muck that he associates with nonhuman filthiness.

Previous to this snowy mountaintop summit, the creature has already discovered what he calls "the fatal effects of this miserable deformity," why he seeks to overcome the species prejudices that facial form maintains by forging a relationship with the blind De Lacey, a person who cannot perforce react as Victor does, because sight is removed from the physical equation (79). Having closely watched the "angelic countenances" of the cottagers near a hovel where he hides, the creature contrasts it to his own "hideously deformed and loathsome" figure, which leads him to a very speciesist conclusion: "I was not even of the same nature as man" (83). "Was I then a monster, a blot upon the earth, from which all men fled, and whom all men disowned?" he asks (83). As he says, "[I] had sagacity enough to discover that the unnatural hideousness of my person was the chief object of horror with those who had formerly beheld me" (92). This realization of both his own physical difference and the speciesist difference that it installs to separate him from human society impels him to a daring and ostensibly smart plan: to avoid the specular economy, Juengel's "ocular wish-fulfillment," that produces such human pride in species prejudice in the first place. Hence, he waits until De Lacey is alone in the cottage before venturing to recount to him a fictionalized version of his own story, cleverly concealing himself within his narrative as himself, a well-meaning, lonely soul in search of those like him who can offer him compassion and sympathy, and vice versa. De Lacey, a kindly and seemingly senescent man, informs him that, "when unprejudiced by any obvious self-interest," humans are kind beings "full of brotherly love and charity" (93). In response, the creature shrewdly details how human kindliness is exactly the problem because it is always controlled by self-interestedness stemming from visual perception, and therefore "a fatal prejudice clouds" the eyes of the family of which he wishes to be a part, causing them to "behold only a detestable monster" rather than his true character, his, as he *sees* it, character of a loving friend (93).

De Lacey, his judgment unclouded by the sightline of prejudice, would seem ideally able to fulfil the creature's wishes, to "see" beyond prejudice because he cannot see, cannot see what there is to be prejudiced about. Nevertheless, while De Lacey is not negatively exemplified as some disabled person or as somehow more than human on account of his disability (another negative version of disability), in the novel he remains, rather, circumscribed within the judiciary tribunal of anthropocentric justice. As De Lacey informs the creature, he cannot "judge of your countenance," which would seem to deviate from the protocols of sympathy's judicial review, but, since he finds harmony and sincerity in the creature's words, he does function as a judge, rendering an opinion on the merits of the case as he hears and "sees" them (94). De Lacey, then, acts as another type of judge, inhering to what he perceives to be the creature's inner character, his benevolence and worth, *without* looking at his face. To De Lacey, the creature, in fact, has no face. With Thomas DuToit, who demonstrates the connection between the novel and the law, we can say that the "monster's face cannot be shown by the monster in such a way that it could be seen by human beings," and this is true even if, as in this scene, they cannot see it.[30] On Smith's and Levinas's terms, then, the creature remains excluded from any sympathy by De Lacey because for sympathy to work the creature's face must be seen, even if – as it will turn out to be the case when Felix sees it – it turns out to be judged not a face. The face must be seen in order to be unseen as a face.

Only if De Lacey could see the creature and not un-see him, that is if he could still accept his physical difference, would he transgress the physically limiting dictates of sympathy that institute alterity and move into a realm where genuine hospitality to the other – and here the creature represents the ultimate other of hospitality, the literal *xenos*, alien and completely strange – becomes possible. De Lacey, on the novel's terms, is thus enabled and not disabled, an enabling that denies him his disability and makes him a negative example of seeing humans and unable to see nonhumans. In other words, the novel forecloses the difference of disability as well as the creature's difference. Shelley's point, *via negativa*, is that only if De Lacey could see the creature, recognize his difference and how that registers the creature as an impossible figure for hospitality, and then, not in spite of but because of this impossibility, *still offer him hospitality would such hospitality not only be possible but fully realized*. Hospitality does not normally exceed the De Lacey family's capacity since "the poor were never turned away from their door" (92).

For hospitality to be truly hospitable, it must invite difference over the threshold in full knowledge of difference's difference, in full knowledge that what it, hospitality that is, is doing is impossible to do. As we saw in Shelley's *The Last Man*, for hospitality to be true hospitality without violence, it needs to be a passivity without passivity, a not-doing, to do, to give that which it cannot but must give, volition and action to the nonhuman.

Therefore, despite the ostensible removal of the speciesist facial prejudice, De Lacey's final words revert back to it as he avers that he is in "any way serviceable to a *human* creature," which requires what is perceived as the heteronormative face (94; my emphasis). In response the creature says, "I trust that, by your aid I shall not be driven from the society and sympathy of your fellow-creatures" (94). Once De Lacey's fellow cottagers see the creature, though, their "seeing" reasserts the explicit exclusionary mechanism of sympathy – "my protectors had departed, and had broken the only link that held me to the world" (94) – in that Felix's attack on the creature declares that they have seen the creature's face and judged it to be no face, in human terms, at all; it is a nonhuman face. This judgment places any hope of hospitality under literal violence (with which it is already entwined), and the creature is cast out, like Satan from heaven, from all that hospitality leads to: ethics, friendship, justice, community, the social in general. Sympathy's speciesist prejudice literally confronts the creature with his fundamental difference, that the face, his own particularly, is ineffaceable. The face's ineffaceability prevents the creature from entering into the social-contract society he yearns for despite his efforts to be a good capitalist subject, acting as (in his own words, which echo Smith's economic theory) "an invisible hand" that gathers wood and so light and warmth and food (the very things that baffled his existence early in the forest when he was unable to spark fire), for the De Laceys (78, 79). He acts without "self-interest," to use De Lacey's word, the key word in Smith's other treatise, *A Wealth of Nations* (1776), because although he wants sympathy, it is not in exchange for his labour. Nor, while committing these actions, does he yet have any hope of recompense; rather, he believes that sympathy should be offered freely, openly, like the family proffers to the poor.

Ian Balfour contends that existence outside of a gift economy, which he notes that thinkers from Mauss to Derrida analyse to show that there is no gift, establishes the creature as "unhuman."[31] In a sense this is correct, but more pressingly problematic for hospitality is the gift economy that the creature eventually wishes to enter: he *wants* his labour valued as a gift, a reservoir of banked goodwill that can accrue the interest of sympathy. He wants to be human, to have self-interest, and, arguably, in the moment he wants this, the wanting gives it to him, and he acquires self-interest if not sympathy – and so the novel is not a total failure of sympathy as Marshall argues but a *success* of sympathy because sympathy is exclusionary in its very heart. The creature becomes human within the various exchange economies (face, capital, gift, sympathy) in operation and so, like De Lacey, achieves a kind of blindness in sight that circumscribes him as human.

Here, the well-known doppelganger theory of the creature and Victor takes on new relevance. Victor is a person, as Mary Poovey argues, controlled by self-interest.[32] Likewise, Felix and family retain their self-interest, and they self-protect from the face of the faceless horror they behold. Such a rejection painfully forces the creature into life as a solitary walker, one who differs from Rousseau in that he finds only misery and desolation in the natural world to which he is reduced for want of the social company he so desires. Alone in both the state of nature and society, an aporia his treatment in the latter realm opens, the creature represents the perfect libertarian, living in a world of anarchy with only his own boot-straps to pull himself up with since no humans can put themselves in his boots.[33] The novel, on the creature's behalf, rejects the linked tenets of sympathy and self-interest entirely while casting suspicion on happiness in both the state of nature and society, much as James O'Rourke argues that Shelley effaces the distinction between Rousseau's love of self (concern for personal preservation in the state of nature) and self-love (egotism conditioned by society).[34] For these reasons we can now read the novel's politics as constitutively post-apocalyptic.

The creature's failure to achieve interspecies affection institutes his turn to nonhuman procreation and the spectre, glimpsed in Victor's non-sympathetic eye, of an attendant rise of a planet of peaceful, alienated, but happy "monsters." Although the creature wishes he could "become linked to the chain of existence and events, from which" he is "now excluded," as he realizes post-encounter with the De Lacey family, "the human senses are insurmountable barriers to our union" (102). He therefore demands that Victor fulfil his newfound sympathetic and sexual desires: "you must create a female for me, with whom I can live in the interchange of those sympathies necessary for my being" (101). While an exit from reflectively homogenous society might seem to break the spell cast by sympathy, the creature actually imprints his boots further into the very mud he cannot escape in his lonesome walk: the Enlightenment postulates of speciesist sympathy. Desiring sympathy, the creature remains firmly wedded to the initial quest that Walton frames as the main plot of the novel: the search for a similar mate who can sympathize with him. The creature is a real "romantic" in Walton's sense of the term. But although the creature again invokes the necessity of sympathy and society for his well-being, he does so in terms that begin to understand the contours of sympathy's exclusionary calculus. In other words, the creature is now able to see what he could not see before: his own face and the face of others, the whole specular economy of the system predicated on the blind spots of monstrosity. Thus, he specifies his needs in similar terms: "one as deformed and horrible as myself would not deny herself to me. My companion must be of the same species, and have the same defects. This being you must create" (97). His mate must have a face that can see his face just as he can see hers – unlike the re-normativized, blind De Lacey. After his meeting with De Lacey the creature knows that without a face sympathy eludes both see-er and seen. With a face, however, the creature believes that their mutual facial monstrousness will enact their actual effacement, their human-deplored deformity made irrelevant, rather than reified, by observation.

For the creature, there is no possibility of sympathy because having no human face, like he does, gives him face enough to be identified as nonhuman, which will leave him mateless. In contrast, having a nonhuman face with another being who has the same nonhuman face will efface both of their nonhuman faces, providing them, metaphorically and effectively, a human face in that now they can sympathize with each other. The creature has learned his lesson well, and, like the representative humanity that confronts him in the novel, he cannot accept difference either. He yearns for a sympathy directed at him but, in so doing, crucially remains bound by the self-referential logic of sympathetic norms; in finding a mate who reflects his face, dwelling in a location far removed from humanity, he will finally look just like everyone else, he will finally be "normal" within the heteronormative modes of his two-person society with his like-faced mate based on anthropocentric parameters. The logical calculus of sympathetic speciesism – wherein the physical regulation of normativity grounds relationships, the axiomatic hinge on which life depends in this far-flung, isolated, deserted, desert love affair – would continue. His education, as others have noted, remains thoroughly humanist: he wants to convert difference into sameness between him and his mate, an Adam and Eve, the last creatures of nonhumanity, and the first creatures of their new species – last men and women made first men and women but, in turn, also last men and women because they would not be subject to the biopolitics of reproduction and extinction.[35] They would be, that is, human in their lastness made firstness.

This homological firstness developed from lastness – the last of his species – is crucial for the creature because this effacement will set him and his deformed mate apart as a new species: "we shall be monsters, cut off from all the world" (102). Achieving this plan would seem to finally complete Victor's original plan of creating "a new species" that "would bless me as its creator," although it would do so in a quite unexpectedly different way, to put it euphemistically, than Victor ever imagined (33). Yet, while the creature still remains locked within the circular logic that demands he occupy the subject position of Enlightenment sympathy, of the Same, Victor foresees that such an effacement would only constitute faces of a different human physiognomy, leading to simply a new replay of old exclusions in this species. Although his knowledge stems from his pride and prejudice, Victor also voices an understanding that an autoimmune effect is possible. Victor is, on McLane's interpretation, an agent of the "ideological biologization of species difference" (biopolitics before the term appeared), whose impulses are completely Malthusian: to guard and proliferate the human (and he is thus something akin to a nation himself, a "Europe" that safeguards against the post-colonial other as McLane says).[36]

Desiring a mate, the creature fits comfortably within Foucault's analytical anatomization of the transition from monarchical power to democratic biopower's control over excess life's reproduction: the proliferation of the monster, or the virus, that exceeds human control. This reproduction of the excess that has been produced is the autopoietic function of biopower, when excess life takes on a life of its own, literally what happens in *Frankenstein* as the creature turns on his creator and, in fact, on the whole human species when his ability to mate gets neutered. Like a virus, excess life replicates itself, creating copies that mirror its originary genetic material. Indeed, the creature, in effect, wants a copy of himself made, a (re)production to which Victor initially accedes. During their confrontation on Mont Blanc, Victor, though unable to sympathize with the creature, to allow him agency as a liberal humanist subject, agrees to harness his creative abilities on the creature's behalf: "I thought, that as I could not sympathize with him, I had no right to withhold from him the small portion of happiness which was yet in my power to bestow" (103). This second act of creation confronts Frankenstein with the biopolitical implications of his actions:

> I was now about to form another being, of whose dispositions I was alike ignorant; she might become ten thousand times more malignant than her mate, and delight, for its own sake, in murder and wretchedness. He had sworn to quit the neighborhood of man, and hide himself in deserts; but

> she had not; and she, who in all probability was to become a thinking and reasoning animal, might refuse to comply with a compact made before her creation. They might even hate each other; the creature who already lived loathed his own deformity, and might he not conceive a greater abhorrence for it when it came before his eyes in the female form? She also might turn with disgust from him to the superior beauty of man; she might quit him, and he be again alone, exasperated by the fresh provocation of being deserted by one of his own species.
>
> Even if they were to leave Europe, and inhabit the deserts of the new world, yet one of the first results of those sympathies for which the dæmon thirsted would be children, and a race of devils would be propagated upon the earth, who might make the very existence of the species of man a condition precarious and full of terror. (118–19)

Because the creature finds his own deformity disagreeably blackballing, Victor reasons that two creatures, when confronted by each other, may find that the other's hideousness proscribes affection and will introduce "the fresh provocation of" the creature's "being deserted by one of his own species." Any such proscription would also prescribe bad medicine; both creatures would convert into state-of-nature beings, solitary, but unlike Rousseau, unhappy in this state because they are ostracized from society, even, eventually, their own duopolistic version of society. Whatever "compact" might exist between them would, in its nullification, also annul the compact that pre-exists them, the one the creature made, and it would, as such, seal their fate, a mandatory expulsion from society and entrance into the *jouissance* of their own return to Paradise.

In Victor's imagination the creatures would truly be a post-apocalypse for humanity because the individualistic anarchy that they would reintroduce into society would dissolve the social contract, placing everyone in the state of nature, the original position from which a contract is drawn up or war is declared. But for Victor it is a "damned if they do and damned if they don't" scenario, for, even if they remain together, their actions will still be post-apocalyptic in the warfare valence of the term because "one of the first results of those sympathies for which the dæmon thirsted would be children … who might make the very existence of the species of man a condition precarious" (119). Frankenstein fears that, if the creature were to act on this reproductive desire – and here we can see how the creature represents the excess of life, the monstrous result of biopower – then his further monstrous reproduction would amount to an act of autopoiesis, the self-creation of life from its own singular genome, fresh oppositional fodder that the creature can field in his war against humanity.[37]

The full post-apocalyptic implications of the novel should now be apparent. On the one hand, the creature desires to fulfil his "romantic" apocalyptic drive to become Adam with his identical Eve in Paradise. On the other hand, his ambition stoppered, the creature transforms into a post-apocalyptic agent that represents humanity's Last Days as he wages war on them. In fact, Victor's thoughts on the annihilation of the human species recall us to the creature's Hobbesian threats on Mont Blanc, the mountain that, as my reading in chapter 1 details, stands as the Romantic instance of the post-apocalypse sublime: "from that moment I declared everlasting war against the species, and, more than all, against him who had formed me, and sent me forth to this insupportable misery" (99). The creature himself becomes War against all. Victor's horrified realization of this potentially species-wide wipe-out effect is ultimately what forces him to destroy the female creature before he completes it.[38] The novel, like Shelley's later *Last Man*, contrasts human Armageddon with the traditional Milton-inflected (a major element of the creature's humanistic education, let us not forget), Romantic narrative of Paradise regained after it has been lost. For the creature, a return to the Edenic prelapsarian paradise remains his ideal, but, when denied such a glorious return, his thoughts turn to giving birth to a post-apocalyptic world, to effectuating the extinction of the human species in the ruins of the world. Since he cannot find love in the ruins he dwells in then no one else can either.

If, as I have been claiming throughout this book, one of the dominant strands underlying Romanticism is the post-apocalyptic, then the creature's prophetic vision of Edenic bliss perfectly captures the turn to the post-apocalyptic sublime. The creature describes his life with his mate as "peaceful and human," but, given his other expostulation – that they will be monsters together – the second half of this rings like false rhetoric that is meant to persuade rather than elucidate, convince rather than explain. In reality the picture he presents is anything but human. It is, in fact, posthuman, all too posthuman:

> If you consent, neither you nor any other human being shall ever see us again: I will go the vast wilds of South America. My food is not that of man; I do not destroy the lamb and the kid, to glut my appetite; acorns and berries afford me sufficient nourishment. My companion will be of the same nature as myself, and will be content with the same fare. We shall make our bed of dried leaves; the sun will shine on us as on man, and will ripen our food. The picture I present to you is peaceful and human, and you must feel that you could deny it only in the wantonness of power and cruelty. Pitiless as you have been towards me, I now see compassion

> in your eyes; let me seize the favourable moment, and persuade you to promise what I so ardently desire. (*Frankenstein*, 102–3)

Unlike the humanity represented by Abel in Byron's *Cain*, but much like Clare's extension of biopolitical frames to animal life in his non-ecopoetic biopolitics, the creature proposes an anti-speciesist agenda, a refusal to sacrifice the lamb and the kid for corporeal satisfaction and species sustenance. He shares more with Cain's metaphorical murdering of the sacrificial economy, an attempt to "sacrifice sacrifice," as Derrida, we recall, puts it. Indeed, the creature and his mate, in his radical utopian fantasy, will adhere to a vegan (not vegetarian, as past critics have claimed) diet of nuts and berries, just as Adam and Eve did in Paradise before the Fall because eating animals would be an act of violence, making Paradise illusory, a social Matrix of reality.[39] However, that Eden did not feature killing does not necessarily mean that it was also posthuman or non-anthropocentric as, indeed, because of Adam's and Eve's sovereignty in Eden, it was not. Eden comes before sacrifice, but Eden was not vegan, since that requires a responsibility and ethics not yet possible. One cannot decide not to eat animals if they have simply not yet been eaten, if there is no choice to make about sacrificing them; it was, after all, a time before good and evil.

Thus the apocalyptic and the post-apocalyptic twist into a double braid. On the one hand, the creature's depiction of life in exile veers towards the apocalyptic, the return of paradise on earth. On the other hand, because of the calculated non-violence of the paradise he describes, his goals turn towards the literally post-apocalyptic, a world without us, a world nonhuman in the sense of not only the absence of human presence but also the absence of the categorical imperative that "thou shalt not kill" other species (the first demand of the face according to Levinas). In this paradoxical logic, the monsters cut off from the world would become more human than human beings in their establishment of a progressive social contract centred on non-violence to humans and nonhumans, a complete contrast to the thanatopolitics of the Anthropocene wherein capitalism remains driven by the speciesist death drive of animal consumption. The creatures would become, instead, posthuman, constructing an ethical road map that Cain himself sought in his quest to understand justice in the tribunal of post-apocalyptic politics.

Yet, Frankenstein's inability to sympathize with the creature also reveals how, even though the novel seems to open a window into a weird world without us wherein the extinction of the human species becomes distinctly possible and palatable, this glimpse of a post-apocalyptic human-less world proves fleetingly evanescent. It is a glimpse that, in reality, paradoxically ensures the security of human life. This is the other facet of Derrida's "autoimmune function." Bio-power curbs, or even destroys, the excess of life made possible by the biopolitical instrumentalization of the reproduction of human life it creates. The hegemonic tenets of liberal humanism expressed by Victor, which finally claim the creature's life, thus postpone any posthuman possibility, serving as a bulwark against the post-apocalyptic worlds imagined by the Shelleys and Byron. Indeed, the novel functions as an exemplar of how autoimmunity works by ultimately rendering the creature (this excess created by biopower) biopolitically inert because he does not get to reproduce. This explains why the novel's final paragraph disappears the creature, as he simply vanishes into darkness – which recalls the novel's Milton epigraph: "Did I request thee, Maker, from my clay / to mould Me man? Did I solicit thee / From darkness to promote me?" (*Paradise Lost*, book 10, lines 743–5) – no longer a representation of sympathy's possible reorientation to nonhuman life: "he was soon borne away by the *waves*, and lost in darkness and distance" (*Frankenstein*, 161). He transitions from representing the posthuman possibility of post-apocalypse to wishing for apocalyptic paradise, like Adam in the epigraph, to being a pre-apocalyptic state of nothingness, not even an atom (Byron's own fantasy as described in his letter quoted in chapter 3).

But in his penultimate speech before he is swallowed in the long bright, cold dark of the Arctic night, like the humans of Byron's "Darkness," the creature offers a romantic eulogy that Enlightenment promises imply for nonhumans: "No sympathy may I ever find" (159). In the novel's world the creature threatens to destroy the established order of society, but, because his face stands outside the window looking in (he literally looks in through the window twice at Victor, once to witness him destroy the second creature and next to be with him on his wedding night), he is faceless and, as a result, outside the social order itself. Yet here, in this scene with Walton, he has climbed in through the window and this reflects the operational closure of the novel: society is always infected by that which lies exorbitant to it, breathing on the other side of the pane of glass *that is also already inside*. Walton looks right at him in this scene, and, despite having now found someone who can see him – "a man who can sympathize with him" perhaps even – in his last utterance to Walton the creature loses all face, all possible face. Contra Sara Guyer, then, the monster is not finally heard, does not enter into reciprocal addressability with humans by his "loss of face" that signals an "almost human voice."[40] Instead, he is silenced as his lastness precludes further existence because it means he is already extinct. To appropriate his earlier words to Victor, he cannot find, with Walton, an exchange of those sympathies necessary for his being – the novel slams the window shut on any possibility of queerness or differential heterosexuality as well. Walton is not a creature like him; the creature is not a man like Walton.

The creature's species of one cannot create anything, cannot reproduce the continuance of his own frame of self-referential life. The creature is literally a viral non–Foucauldian monster that cannot replicate and hence cannot spread virally. By stymying the creature's reproduction, the novel recuperates the established social order of human procreation and therefore the continuance of the human species is no longer "a condition precarious" as the extinctual threat represented by the creature gets squashed. Enlightenment classical liberal humanism has "built the monster," to hearken back to Foucault's phrase, but in the process his existence reinforces the aesthetic and biological heteronormative procedures, categories, and mores of human society rather than overcoming or overpowering them. "Monstrosity" is contained, quarantined, and finally disposed of. Post-apocalyptic, posthuman possibility is prevented by the autoimmune internal workings of a sympathetic society that will always destroy different, non-normative life in the pursuit of its own species' biopolitical advancement, its own sympathetic narcissism. Like the kindly blind De Lacey and the society that cannot accept his blindness as anything other than a type of reverse special sight, society cannot see and accept difference, because it cannot see the faces of what are, to society, the faceless.

As in *Frankenstein,* where the dialectic of normalcy and deformity governs the state of nature and society, the recognition of physical likeness and the exclusion of dissimilar forms also power the courtship rituals of *Pride and Prejudice.* What differentiates Austen from Shelley is *Pride and Prejudice*'s insistence on enacting the audacious paradisiacal finis proposed by the creature: the novel installs each character in a relationship with someone exactly like them at novel's end, but it does so – and here is the difference that its difference makes – between Elizabeth and Darcy and their openness to the nonhuman other *in the other.* They accept the other's difference, accept the other's exclusion from society, rather than trying to incorporate it into society and erase its difference. Outsiders are in. Whereas, in *Frankenstein,* external features directly control species differentiation, in Austen, species form dictates how internal character is understood. These sympathetic boundaries become a type of impossible hospitability that socially contracts humanity into a closed social system composed of appropriately appropriated pairs – but only one of which, that is, Darcy and Elizabeth – models love.[41] In this sense, *Pride and Prejudice* implicates its lovesick courters in a marital comedy where love depends on material as well as internal character rather than station; this is why all of the characters, in defiance of conventions, marry outside their stations. Lady Catherine de Bourgh summarizes this nicely in her description of the intended marriage of Darcy and her daughter: "'my daughter and my nephew are formed for each other. They are descended on the maternal side, from the same noble line; and, on the father's, from respectable, honourable, and ancient, though untitled families'" (232). On this model the same speciesist wheels of sympathy turn: each character thinks of each of the other characters in the novel as the creature, looking for sympathetic affiliation. In the subsequent inclusion in marriage that the characters achieve from those unlike them, the novel's romance no longer consists of matchmaking alliances. These alliances are based, rather, on invisible traits that are discerned by reading the visible countenance, traits that emphasize deformity and normalcy and that allegorize species. Just as the creature can never see anyone sympathizing with him because the specular nature of sympathy bars the nonhuman form as an excitation to sympathize, so the characters in Austen's novel will strive to see that they too, in a Levinasian fashion, excite sympathy with and from someone whose physical and emotional landscape resembles theirs, someone who shares their face, inside and out. However, Elizabeth and Darcy's marriage is not based on achieving sympathy with and from someone – rather, they can look at the face of the other not like them and see difference, see what cannot be seen in what they see. They give and get what they do not give and get: pure hospitality and, in that, post-apocalyptic love.

In *Pride and Prejudice*, unlike and like in *Frankenstein*, humans are construed as nonhumans in humanoid shape. But in Austen's novel, exclusionary mechanisms also prove inclusive, as physical form brings together unlike people, even while it encourages difference among human beings. In its pairing of Elizabeth and Darcy the novel finally argues that love is only possible through the open-armed reception of difference. Elizabeth and Darcy welcome rejection of each other and, in the process, demonstrate their similarity: an acceptance of rejection is the acceptance of difference. They do not need likeness, but rather likeness in difference, which is not likeness at all. Without the possibility of rejection, they tell us, no acceptance of difference is itself possible because difference demands that one either accept or reject. In doing so, they model how love prevails from the face of the other whose face presents as nonhuman, a difference whose face allows for love's possibility. Elizabeth and Darcy can see what the creature cannot – their differences, that everyone is a nonhuman in someone's eyes – *and they accept each other, not in spite of, but because of, that.*

Although they do not initially know it, they both exist outside of the society inside of which they think they reside. The Luhmannian "operational closure" of the novel opens society outward to that which it must constantly strive to protect its own borders from: the presence of the nonhuman other. Elizabeth and Darcy preview how to love the other in the Anthropocene, when humans face the end of their world, personally and collectively, and this is the final hope for life amidst the political ashes of the post-apocalyptic whose burning embers we have never successfully escaped.

The need for sympathetic identification that enforces and is enforced by species boundaries overrides class confines in *Pride and Prejudice.* When the novel first introduces Darcy at a Derbyshire ball, "his fine, tall person, handsome features, noble mien, and the report, which was in general circulation within five minutes after his entrance, of his having ten thousand a year" draw the attention of the room (7). Although his moneyed estate would, one might think, define his social standing, his impassive façade – which we later learn is due to both his pride and his social awkwardness – lead the company to mark him as proud with "a most forbidding, disagreeable countenance" (7). Henceforth, his wealth, though it intimidates, is overpowered by this reading of his face, in contrast to the character of Wickham who is always described as having an "amiable" countenance. Class, in other words, draws lines of social stratification, but, as with Elizabeth's initial attraction to the fine features of the impoverished Wickham, external form and its purported relation to character render class of secondary importance – "his appearance was greatly in his favour; he had all the best part of beauty, a fine countenance, a good figure, and very pleasing address" (49).

Construed as nonhumans in human shape via the same visual dynamics at play in *Frankenstein*, the characters are creatures looking for love in all the wrong faces. Darcy, for instance, when he first sees Elizabeth, describes her as "not handsome enough to tempt me" (9). She is not beautifully formed enough for his taste; she is de-formed. His surface reading of her, he will reluctantly learn, does her no justice – is pre-judice – for he eventually sees in her face a blistering wit and a sparkling mind, which is not at all like his "face." His reading viciously others her as a nonhuman and exiles her from his patristic realm. To Darcy, it is not station that marks Elizabeth as unacceptable marriage material, but her facial nonhumanness. Likewise, he is unacceptable to her, "the last man" she would ever marry, for the same reason (as we will see).

Crucially, all of the people in the novel are committed to the study of character, which informs the face-to-face economies of the novel – identical to *Frankenstein*'s reminder that we should not seek identity, our own or the other's, by looking in the mirror.[42] According to the *OED* character can mean "to stamp or engrave," "the aggregate of distinctive features of any kind of thing," "the face or features as betokening moral qualities," and, in eighteenth-century natural history, "one of the distinguishing features of a species." In the eighteenth century, character also meant a person's reputation and their innate, inner traits. All of these ideas are at play as discovering someone's character is at the heart of the novel's idea of romance:

> "Your plan is a good one," replied Elizabeth, "where nothing is in question but the desire of being well married; and if I were determined to get a rich husband, or any husband, I dare say I should adopt it. But these are not Jane's feelings; she is not acting by design. As yet, she cannot even be certain of the degree of her own regard, nor of its reasonableness. She has known him only a fortnight. She danced four dances with him at Meryton; she saw him one morning at his own house, and has since dined in company with him four times. This is not quite enough to make her understand his character." (*Pride and Prejudice*, 16)

According to Elizabeth, on the one hand, if the character of the other cannot accurately be understood, then marriage will occur only on account of the "desire of being well married" without considering the "regard" of those involved. On the other hand, as Elizabeth reads the social space around her, coming to grips with character does allow for people like her sister, Jane, who wishes to marry someone like herself, to discover a mate whose character corresponds to hers. Charlotte Lucas, of course, proceeds to disagree with this argument in a declaration that, while apparently contradictory to whether or not character likeness matters, actually supplies the full force of how the novel deals with both likeness and unlikeness: "If the dispositions of the parties are ever so well known to each other, or ever so similar before-hand, it does not advance their felicity in the least. They always continue to grow sufficiently unlike afterwards to have their share of vexation; and it is better to know as little as possible of the defects of the person with whom you are to pass your life" (16).

Her statement asserts that romance in the novel depends on living with the unlikeness of a mate because even if, like Jane and Bingley, a couple begins in likeness, they will diverge, grow more unlike as they go along: likeness in character is only possible, to faintly recall the famous opening sentence, between single men and women. But the novel is at great pains to disprove the argument Charlotte makes in this passage, as all of the characters who marry are "similar beforehand," which, for those whom the novel classes as moral, eventually non-prejudiced, exemplars, does advance their felicity (Jane and Mr Bingley). For Wickham and Lydia, who are alarmingly similar beforehand in their thoughtless vacuity for materialistic aesthetics and stratospheric social status, their felicity is not advanced, precisely because they are alike in the fragility of their domestic dispositions: mutual regard for one another is only a superficial affair for them, a by-product of their shallow natures.

In this sense, what the characters discover throughout the novel by marrying and mating are exactly these defects that Charlotte believes will eventually emerge but nonetheless be voided of meaning because character is itself irrelevant to domestic happiness. However, Charlotte captures a key aspect of how the novel thinks marriage should work: characters should accept this unlikeness once it materializes. Problematically, because they "grow … unlike" in marriage, they cannot accept this difference, hence dissimilarity overrides any previous similarity, leading to complete separation in togetherness: again, Wickham and Lydia; Charlotte herself and Mr Collins. Marriage, for Charlotte, renders likeness and unlikeness superfluous; all that matters is that one is married; happiness is therefore also irrelevant and, indeed, on her analysis, impossible.

Yet, the novel rejects this thesis. Charlotte does not heed her own advice, as we see when Elizabeth visits her; she knows exactly what Mr Collins's defects are and, in truth, saw them with eyes wide open beforehand and manages quotidian household affairs by totally ignoring Mr Collins's self-assured, obsequious buffoonery and intellectual ineptitude. But she never accepts him as anything other than a husband; she never accepts him and his otherness, even though she can see it – she never loves him. Hers is a rejection miming acceptance, which maintains their differences in marriage to the extent that it ignores them: they can look right at each other without seeing each other, eyes wide open because they are closed. Neither of them has a face to and for the other; hence they are two lonely creatures who disavow each other's mutual otherness, just as Victor fears the imagined creatures in *Frankenstein* will do.

One of the liveliest exchanges in the novel is quite different. Elizabeth and Darcy conceptualize character defects as innate human corruption, even as this scene establishes how Elizabeth's and Darcy's defects prompt them towards understanding and accepting such "defects" in each other without their own conscious realization. On Elizabeth's part, she jestingly (though she appears to actually believe it) remarks that she is "perfectly convinced by it [that is, her examination of Mr. Darcy] that Mr. Darcy has no defect. He owns it himself without disguise" (39). Elizabeth's use of the word "disguise" pivots back to the idea of character as it relates to the face, but does so by revealing the face itself as what is not revealed, but that is instead a handy disguise that shields one's true features. What David Sigler calls "True Darcyness," his hidden nature underneath his disguise, requires Elizabeth's unearthing.[43] Darcy's face in this scene, however, on Elizabeth's reading, proves transparent, unshielded, allowing for her examination of it and her conclusion that he has no defects; if he had worn a disguise, had a face, her reading implies, his defects may have been hidden from her powers of penetration. Instead, in Elizabeth's eyes he has no human face, is entirely other, because he is a being defectless and faceless, the very qualities, in this discussion, that qualify humans as human. He is therefore totally outside the realm of sympathy, a creature. The task of their love will be, oppositely from *Frankenstein*'s creature and his imagined mate, to in-efface this effaceability, to give character to their faces without erasing the face and thereby negating difference.

Darcy, meanwhile, refuses her clever facial explication and claims his share of defects: "I cannot forget the follies and vices of others so soon as I ought, nor their offences against myself. My feelings are not puffed about with every attempt to move them. My temper would perhaps be called resentful. My good opinion once lost is lost for ever" (39). Elizabeth is shocked by this defect, describing "implacable resentment" as "a shade in a character," especially as it entails him viewing others as nonhuman (39). On her reading, every character harbours a defect that cannot be easily understood, because it is no more than a shade, a nebulous, durational penumbra whose transitory fleetingness is difficult to isolate. For Darcy, though, these shades dapple "every disposition" as "a tendency to some particular evil – a natural defect, which not even the best education can overcome" (40). Character, in this disquisition, features an innate tendency towards a moral or normative irregularity that cannot be regulated, a type of always already reducibility between human and irregular, or nonhuman, categorization.

The society in *Pride and Prejudice* needs to contain the nonhuman shade disordering normative stability. Character is explicitly tied to the face in two conversations that reveal the novel's physiognomical architecture and exemplify the ethical stakes of this architecture. In the first,

Bingley describes himself as "easily seen through," to which Elizabeth responds, "It does not necessarily follow that a deep, intricate character is more or less estimable than such a one as yours" (29). The reference to seeing through his façade suggests, in accord with the work of the famous eighteenth-century physiognomist Johann Lavater, that external form transparently reflects the inner nature of a person.[44] We learn from this conversation that, as Bingley says, Elizabeth is "a studier of character" (29). But more than simply a student, Elizabeth is also a composer of character since, in the novel, to study character also entails a creative poiesis: ascribing meaning to the face of the other and thereby not only socially but somatically constructing that person.

The metaphorical language on display between Darcy and Elizabeth during their dance at the Netherfeld ball equates this study with the visual culture of portraiture:

> "I have always seen a great similarity in the turn of our minds," [Elizabeth says]. "We are each of an unsocial, taciturn disposition …"
>
> "This is no very striking resemblance of your own character, I am sure," said he. "How near it may be to mine, I cannot pretend to say. – You think it a faithful portrait undoubtedly." (63)[45]

Elizabeth proceeds to question Darcy, provoking him to ask, "to what these questions tend?" "Merely to the illustration of your character," she says (64). Darcy's response, asking her "not to sketch my character at the present moment, as there is reason to fear that the performance would reflect no credit on either," indicates the clear creative impulses crucial to the interpretation of facial social, aesthetic, moral, and emotional economies (64). But Elizabeth discounts this because she wants to "take his likeness" now (64). The dance allows her this opportunity because they are, literally, face to face in an estranging embrace of otherness. The reference to his "likeness" emphasizes the similitude between his external and internal form that Elizabeth wishes to produce in her "sketch." That her study of his face requires her to perform – she who never performs to strangers! – amounts to a tacit acknowledgment that reading the face is an active art, one that imparts characteristics to the object of inquiry in the act of explicating it. Reading the face is also writing the face, an act of poiesis; Darcy and Elizabeth literally write each other into existence from their own inexistence; they exist only once they co-write their own production. And because studying character is interactive, it thus also incorporates the interpreters into social networks and places ethical obligations on them, for it is the accuracy, or inaccuracy, of these interpretations that guide their responses to others in this network.

As part of this ethical co-writing, Elizabeth and Darcy's exchanges throughout suffice to showcase how alike their characters are via their non-normative natures and their dissimilarity. They are alike because of and not in spite of their understanding of their different defects, alike in being unlike each other, alike in being different, from each other and from society: Elizabeth: "And your defect is a propensity to hate everybody"; Darcy: "And yours … is willfully to misunderstand them" (40). But there is a great deal of understanding in their misunderstanding, for what they agree on is that innate defects in character do exist and should be explicated – just as they try to manage in their discourse, despite the fact that each believes the other has failed in the other's explication. This mutual reading misfire points again to their similarity in that they even fail in the same way concerning the same subject: misunderstanding their misunderstanding of each other. To put it differently, the scene's subtle irony resides in the unspoken conclusion that they do perfectly understand each other to the extent that they understand their misunderstandings – they understand that they are misunderstanding their own differences by taking the other's likeness. And, ironically enough, this mutual understanding of misunderstanding guides them throughout the rest of the novel as they work to alleviate these misunderstandings by explicating, by interpreting and writing, each other's understanding of their own perfectly misunderstood characters.

The famous letter scene reveals how the circumvolutions of Elizabeth's and Darcy's readings of countenance and character are tied to the novel's conception of romantic misconception.[46] Their initial sight of each other, before Darcy gives her his letter, cements this: she fears she will meet him on her walk and, to avoid this face-to-face transactional possibility, pivots into a different walk – only to be unexpectedly confronted by his indistinct shape. As he comes nearer to her, he comes into sharp focus: "but the person who advanced was now near enough to see her, and stepping forward with eagerness, pronounced her name" (129). Darcy claims that he wrote the letter to redeem his character, even as his address to her also recalls her to the world of difference they both represent: "the effort which the formation, and perusal of this letter must occasion, should have been spared, had not my character required it to be written and read" (129). By giving voice to the privilege of character, Darcy reveals that his ability to read character has created all of the problems: "But I shall scruple to assert, that the serenity of your sister's countenance and air was such, as might have given the most acute observer, a conviction that, however amiable her temper, her heart was not likely to be easily touched" (130). Later in the novel, Darcy will again observe Jane in Bingley's presence and take a more accurate sounding of her face (or so he claims), but his initial interpretation leads him to suspect her of being indifferent to Bingley, which in turn impels Darcy to head off the engagement by sharing his reading with Bingley, whom he easily converts to his facial explication of Jane's lack-thereof of love.

In one of the novel's many ironies, Darcy proves as poor a reader as Elizabeth herself, who, when reading about Wickham, fails initially to realize her mistake. They both misunderstand the faces of other humans. Wickham's face immediately brokers his social position: "as to his real character, had information been in her power, she had never felt a wish of enquiring. His countenance, voice, and manner, had established him at once in the possession of every virtue" (135). Darcy's reading, supplied logical ballast by Elizabeth's own searchingly critical nature, completes, at least at this point in the novel, a full-ish picture, and Elizabeth sees what she could not see before: "[she] could see him instantly before her, in every charm of air and address; but she could remember no more substantial good than the general approbation of the neighborhood, and the regard which his social powers had gained him in the mess" (136). Elizabeth virtualizes a copy of Wickham to study his face anew, a representation that overmasters empirical facial recognition and representation, signalling that a turn in how accurately she adduces her interpretive abilities has occurred in the novel. That Elizabeth's and Darcy's becoming accurate readers should hinge on re-reading Wickham's countenance is also ironic but also indicative of how the novel itself backgrounds physiognomy as its paradoxical foundational base – you have to read it accurately to see it, but only in not seeing it can you read it accurately, because it is not there to see.[47]

The difficulty for Elizabeth and Darcy lies in that they must learn to accept that they cannot see the other's face as internal character and instead must accept the faces of the other as disconnected from inner character. It is this acceptance that allows for their co-authorship of a new, so to speak, face between the two of them, the very thing that no two humans or nonhumans can do in *Frankenstein*.

It is the later portrait scene at Pemberley where Elizabeth and Darcy realize their physical and emotional compatibility as a mating couple.[48] When the housekeeper gives a tour of Pemberley to Elizabeth and her aunt and uncle, the Gardiners, the portrait of Darcy "arrested her – and she beheld a striking resemblance of Mr Darcy, with such a smile over the face, as she remembered to have sometimes seen, when he looked at her" (162). Elizabeth's interpretive, creative abilities are evident here; she interprets the nonhuman portrait even as it interprets her. This portrait rouses her feelings: she experiences "a more gentle sensation towards the original, than she had ever felt in the height of their acquaintance" (162). The housekeeper, meanwhile, busily provides them with details of Darcy that are "favourable to his character" (162). Yet, surprisingly, it is not the social generosity of Darcy that convinces Elizabeth of his goodness and attracts her, but rather his physicality, as the famously strange syntax in this scene makes clear (what Susan Fraiman calls "the self-consciously strange" description): "Every idea that had been brought forward by the housekeeper was favourable to his character, and as she stood before the canvas, on which he was represented, and fixed his eyes upon herself, she thought of his regard with a deeper sentiment of gratitude than it had ever raised before; she remembered its warmth, and softened its impropriety of expression" (162).[49] As Kate Singer puts it, "Elizabeth's coming to terms with Darcy occurs not so much through his own acts as her continual re-picturing of him, from the first proposal scene to her visit to Pemberley – in other words, through a complex, multi-tiered remediation of Darcy."[50] And to follow Singer, suddenly the syntax twists, and the image on the canvas attains medial agency through its pictorial gaze, as the Darcy representation can be read to have "fixed his eyes upon herself," as if human form in nonhuman media triumphs over "every idea brought forward by the housekeeper."

This portrait scene has received much critical attention, justly so. But the housekeeper, in taking Elizabeth and the Gardners out of doors, reminds us that the aftermath of the portrait scene is just as crucial. It reveals Elizabeth's and Darcy's acceptance of their own similarly different nonhuman status – here they look at each other and see what they could not see before, but without looking away, and in this moment become the other for the other.

Immediately following their virtual encounter in the painting, physical reality mirrors it as Darcy and Elizabeth come face to face in the yard: "They were within twenty yards of each other, and so abrupt was his appearance, that it was impossible to avoid his sight. Their eyes instantly met, and the cheeks of each were overspread with the deepest blush. He started, and seemed for a moment immovable from surprise" (163). Darcy is "immovable," like the portrait, but also starts, an involuntary physical jerk that signals this meeting's important disruption of his inscrutable façade and marble immovability. Previously, when he had made his haughty marriage proposal, he "was leaning against the mantle-piece with his eyes fixed on her face," and "his complexion was pale with anger" (132). Subsequently, during her final expostulation against him, "she saw him start at this" (134). Even earlier, reflecting on his supposed behaviour to Wickham, Elizabeth, in characterizing Darcy, "had supposed him to be despising his fellow-creatures in general" but then found that he was capable, as she put it, "of descending to … inhumanity," a description that suggests she viewed him as another species entirely (55).

This scene presents a marked contrast to those earlier scenes. Here his statuesque movement evokes Darcy's nonhuman side as Elizabeth reads it, but it also, on her reading, evokes his loathing of human non-normativity, even as the unleashed mutual emotion of the blush on both of their parts alerts us to his, and her, suffused (non)human nature. He is moving while standing still, just like his roving feelings are, as she is moving to him by waiting on him to walk to her. The scene is therefore a signal that the old familiar faces have become new faces produced by both of them. Elizabeth and Darcy have literalized the metaphor of sketching each other's likeness at last, and the two blush in accord, a figural example that indicates their physical and emotional correspondence, accepting rather than obsessing over their alien otherness, much like Mulder and Scully finally do in *The X-Files* when they ultimately accept such otherness in their love.

They have in-effaced the effaceable. Henceforth in the novel they share the same unity of understanding. Elizabeth believes that her aunt and uncle have "entirely mistaken his character," by which she means that they have failed to accurately read his face, which Elizabeth herself can now read, because Elizabeth and Darcy have interpreted and constructed each other, an act of writing, de-picting, the other in that they have seen each other's face by giving each other a face. They have created each other – but they have done so mutually, as a gift without a gift, hospitality to and from the other. Whereas the creature wanted to efface his face by finding it in the face of a female replication of himself, Elizabeth and Darcy in-efface effacement; they steadily gaze at difference without wishing for sameness – and this acceptance of difference allows for similarity without sameness. Elizabeth articulates it in a later moment of hopelessness in the novel: "She began now to comprehend that he was exactly the man who, in disposition and talents, would most suit her. His understanding and temper, though *unlike* her own, would have answered all her wishes. It was an union that must have been to the advantage of both; by her ease and liveliness, his mind might have been softened, his manners improved; and from his judgement, information, and knowledge of the world, she must have received benefit of greater importance" (212; emphasis mine). The difference they recognize is that they are both different in each other's eyes.

Darcy's miraculous-seeming change in manners is made manifest only after the face-to-face identificatory moment in the yard because he and Elizabeth have embraced difference, which means they have embraced the nonhumanity of their humanity. Elizabeth is finally able to offer not sympathy but pure hospitality of and with Darcy, and he with her, to place themselves in corresponding places of alterity, outside of their own kinship networks, to which, the novel now makes clear, neither belongs. As Nina Auerbach argues, there is a prevailing anti-familial strain in the novel – both Jane and Elizabeth, for instance, are evacuated from their familial life of folly because they are ill suited to it, whereas Lydia remains wedded to it as she remains wedded to the idea of wedding.[51] Indeed, in the rearrangement of characters into fitting marriages in *Pride and Prejudice,* the traditional bloodlines and the marriage alliances that sustain them take on new contours because forging a marriage alliance, as it turns out, requires accurately reading and writing the face of the other to discover someone of the same "species," someone with a different character whose likeness is secured by this difference. The novel accustoms us, in other words, to view some characters, like Mr Collins and Mr Wickham, as monsters, as deformed in some way, the former as an unregenerate blatherskite, the latter as an amoral degenerate, while it meanwhile presents Darcy and Elizabeth as a species capable of performing reproduction of their own family that is closed off from society. That is, Collins and Wickham at first seem more human because they can easily reproduce whereas Darcy and Elizabeth, while on the surface more appealing, are less reproductively attractive until they meet each other. But once the characters have been satisfactorily established with their appropriate mates, when other dissimilar forms – Wickham's, for example – have been established with theirs, it becomes a society of humans and nonhumans in which some are included and others excluded. After all, the gates of Pemberley are shut to Wickham who has proved himself to be not a monster but a real human in his incessant self-regard. And yet, nonetheless, Darcy and Elizabeth prove themselves more than human in their lack of self-regard since they continue to help Wickham in his profession. They are not embowered in an apocalyptic paradise but a post-apocalyptic world without us.

Darcy's and Elizabeth's paradoxical removal from and selfless inclusion in the world of their fellow creatures demonstrate the biopolitical agendas moving on and under the surface of moneyed country life: what a person is as a biologically legible body, how that body relates to other bodies in social network spheres, and where exactly such a body belongs in a world where biorhythms unite through processes of exclusion and division. According to *Frankenstein*, social networks founded on speciesist sympathy create and reinforce exclusionary methods before recuperating heteronormative human reproduction. This same epistemic speciesism is the crucial axiomatic at work in the country-gentry systems of social life in *Pride and Prejudice* as Darcy's and Elizabeth's secluded paradise mirrors the paradise envisioned by the creature and his fantasized female mate – except Darcy's and Elizabeth's is post-apocalyptic Romanticism. Darcy's and Elizabeth's match-up illustrates what I above referenced as the autoimmune structure of society, the ways in which the most routine matters of life, like courtship, implement divisionary partitions that enact the continuance of life by buffering human subjects from differences that exceed societal parameters, thereby defending the social order from those others who operate within society from outside of those normative social structures. It is worth recalling again that Darcy and Elizabeth, due to their various eccentricities, are initially seen as nonhuman, as social misfits, by others around them. Designating and excluding people as nonhuman others provides the social boundaries that must be maintained, just as, in a turnabout perspectival shift in the novel, the boundaries of Pemberley are maintained by those who are excluded by their inclusion – again, Wickham.

In Luhmann's terms this is a closed social system, a system that runs only according to its own internal protocols and filters out dangerous malware that can disrupt it. But for Luhmann, a closed system also requires this filtration process – an openness to what is outside the system and can potentially corrupt it is necessary for the system to maintain its closure. Since a social system always runs up against its own boundaries, it is always, therefore, exposed to what lies outside of it as this establishes the boundaries to be protected and, in turn, this exposure saturates that system with systems that exist outside of it. In essence, a closed system needs Michel Serres's "parasite" to constantly retrofit its protective boundaries from the penetration of the very other that allows for this retrofit.[52] Contrary to Foucault, then, an excess of biopower has always been in evidence in the sense that defining "the human" has always entailed an operational speciesist closure – a process that defines who and what counts as a social subject – involving nonhuman life and those humans regarded as nonhuman monsters. Indeed, the post-apocalyptic imaginary working behind the scenes in these two novels allows us to identify how the frictional speciesist limits of sympathy both conserves the concept of the human from radical otherness – as in *Frankenstein* – even while sympathy's margins situate the nonhuman at the heart of this concept – as in *Pride and Prejudice*.

Defamiliarizing the biopolitical narrative of reproduction as a form of operational closure in *Pride and Prejudice* also helps to make sense of the great conundrum of Austen's novels: whether her matchless irony has a concrete ethical and political texture, or is merely Austen's way of gently satirizing her own contemporary, gentry social circle. For Marvin Mudrick, who set the tone for much of the scholarship that would follow him, Austen's irony allowed her to distance herself from the socio-political entanglements of her time and evade taking a stand on any issue.[53] In contrast, Marilyn Butler and Alistair Duckworth read her as a conservative who uses the happy resolution of the marriage plot in her novels to reinforce the patriarchal anti-Jacobin ideology of her time. Contrastingly, Mary Poovey and Claudia Johnson, on the one hand, see her as an ironist so subtle and superb that she paradoxically manipulates the marriage plot to undermine the resolutions of her own novels as a political protest against gender inequality.[54] David Sigler, on the other hand, astutely finds the novel's conservatism generative of a destabilization of the human subject.[55] Austen's novel does, in fact, react to the authoritarian patriarchal and class divisions that have long been under assault since the revolutions in society in the late eighteenth century. Poovey is right then that the novel exposes the tensions between patriarchal hierarchy and individual liberty, but wrong in that it does not resolve them.[56] It does – by nullifying patriarchal hierarchy. Although the entail – that which confers the property on the oldest living male descendant to perpetuate a patrilineal line – on the Bennet estate remains at novel's end, Austen's novel, in its refusal to abide by traditional patriarchal alliances, breaks the entail, metaphorically speaking.

Thus the novel dramatizes how species difference can override social conventions that fail to contain the biohazardous material of the nonhuman. By allowing Elizabeth and Darcy to find their identically nonidentical other outside of the bounds of propriety, class, station, and convention, Austen envisions a society structured by the inclusion of contaminating pollutants, a society where coupledom is predicated on accepting rejection, as Elizabeth and Darcy do when they give themselves up to the ode to dejection rejection begets.[57]

But strangely, albeit obviously, this insistence on materiality seems to eradicate a most important aspect of the marriage plot, love. In many ways the novel itself shows how species distinctions already do this: many of the characters in the novel, as we have seen, are perfectly happy to marry not for love but simply to carry on, to breed, to extend their own "hideous progeny" (to borrow from Shelley). Yet, perhaps one way of thinking about Austen's novels is to ask whether they even think love is possible. More pressingly, we can ask, what would it matter if love is possible in the Anthropocene, the time when humans usher in their own extinction via the climate change they have created in their biopolitical attempts to extend the human species?

In answer, Elizabeth and Darcy, by embracing passivity without passivity, augur a version of love wherein one must accede to the hopelessness of love's impossibility for love to ever be possible. Darcy's letter does part of the work of this co-writing of the other, even despite his hopelessness. But Elizabeth does much the same. In the scene with Lady Catherine, where Elizabeth stands her ground and insouciantly denounces Lady Catherine's insulting demands, we later find out that her replies return to Darcy as a verbal letter. He tells Elizabeth, "I knew enough of your disposition to be certain, that, had you been absolutely, irrevocably decided against me, you would have acknowledged it to Lady Catherine, frankly and openly," but it also, he says, "taught me to hope" (251). Both Elizabeth and Darcy relinquish the hope of love – but, crucially, they relinquish it only in relation to each other, which paradoxically affirms its arrival from the ruins, from hopelessness.

Austen's arrangement of the future foregrounds this feature of her work.[58] Darcy's and Elizabeth's lives at Pemberley are presented as if in a beautiful snow globe, perpetually suspended like the lovers on Keats's urn, always about to kiss but forever frozen. Timelessly frozen at novel's end, made immovably nonhuman once again, the impossibility of physical consummation depicted here indicates how love might lead to a world without us by voicing a song about the end of the world as we know it. Frozen in paradise, Darcy and Elizabeth appear to have no present, no way to live on, because the novel suspends their future, the temporal never arrival that paradoxically grants us a present by the future's infinite deferral and flickering presence.

If the future cannot arrive in any other sense than as a perpetually evanescing trace in the present, then love can only occur in the temporal distortion of the future's constantly present absence. We can see this with Darcy and Elizabeth, who, for love to be love, must strive to be unconditional in that temporally unforgiving yet hospitable sense. For a total giving of oneself to the other moves beyond any human condition of love that is based on the conditions of a fully present human self prior to love. That type of love requires a temporal stasis that prevents humans from becoming other than human, a temporal stasis that verifies and reifies its anthropocentric terms and conditions. Unlike Darcy and Elizabeth, the other characters in the novel continue to think in selfish, human terms, about the human self's needs and wants and not those of the other – Wickham and Lydia provide the most obvious examples of this selfishness. This type of human egocentricity is deeply linked to anthropocentrism, the human species' belief in its status as masters of the universe, as if they are Wall Street brokers insider-trading tips on biopolitical species on a cosmic scale. In seeking an unconditional love freed from sympathy's ego- and anthropo-centrism and its imaginative projection of the self in the other's shoes, Elizabeth and Darcy model how love must move beyond perceived similarities to difference, which must itself incorporate exclusion and rejection, the nonhuman.

The movement from love as conditioned by selfish desire to love conditioned by the nonhuman begins when Elizabeth rejects, with stunning vitriol, Darcy's initial proposal:

> From the very beginning, from the first moment I may almost say, of my acquaintance with you, your manners, impressing me with the fullest belief of your arrogance, your conceit, and your selfish disdain of the feelings of others, were such as to form that ground-work of disapprobation, on which succeeding events have built so *immoveable* a dislike; and I had not known you a month before I felt that you were the last man in the world whom I could ever be prevailed on to marry. (134; emphasis mine)

Of course, the dislike proves precisely the opposite of "immoveable" as both Elizabeth and Darcy are continually moved by and towards each other, both physically and emotionally, as in the post-portrait scene in Pemberley's yard above where the "immoveable" moves by jerks, starts, and blushes. What is interesting in this rejection, though, is that, for Elizabeth and Darcy, love, when true and unconditional, is post-apocalyptic because it ends the world by establishing two people as the first two in the world for each other – but not in a kind of hoary romantic cliché. Rather, it allows for the two, as lasts made firsts, to find love in rejection, the opposite of love, in a space – the end of the world – where hope for love, and hope in general, are no longer feasible. For love to work, they must be able to reject the other person, otherwise there is no decision for them but instead only universal acceptance of anyone by anyone, which is a totalitarian union that simply adheres to biopolitics' heedless species goals, affixing the same face to all humans in a marriage plot meant to reproduce human lineages. Brought into existence as firsts, the lasts that they were, they are now extinct, the end of a lovelorn species.

Darcy and Elizabeth, because they love each other, are hospitable to each other in the sense that post-apocalyptic Romanticism means – they must make choices. To choose, to choose each other implies exclusion because any choice must exclude – for that is the nature of choice. Something must be left out and something must be included, often in the same moment, the same breath. Understanding choice in this way, as a kind of working through understood misunderstandings, as Elizabeth and Darcy do, proves key to how they come to each other. A late scene in the novel when Darcy and Elizabeth finally reveal their love to each other – a moment starkly in contrast to Darcy's earlier proposal scene where verbally slung arrows hit their targets with deadly accuracy – matchmakes them via their mutual dismissal.

> Elizabeth was too much embarrassed to say a word. After a short pause, her companion added, "You are too generous to trifle with me. If your feelings are still what they were last April, tell me so at once. *My* affections and wishes are unchanged; but one word from you will silence me on this subject for ever."
>
> Elizabeth, feeling all the more than common awkwardness and anxiety of his situation, now forced herself to speak; and immediately, though not very fluently, gave him to understand that her sentiments had undergone so material a change since the period to which he alluded, as to make her receive with gratitude and pleasure his present assurances. The happiness which this reply produced was such as he had probably never felt before, and he expressed himself on the occasion as sensibly and as warmly as a man violently in love can be supposed to do. (250)

By giving him "to understand" her sentiments, they now understand that they understand their misunderstandings of each other and that they can, now, welcome that misunderstoodness. Welcoming this gift of love, silence becomes them. Called upon to express their love, the characters do so, but Austen drops a curtain over the actual articulation of this feeling, closing the fairy tale from our view. This refusal to let us hear anything but a description of their description of their feelings suggests that love, for Austen, is not merely linguistic in nature, not another language game. It cannot be verbalized. Nor is it simple emotion. For Austen, love exists as an ontological force in and of itself. Whatever this ontological love consists of, it goes beyond words and also beyond any human witness outside of the two persons whom it involves, as if the world of love existed, romantically enough, well outside of any human epistemology or linguistic virtuosity, an affect much more posthuman, as Kate Singer suggests, than we have heretofore realized.[59] If, for Levinas, the face consists of the human body and human linguistic addressability to other humans, then love, as theorized by Darcy and Elizabeth, is nonhuman, an exemplar of love and how it gives face by its in-effacement of not only face but voice.[60] It welcomes the different face. It is as if Darcy and Elizabeth disappear behind the words of the text on the page into their own world, an ontological world without us, a world outside of human ken. To write it would be to give it face, human face, and so Darcy and Elizabeth need no longer send written or verbal missives to each other. Love is a thing no longer written between lovers, something that we cannot see, as in this passage, for if it could be seen, it would not be seen by us, for that is their world, that they make, in loving.

Elizabeth's and Darcy's union, which has been read as preserving a conservative stasis, bringing Elizabeth under Darcy's umbrella, might reify the heteronormativity that they ostensibly represent, another biopolitical goal checked off as Darcy's paternal lineage reproduces itself. This recurs to the conundrum above: is this a novel arguing that this society needs progressive change – that women can achieve equality with men if they break the rules, but only within the master's house? Or does Elizabeth ultimately only become one more vessel for the continuance of hierarchy and patrilineal biopolitics? According to the novel, on the one hand, unsuccessful marriages occur between people with different characters – they do not see that they see and still cannot accept, cannot love, each other – like Mr Collins and Charlotte. Elizabeth and Darcy, on the other hand, in counterpoint, are successful because they co-create; they bring each other into being, for the first time, as they bring love into being. Perforce the novel argues that society needs wholesale progressive change as regards marriage because women do not have equality with men, and this leads to loveless marriages that render women objects of single men's wife-wanting. Elizabeth and Darcy work through their pride and prejudice together, a process that inaugurates an alterity that, in its alienation, welcomes the other and does justice to who that person really is, an acceptance of unlikeness, and so an acceptance of the likeness of unlikeness, of difference, which demands unlikeness to be difference and that demands the rejection inhering in difference to be acceptance. By being able to see each other for who they truly are not, they see each other for who they are in their textual writing of creaturely ontology. By finding their person, and their own person, in this ontological genesis, Elizabeth and Darcy articulate a form of love that spreads its arms to the nonhuman that activates humanity. Society, they claim, can be altered, achieving a vision of progress wherein happiness, even the paradoxically destructive desire for happiness, as Joel Faflak terms it, is the basis of life.[61]

What the monsters in *Frankenstein*, and the entrenchment of the nonhuman within human social systems inhering in the circumscribed world in *Pride and Prejudice*, both illuminate is that humans are not, in fact, wholly human, a distinct species entirely closed off from the nonhuman. Even more importantly, when juxtaposed to Shelley's redirection of sympathy's broken promise towards the creature, these novels teach us that what is ontologically nonhuman is not necessarily inhuman. Taking seriously Austen's famous comment in her letters, that *Pride and Prejudice* "is rather too light, and bright, and sparkling" and needs "a contrast," and by placing the novel as the monstrous other to *Frankenstein*, we can ultimately see that we can be a species if we want, but only at the cost of being the monsters we think we are not.[62]

This is what Darcy and Elizabeth vow in their unstated vows. In the final scene inside Pemberley, we see that Darcy and Elizabeth deconstruct love as biopolitical power relation. Indeed, the hospitality of love, giving oneself to the other, breaks down patriarchal social structures: Darcy, the master of Pemberley, and master as Regency-era man, and host to Elizabeth, becomes her guest in his own home, a form of passivity without any passivity. As Derrida puts it regarding the liminality of hospitality – that is, the paradox of its threshold – "the master thus enters from inside as if he came from outside."[63] Elizabeth, in this sense, is the master of the house who enters from outside as if she comes from inside, and Darcy the master who enters from inside as if he comes from outside. Because it is Elizabeth who takes charge, who breaks down Darcy's immovable façade by teasing him, taking (the text says) "liberties" with him, a fully loaded word indicative of the social and gendered transgressions of Elizabeth. By welcoming each other unconditionally, and allowing for, accepting, the trespass and rejection that must accompany any liberty, Elizabeth and Darcy, with these liberties, enact a form of love that does not require reciprocity but is instead purely gifted, purely given, purely thought without sense of preservation or self-regard, the defining feature of humans, as *Frankenstein* argues.

Love as Elizabeth and Darcy experience it and live it enacts a hospitality that avoids the exclusionary mechanisms of species production, which lead to the end of the world and of self-regard, the personal drive to protect ourselves from the nonhuman other. The nonhuman species must be *included through a passivity without any passivity* that maintains its exclusion to avoid the violence of hospitality and the erasing of difference, to become a collective member *like us*. The nonhuman must be able to take liberties to maintain its liberty from the society of which it is not a part. Elizabeth must take liberties with Darcy, otherwise their unlikeness will become their likeness, their differences become sameness, their faces a human face.

In the end they teach us that thinking like a species, like masters of the universe, leads to the climate change of the Anthropocene. If we allow ourselves to think like a species, even at the interpersonal level of love, we will only affirm a return to Hobbesian anarchism, as every person will be against every person in a survivalist fight in a world with scant resources. Moving to what we might call a posthuman consciousness of love gives up this sense of human mastery, this belief in our own human centrality to the world, gives ourselves unconditionally to the other. Such generosity at last configures us as truly last men and women because we are no longer anthropocentric and hence no longer just a species, just gendered, just men and women. The final irony of post-apocalyptic Romanticism is that turning to face the nonhuman other turns us to face ourselves as the nonhuman other. This will be an act of generosity that gifts to us from a world without us, life. It will be a form of love in the ruins that does not ruin.

Coda: After Extinctualism: Hope for Life

In post-apocalyptic Romanticism we can begin to glimpse how love can anchor a nonhuman ontological social contract that is an alternative to the anthropocentric political models that have proven irreducible. As I have been arguing, despite its apparent nihilist or pessimistic view of humanity's future, post-apocalyptic Romanticism theorizes hope. For these texts, hope is a possibility that can only be gleaned when there is no hope. For hope to exist, it must do so under the conditional limits of its opposite, hopelessness, because hope must be able to traduce the worst, the lack of any hope, or otherwise hope itself is hopeless. We can see this play out in the anecdote with which I opened this book. Shortly after Lady Catherine de Bourgh's visit to Elizabeth, Darcy says that Elizabeth's decisive denial to his aunt of their engagement "taught me to hope." Elizabeth has the same thought after Lydia marries Wickham: "she became jealous of [Darcy's] esteem, when she could no longer hope to be benefited by it" (212). Only then does she "comprehend that he was exactly the man who, in disposition and talents, would most suit her" (212). More than an urge for what she cannot have, it is specifically the extinction of hope, and hope of and for love, its possibility, that inspires love with breath because the hopelessness of it moves her into the gift without a gift of hospitality – beyond human self-regard – that structures real love. Like Darcy, in whom hope arises precisely once his expectations seem hopeless, Elizabeth begins to hope for their union because their dissimilarity proves their suitability as those who can selflessly give the gift of love to even the most nonhuman from the most nonhuman.

If predictions about the Anthropocene are correct, then there is no hope for the human species' survival. We may shortly become, as that other Elizabeth, Elizabeth Frankenstein, says, "monsters thirsting for each other's blood" in a circulatory vampiric war for sanguine subsistence on a post-apocalyptic world. If we are to follow Elizabeth's and Darcy's example, seeing the other by passively opening ourselves to the nonhuman within the other who might come, we might find a love whose progeniture depends on more than blood. We might enter into a new form of life, post-species, wherein a social contract that prevents war includes all creatures by rejecting them from any homogenous totality. This social contract accepts, respects, and multiplies difference, as Darcy and Elizabeth's mismatched match does. Such a world might depend on allowing ourselves to be written by the one who is for us, the impossible one who extinguishes us and in the same breath gives us hope, extinction, and what comes after, life and love. And while Elizabeth and Darcy cannot verbally inscribe their love in a textuality we can read without betraying its ontological future-to-come, we find *Persuasion* echoing what their love would say if it could: Elizabeth and Darcy are those who are post-apocalyptically "loving longest, when existence or when hope is gone."[1] They are living, and loving, on.

Notes

Introduction

1 Jane Austen, *Pride and Prejudice*, ed. Donald Gray and Mary Favret (New York: Norton, 2016), 134.
2 Mary Shelley, *Frankenstein*, ed. J. Paul Hunter (New York: Norton, 2013), 161.
3 This is Foucault's famous pronouncement at the end of *History of Sexuality*, which he expands upon in his late lectures. Foucault, *The History of Sexuality*, vol. 1, *An Introduction*, trans. Richard Hurley (New York: Vintage, 1990), 135–59. Foucault, *"Society Must Be Defended": Lectures at the College de France, 1975–1976*, trans. David Macey (New York: Picador, 2003), 239–63.
4 It is worth noting, though, that the human species is not extinguished in the novel; Lionel lives. Anne Mellor, *Mary Shelley: Her Life, Her Fictions, Her Monsters* (New York: Routledge, 1989), 166.
5 Jerome McGann, *The Romantic Ideology* (Chicago: University of Chicago Press, 1983), 1.
6 See for example: *#Accelerate: The Accelerationist Reader*, ed. Robin Mackay and Armen Avanessian (Falmouth, UK: Urbanomic, 2014). Steven Shaviro, *No Speed Limit: Four Essays on Accelerationism* (Minneapolis: University of Minnesota Press, 2015).
7 M.H. Abrams, *Natural Supernaturalism: Tradition and Revolution in Romantic Literature* (New York: Norton, 1971), 57.
8 Abrams, *Natural Supernaturalism*, 38.
9 Morton D. Paley, *Apocalypse and Millennium in English Romantic Poetry* (Oxford: Clarendon Press, 1999). Other recent writers on related topics are Ian Balfour, *The Rhetoric of Romantic Prophecy* (Stanford, CA: Stanford University Press, 2002); Tim Fulford, ed., *Romanticism and Millenarianism* (Houndmills, UK: Palgrave Macmillan, 2003).

10 For green writers see James McKusick, *Green Writing: Romanticism and Ecology* (Houndmills, UK: Palgrave McMillan, reprinted 2010); Jonathan Bate, *The Song of the Earth* (Cambridge, MA: Harvard University Press, 2000); Onno Oerlemans, *Romanticism and the Materiality of Nature* (Toronto: University of Toronto Press, 2002); Timothy Morton, *Ecology without Nature* (Cambridge, MA: Harvard University Press, 2009). Heidi C. Scott offers a different take on Romantic ecology in relation to chaos theory, but she also reads Romantic ecocriticism as indebted to a pure and pristine vision. *Chaos and Cosmos: Literary Roots of Modern Ecology in the British Nineteenth Century* (Pennsylvania: Penn State University Press, 2015).

11 For writers of Romantic disaster see the cluster of essays in *Romanticism and Disaster*, ed. Jacques Khalip and David Collings, Romantic Circles Praxis. https://www.rc.umd.edu/praxis/disaster/; David Collings, "After the Covenant: Romanticism, Secularization, and Disastrous Transcendence," *European Romantic Review* 21, no. 3 (2010): 345–61.

12 Jacques Khalip, "Contretemps: Of Extinction and Romanticism," *Literature Compass* 13, no. 10 (2016): 629.

13 Khalip, "Contretemps," 629.

14 Steven E. Goldsmith's book offers a thorough account of Romantic apocalypse in the works of Blake and the Shelleys as it relates to biblical prophecy. *Unbuilding Jerusalem: Apocalypse and Romantic Representation* (Ithaca, NY: Cornell University Press, 1993), 23.

15 Claire Colebrook, *The Death of the Posthuman: Essays on Extinction*, vol. 1 (Ann Arbor, MI: Open Humanities Press, 2014), 634. https://quod.lib.umich.edu/o/ohp/12329362.0001.001/1:3/ – death-of-the-posthuman-essays-on-extinction-volume-one?rgn=div1;view=fulltext.

16 Colebrook, *The Death of the Posthuman*, 634.

17 Khalip, "Contretemps," 629.

18 The reference here is, of course, to Harold Bloom's phrasing of this apocalyptic urge in Romantic writers. Bloom, *The Visionary Company* (New York: Norton, 1971).

19 William Wordsworth, "The Prospectus, " *The Excursion*, edited by Sally Bushell, James A. Butler, Michael C. Jaye, and David Garcia (Ithaca, NY: Cornell University Press, 2007).

20 Frye offers an exemplary instance of apocalypse as the human not only connected to nature but subsuming nature: "by an apocalypse I mean primarily the imaginative conception of the whole of nature as the content of an infinite and eternal living body which, if not human, is closer to being human than to being inanimate" (*Anatomy of Criticism,* 119). M.H. Abrams, "English Romanticism: The Spirit of the Age," *Romanticism Reconsidered*, ed. Northrup Frye (New York: Columbia University Press,

1966). Northrup Frye, *Anatomy of Criticism: Four Essays* (Princeton, NJ: Princeton University Press, 2000). See also Geoffrey Hartman, *Wordsworth's Poetry, 1787–1814* (Cambridge, MA: Harvard University Press, 1964); Northrop Frye, *Fearful Symmetry: A Study of William Blake* (Princeton, NJ: Princeton University Press, 1969); Bloom, *Visionary Company*; Alan Liu, *Wordsworth: The Sense of History* (Stanford, CA: Stanford University Press, 1991); Paul de Man, "Autobiography as De-facement," in *The Rhetoric of Romanticism* (New York: Columbia University Press, 1984), 67–82; Mellor, *Mary Shelley*.

21 Abrams, *Supernatural*, 91.

22 William Wordsworth, *The Prelude, 1799, 1805, 1850*, ed. Jonathan Wordsworth, M.H. Abrams, and Stephen Gill (New York: Norton, 1979), 29–484.

23 William Blake, "And Did Those Feet in Ancient Times," in *Milton, A Poem*, ed. Robert N. Essek and Joseph Viscomi (Princeton, NJ: Princeton University Press, 1998). I do not deal with Blake at length in this book because I find myself agreeing with Kir Kuiken that Blake's thinking on questions of sovereignty remained enmeshed in theology. Kuiken meanwhile offers an alternative view of how the Romantics develop a notion of sovereignty. For him, the Romantics "invested in a fundamentally modern form of sovereignty, one that would no longer rely on the absolute notion of the divine." His book "makes the case that the vague and still much misunderstood term 'the imagination' is the site where this task is pursued," and finds that for the Romantics "the imagination" is "an aesthetic principle" and "a political one" (*Imagined Sovereignties*, 2–3). While I agree with the former disposal of the divine, the imagination, as I argue in chapter 2, is largely under attack in these later Romantic writers. But, ultimately, I think that Kuiken and I are discussing different notions of sovereignty that are nonetheless in sympathy with each other. He refers to the sovereign of a state, the figure who is determined by a ground that precedes it, even as it also must remain wholly ungrounded because it is itself unique. The political sovereign derives its power from its own individuality, its own exception from the state that founds it, an exception that nevertheless empowers its very sovereignty. When I talk of anthropocentric sovereignty, the connections to this political sovereign should be clear in that the sovereign, though he functions, as Derrida points out, like a beast, remains a human, and thus political sovereignty is also anthropocentric sovereignty. But anthropocentric sovereignty supersedes the nation-state; it is a species-wide, universal categorical imperative. On my reading, the Romantics seek to depose both forms of sovereignty. Kuiken, *Imagined Sovereignties: Towards a New Political Romanticism* (Brooklyn, NY: Fordham University

Press, 2013). Derrida, *The Beast and the Sovereign*, trans. Geoffrey Bennington (Chicago: University of Chicago Press, 2009).

24 Goldsmith provides a helpful trajectory of apocalyptic criticism in Romanticism and notes that it often equates apocalypse with the human either in triumph or in ruin. Goldsmith's illuminating study nonetheless seems to identify apocalypse, even once he connects it back to historical events and politics, as a human affair, even when what Goldsmith means by *apocalypse* is more properly "post-apocalypse" as in his reading of Shelley's *The Last Man*. As I show in this study, post-apocalypse is about what comes after the human and about the politics generated by the nonhuman. *Unbuilding Jerusalem*, 6–19.

25 The line appears in Walt Kelly's 1971 Earth Day poster that depicts Pogo and Porky Pine looking on at the garbage and pollution that has piled up high in their home, the Okeefenokee Swamp. Porky Pine famously declares, "We have met the enemy, and it is us."

26 Samuel Taylor Coleridge, "Kubla Khan," in *The Complete Poems*, ed. William Keach (New York: Penguin, 1997), 249–51.

27 Bate, *Song of the Earth*, 283.

28 Orrin Wang, *Romantic Sobriety: Sensation, Revolution, Commodification, History* (Baltimore, MD: Johns Hopkins University Press, 2011), 1.

29 Percy Bysshe Shelley, "Mont Blanc," in *The Complete Poetry of Percy Bysshe Shelley*, vol. 3, ed. Donald H. Reiman, Neil Fraistat, and Nora Crook (Baltimore, MD: Johns Hopkins University Press, 2012), 79–90.

30 Mary Shelley, *The Last Man*, ed. Morton D. Paley (Oxford: Oxford World's Classics, 2008), 412–13.

31 Much recent work on animals in the period has appeared: Christine Kenyon-Jones, *Kindred Brutes: Animals in Romantic-Period Writing* (New York: Routledge, 2001); David Perkins, *Romanticism and Animal Rights* (Cambridge: Cambridge University Press, 2007); and Ron Broglio, *Beasts of Burden: Biopolitics, Labor, and Animal Life in British Romanticism* (New York: SUNY, 2017). Zoe Beenstock offers an overview of the social contract in Romanticism, in *The Politics of Romanticism: The Social Contract and Literature* (Edinburgh, UK: Edinburgh University Press, 2016).

32 Jacques Derrida, *The Animal That Therefore I Am*, ed. Marie-Lousie Mallet, trans. David Wills (New York: Fordham University Press, 2008). Morton, *Ecology without Nature* (Cambridge, MA: Harvard UP, 2009).

33 Regarding this point on animals, what he calls "*animaux*," see Derrida, *The Animal That Therefore I Am*, 32–41.

34 Nicole Shukin, *Animal Capital: Rendering Life in Biopolitical Times* (Minneapolis: University of Minnesota Press, 2009), 7–14.

35 Gillen D'Arcy Wood's magnificent book lays out the results of Mount Tambora's eruption and its devastating effect on the earth in stunning

detail. These events serve, he says, as a preview of how climate change will impact the earth. D'Arcy Wood, *Tambora: The Eruption That Changed the World* (Princeton, NJ: Princeton University Press, 2015).

36 Edmund Burke, *A Philosophical Enquiry into the Origin of our Ideas of the Sublime and the Beautiful* (Oxford: Oxford University Press, 2015).

37 John Keats, "Letter to Richard Woodhouse, October 27th, 1818," in *Selected Letters*, ed. Robert Gittings (Oxford: Oxford University Press, 2009), 147.

38 Anahid Nersessian, *Utopia, Limited: Romanticism and Adjustment* (Cambridge, MA: Harvard University Press, 2015).

39 Anne-Lise François, *Open Secrets: The Literature of Uncounted Experience* (Stanford, CA: Stanford University Press, 2008), 33, 32. Derrida discusses passivity in his lecture on Levinas: *Adieu to Emmanuel Levinas*, trans. Pascale-Anne Brault (Stanford, CA: Stanford University Press, 1999).

40 François, *Open Secrets*, 34, 47.

41 Jacques Khalip, *Anonymous Life: Romanticism and Dispossession* (Stanford CA: Stanford University Press, 2008), 14, 1.

42 This links, in part, to what Kuiken says of Romantic notions of sovereignty: they are always exterior to the subject (*Imagined Sovereignties*, 18).

43 Michel Serres, *The Natural Contract*, trans. Elizabeth MacArthur and William Paulson (Ann Arbor: University of Michigan Press, 1995).

44 Ray Brassier, *Nihil Unbound: Enlightenment and Extinction* (Houndmills, UK: Palgrave Macmillan, 2007), 239.

45 Timothy Morton, *Hyperobjects: Philosophy and Ecology after the End of the World* (Minneapolis: University of Minnesota Press, 2013), 2–3, 6–7.

46 Quentin Meillassoux, *After Finitude: An Essay on the Necessity of Contingency*, trans. Ray Brassier (New York: Continuum, 2008). See Greg Ellermann's "Speculative Romanticism" for a different reading of Shelley's "Mont Blanc" as well as a different view of how speculative realism and Romanticism engage. Evan Gottlieb's is the first book to explicitly illustrate the links between Romanticism and speculative realism. *Romantic Realities: Speculative Realism and British Romanticism* (Edinburgh, UK: Edinburgh University Press, 2016). Anne McCarthy also draws on speculative realism to think through Romanticism, and vice versa; *Awful Parenthesis: Suspension and the Sublime in Romantic and Victorian Poetry* (Toronto: University of Toronto Press, 2018). See also Chris Washington and Anne C. McCarthy, eds., *Romanticism and Speculative Realism* (London: Bloomsbury, 2019).

47 Meillassoux, *After Finitude*, 5.

48 The differences between Meillassoux's and Harman's work are lengthy in terms of the details, but the larger difference is that Meillassoux believes there is no way to escape the correlationist circle; he agrees with the typical

attack against Speculative Realism, that one cannot think an unthought without it becoming a thought. Meillassoux, however, wants to push past Kant's notion that human thought is finite; hence the title of his book *After Finitude*. Harman denies that both positions are desirable or possible, and he offers a quick distinction here: "That is to say, Meillassoux rejects Kantian finitude in favor of absolute human knowledge, while I reject absolute knowledge and retain Kantian finitude, though broadening this finitude beyond the human realm to include all relations in the cosmos – including inanimate ones" (185). Graham Harman, "The Well-Wrought Broken Hammer," *New Literary History* 43, no. 2 (2012): 183–203.

49 Meillassoux, *After Finitude*, 10.

50 Meillassoux, *Time without Becoming*, ed. Anna Longo (Haverton, PA: Mimesis International, 2014), 23.

51 Meillassoux, *After Finitude*, 10.

52 Meillassoux, *After Finitude*, 112.

53 Meillassoux, *After Finitude*, 127.

54 Meillassoux, *After Finitude*, 127.

55 Eugene Thacker, *After Life* (Chicago: University of Chicago Press, 2010), 256.

56 Thacker, *After Life*, 256.

57 For the earliest example of speculative realism's hostility to Derrida, see Graham Harman, *Prince of Networks: Bruno Latour and Metaphysics* (New York: re:press, 2009).

58 Jacques Derrida, "Living On," in *Deconstruction and Criticism*, ed. Harold Bloom (London: Bloomsbury, 2004), 62–142.

59 Jacques Derrida, *Rogues: Two Essays on Reason*, trans. Pascal-Anne Brault (Stanford, CA: Stanford University Press, 2005).

60 Mary Shelley, *The Last Man*, 85.

61 I have worked out elsewhere the differences between Paul de Man's irony and allegory in this regard. See Chris Washington, "Romanticism and Speculative Realism," *Literature Compass* 12, no. 9 (2015): 448–60.

62 See Ron Broglio's *Beasts of Burden* for a reading of biopolitics at work in the English countryside.

63 Thomas Hobbes, *Leviathan*, ed. Edwin Curley (New York: Hackett, 1994). Jean-Jacques Rousseau, *Discourse on Inequality*, trans. Franklin Philip (Oxford: Oxford University Press, 1994). Jean-Jacques Rousseau, *The Social Contract*, trans. Christopher Betts (Oxford: Oxford University Press, 1994).

64 Hobbes, *Leviathan*, 76.

65 Katey Castellanno argues that Burke's conservatism in the period was a positive force for environmental conservation. Castellanno, *The Ecological Roots of British Romantic Conservatism, 1790–1837* (Houndmills, UK: Palgrave Macmillan, 2013).

66 Jared McGeough, "Romanticism after the Anarchist Turn," *Literature Compass* 13, no. 1 (2016): 3–12.

67 William Godwin, *An Enquiry Concerning Political Justice*, ed. Mark Philp (Oxford: Oxford University Press, 2013), 51–81.

68 Jerome Christensen, *Romanticism at the End of History* (Baltimore, MD: Johns Hopkins University Press, 2004), 2.

69 Goldsmith quotes from Irigaray, *This Sex Which Is Not One*, in his *Unbuilding Jerusalem*, 21–2.

70 Jacques Derrida, *Of Hospitality*, trans. Rachel Bowlby (Stanford, CA: Stanford University Press, 2000).

71 Peter Melville, *Romantic Hospitality and the Resistance to Accommodation* (Waterloo, ON: Wilfrid Laurier University Press, 2007). Derrida, *Adieu to Emmanuel Levinas*.

72 Derrida, *The Animal That Therefore I Am*, trans. Marie-Louis Mallet (Stanford: Stanford University Press, 2008.

1. The Mind Is Its Own Place

1 Scholars have long been vexed concerning these diverse, conflicting apocalyptic strains in Shelley's work. Ross Greig Woodman writes that "Shelley's apocalyptic vision … belongs within a verbal universe; it is not an earthly kingdom that will one day be established among men." Woodman, *The Apocalyptic Vision in the Poetry of Shelley* (Toronto: University of Toronto Press, 1964), 20. Stuart Curran seems to agree with M.H. Abrams on this point, though he sees this paradise as decidedly secular rather than Christian. Curran, *Shelley's Annus Mirabilis: The Maturing of an Epic Vision* (San Marino, CA: Huntington Library, 1975), 40, 65. Still other critics, such as Earl Wasserman and Michael O'Neil, have noticed how the apocalyptic urges in Shelley arrive at a paradisiacal terminus but remain deeply, even confusingly and paradoxically, complicated via their imbrication in his theories of epistemology and ontology. Wasserman, *Shelley: A Critical Reading* (Baltimore, MD: Johns Hopkins University Press, 1977). O'Neill, *The Human Mind's Imaginings: Conflict and Achievement in Shelley's Poetry* (Oxford: Clarendon Press, 1989). Harold Bloom reads Shelley as crafting a mythopoetic apocalypse that is visionary though not paradisiacal. Bloom, *Shelley's Mythmaking* (Ithaca, NY: Cornell University Press, 1969). Judith Chernaik similarly notes both Shelley's "millennial optimism" and his apocalyptic ambivalence. Chernaik, *The Lyrics of Shelley* (Cleveland, OH: Press of Case Western Reserve University, 1972), 4–6. Michael Henry Scrivener also connects Shelley's anarchism to nineteenth-century millennialism. Scrivener, *Radical Shelley: The Philosophical and Utopian Thought of Percy Bysshe Shelley*

(Princeton, NJ: Princeton University Press, 1982), 35–76. Ann Wroe, Shelley's most recent biographer, suggests that *The Triumph of Life* might be read as apocalyptic as well: "having acquired Dante's music, he too might be able to progress from his Inferno to his Paradise. As he broke off from the *Triumph* a boat was edging its way on the folded page, his perennial hope of rescue and transfiguration" (61). Wroe, "Resolutions, Destinations: Shelley's Last Year," in *The Oxford Handbook of Percy Bysshe Shelley*, ed. Michael O'Neill, Anthony Howe, and Madeleine Callaghan (Oxford: Oxford University Press, 2013), 48–64.

2 Meillassoux, *After Finitude*, 5. Steven Goldsmith has argued that detaching apocalypse from its socio-historical milieu creates an aesthetics that is often used to quash political dissent and affirm unjust societies. Like Goldsmith, I think Shelley challenges this version of apocalypse as an aesthetic tool used to forward injustice. Only, on my reading, Shelley does so from a post-apocalyptic angle that revises apocalyptic aesthetics like the Romantic sublime. Goldsmith, *Unbuilding Jerusalem*, 209–60.

3 Percy Bysshe Shelley, *Prometheus Unbound, Shelley's Poetry and Prose*, ed. Donald H. Reiman and Neil Fraistat (New York: Norton, 2002), 202–85. Cited by act and line number.

4 Ian Balfour derives a similar point from Walter Benjamin: "Benjamin is not remotely advocating some historical stance that simply turns to the past (nostalgically or otherwise) and suspends any interest in the future. But he is deeply suspicious of any notion that one can somehow know the future and then guide one's actions accordingly. Hence, the importance of the prophetic though quite apart from any knowledge that it is supposed to provide of the future. Prophecy is a call and a claim much more than it is a prediction, a call oriented toward a present that is not present" (*Rhetoric of Romantic Prophecy*, 18). Balfour's own argument is that the Romantic prophetic text, because of the nature of textuality as constantly iterable, can tell us something about times beyond its own: "And so the point of the readings will not be simply to determine the sense of these Romantic texts in and for their own time; the logic of prophetic discourse itself may help us glimpse the poverty of such historicism. The prophetic text, perhaps more than any other, resists being confined to one and only one moment, and in that respect too it may tell us – in extreme fashion – something about textuality as such. The prophetic moment has momentum. Even if a text, prophetic or otherwise, were *produced* in a single historical moment, the text, as text, resists ascription to that single moment. To acknowledge this fact is not to deny the text's historicity but to recognize its complexity" (3).

5 Alan Bewell, *Romanticism and Colonial Disease* (Baltimore, MD: Johns Hopkins University Press, 1999), 205–41.

6 Percy Bysshe Shelley, "A Defence of Poetry," in *Shelley's Poetry and Prose*, ed. Donald H. Reiman and Neil Fraistat (New York: Norton, 2002), 509–35, 535.

7 Percy Bysshe Shelley, "Essay on a Future State," in *Shelley's Prose: The Trumpet of a Prophecy*, ed. David Lee Clark (Albuquerque: University of New Mexico Press, 1954), 178.

8 I take the phrase "living on" from Derrida's "Living On," an essay partially about Shelley. A version of the phrase occurs in Shelley's "On Life": "What is life? Thoughts and feelings arise, with or without our will, and we employ words to express them. We are born, and our birth is unremembered, and our infancy remembered but in fragments; we live on, and in living we lose the apprehension of life." Percy Bysshe Shelley, "On Life," in *Shelley's Poetry and Prose*, ed. Donald H. Reiman and Neil Fraistat (New York: Norton, 2002), 506. Ross Wilson defines "living on" in this passage as "mere enduring" (*Shelley and the Apprehension of Life*, 10). Hence, on Wilson's reading, Shelley is against "living on," and against life, unless it is qualified. "He hates life," Wilson writes, "lived under conditions of suffering, injustice, and oppression" (10). I read "living on" in Shelley as what it means to live not as mere endurance – remaining alive – but as living in the presentist time. This type of living, as I will show below, restores to us an apprehension of life that non-ontological pictures of life, with which Shelley opens this essay, obscure. Derrida, "Living On," 62–142. Wilson, *Shelley and the Apprehension of Life* (Cambridge: Cambridge University Press, 2013).

9 Meillassoux, *After Finitude*, 7.

10 Cian Duffy, *Shelley and the Revolutionary Sublime* (Cambridge: Cambridge University Press, 2005), 5.

11 Thomas Weiskal writes in his classic study that "the essential claim of the sublime is that man can, in feeling and in speech, transcend the human" (3). Weiskal, *The Romantic Sublime: Studies in the Structure and Psychology of Transcendence* (Baltimore, MD: Johns Hopkins University Press, 1976).

12 Duffy is correct in what he says even as he ultimately draws significantly different conclusions than my own: "After all, to follow Kapstein's claim that 'Mont Blanc''s 'subject matter is ontology,' the 'nature of the mind, the nature of knowledge, the nature of reality, and the relation of the human mind to the universe,' is to risk forgetting the poem's ostensible object: the mountain itself. Conversely, a satisfactory account of 'Mont Blanc''s 'ambigious' ontology can only be provided within the context of Shelley's revision of the discourse on the sublime" (Duffy, *Shelley and the Revolutionary Sublime*, 87). Matthew C. Borushko claims that "'the sublime' stands at the point of separation between man and Nature. It marks the originary violence of discourse, the moment when man and Nature were

first riven into two realms, two 'separate fantasies,' that, according to the poem, might one day be reconciled" (244). Borushko's conclusion aptly summarizes the critical conclusion from which I diverge in this chapter: "That the 'vacancy,' the silence and solitude atop Mont Blanc, is not, in the end simply an empty void means that the 'adverting mind' has learned well its own agency in the making of the world for it no longer pays tribute: it has filled the vacancy with the beauty of the earth, the stars, and sea" (249). Borushko, "The Politics of Subreption: Resisting the Sublime in Shelley's 'Mont Blanc,'" *Studies in Romanticism* 52, no. 2 (2013), 225–52. Duffy and Borushko ultimately read the sublime in "Mont Blanc" as instancing, respectively, violent and non-violent progressive politics, with which I am largely in paradoxical agreement. See also William Keach, *Shelley's Style* (London: Methuen, 184), 42–78. Louise Economides offers a reading of "Mont Blanc" materiality through the systems theory of Niklas Luhmann, whose work I take up in chapter 5. Economides, "'Mont Blanc' and the Sublimity of Materiality," *Cultural Critique* 61 (2005): 87–114.

13 On Anahid Nersessian's reading of *The Revolt of Islam*, Shelley suggests that the best of all possible worlds might be one without the human race (Nersessian, *Utopia, Limited*, 75–109). But her reading of Shelley also makes possible what she calls "Rcsm," the limited utopia of Romantic futures focused on conservation and making do with less. My argument does not oppose this reading of Shelley (they are complementary) so much as it takes a different tack. As I claim in the introduction, we already live in a world without us if by this we understand a world moving on independent of us that we can nevertheless affect (and that can, and does, affect us).

14 A classic essay in "Mont Blanc" criticism claims that the subject matter of the poem is not only ontology but also "the nature of mind, the nature of knowledge, the nature of reality, and the relation of the human mind to the universe" (1046). I.J. Kapstein, "The Meaning of Shelley's 'Mont Blanc,'" *PMLA* 62, no. 4 (1974): 1046–60. Kapstein offers two possible readings of the poem similar to the ones I trace out below, but sees them as instances of a materialism that Shelley overcomes in his later idealism. This idealism is, according to Kapstein, an instance of how the mind can create the world (1058–9).

15 Goldsmith, *Unbuilding Jerusalem*, 1–26.

16 Percy Bysshe Shelley, "Speculations on Metaphysics and Morals," in *Shelley's Prose: The Trumpet of a Prophecy*, ed. David Lee Clark (Albuquerque: University of New Mexico Press, 1954), 182.

17 In a letter to Godwin dated 29 July 1812. Percy Bysshe Shelley, *The Letters of Percy Bysshe Shelley*, vol. 1, ed. Frederick L. Jones (Oxford: Clarendon Press, 1964), 315–18.

18 Shelley, *Prometheus Unbound*, 202–85.
19 Alan Richardson, *A Mental Theater: Poetic Drama and Consciousness in the Romantic Age* (University Park: Pennsylvania State University Press, 1988).
20 Shelley, *Prometheus Unbound*, 209.
21 Hugh Roberts, *Shelley and the Chaos of History* (University Park: Pennsylvania State University Press, 1997).
22 Roberts, *Shelley and the Chaos of History*, 467.
23 Shelley's long passage on ruin, in which he draws on James Parkinson's *Organic Remains of a Former World*, anticipates Byron's Cuvierian depiction of former stages of life on the planet in his *Cain* that I explore in chapter 3. For now it is worth noting how both poets are invested in natural-history theorizations of a world hurdling towards catastrophe. Georges Cuvier, *An Essay on the Theory of the Earth*, 1813.
24 As Abrams sees it, the "marital reunion" of Prometheus and Asia ushers in "a paradise of this earth" (*Natural Supernaturalism*, 306).
25 Curran, *Shelley's Annus Mirabilis*, 64.
26 Shelley, *Prometheus Unbound*, 209.
27 Shelley, *Prometheus Unbound*, 209.
28 David Lee Clark publishes "Speculations on Metaphysics and Morals" under a different title. Percy Bysshe Shelley, "A Treatise on Morals," in *Shelley's Prose: The Trumpet of a Prophecy*, ed. David Lee Clark (Albuquerque: University of New Mexico Press, 1954), 182.
29 Shelley, "Speculations on Metaphysics and Morals," 182. It is perhaps not for nothing that in Mary Shelley's *The Last Man*, Lionel, under the tutelage of Adrian, "studied the metaphysics of Plato and Berkeley" (287).
30 Shelley, "Speculations on Metaphysics and Morals," 182.
31 Meillassoux, *After Finitude*, 3. See also Steven Shaviro, *The Universe of Things: On Speculative Realism* (Minneapolis: University of Minnesota Press, 2014), 108–9.
32 Shelley, "Speculations on Metaphysics," 182–3.
33 Shelley, "Speculations on Metaphysics," 185.
34 Shelley, "Speculations on Metaphysics," 186.
35 Shelley, "On Life," 505–9.
36 Shelley, "On Life," 507.
37 Shelley, "On Life," 506.
38 See D'Arcy Wood, *Tambora*.
39 For another speculative account of this poem, see Ellermann, "Speculative Romanticism."
40 For that matter, Kate Singer's forthcoming book re-maps the subject of Romantic vacancy altogether. Singer, *Romantic Vacancy: The Poetics of Gender, Affect, and Radical Speculation* (New York: SUNY, 2019). Noah Heringman explores how the poem begins to mobilize the analogy

between "geological and political revolution." *Romantic Rocks, Aesthetic Geology* (Ithaca, NY: Cornell University Press, 2010), 14. Nigel Leask explores similar issues by examining the competing attitudes of Neptunists – followers of Cuvier – versus Vulcanists – followers of Hutton. Leask, "Mont Blanc's Mysterious Voice: Shelley and Huttonian Earth Science," in *Third Culture: Literature and Science*, ed. Elinor S. Shaffer (New York: Walter de Gruyter, 1998), 182–203.

41 Wasserman identifies this as the central problem in Shelley's "intellectual philosophy" as it relates to his idea of the "One Mind" throughout his poetry. He finds that Shelley collapses the distinction between thought and thing, subject and object, though his ontology does so ambiguously, and the end goal is to elucidate human delusions about reality (Wasserman, *Shelley: A Critical Reading*, 131–254). See also Frances Ferguson, "Shelley's 'Mont Blanc': What the Mountain Said," in *Romanticism and Language*, ed. Arden Reed (Ithaca, NY: Cornell University Press, 1984), 202–14; Christopher Hitt, "Shelley's Unwriting of 'Mont Blanc,'" *Texas Studies in Literature & Language* 47, no. 2 (2005): 139–66; Economides, "'Mont Blanc' and the Sublimity of Materiality."

42 Wasserman, *Shelley: A Critical Reading*, 223.

43 Anne C. McCarthy, "The Aesthetics of Contingency in 'The Universe of Things,' or, 'Mont Blanc' without Mont Blanc," *Studies in Romanticism* 54 (2015): 359.

44 McCarthy, "The Aesthetics of Contingency," 360.

45 Given the line's anthropomorphism, it shares something with Shelley's description of the mountain in a letter written to Thomas Love Peacock while Shelley and Mary were there in July 1816. "One would think that Mont Blanc was a living being & that the frozen blood forever circulated slowly thro' his stony veins." Percy Bysshe Shelley, "Letter to Thomas Love Peacock, December 22nd, 1818," in *The Letters of Percy Bysshe Shelley*, vol. 1, ed. Frederick L. Jones (Oxford: Clarendon Press, 1964), 500.

46 Gottlieb, *Romantic Realities*, 166.

47 Both Leask and Heringman explore how deep time connects to the poem.

48 My conclusion is somewhat different from Frances Ferguson's: "Rather, because the human mind can attribute destructiveness to nature, nature needs us for it to be destructive in any significant way. Thus Mont Blanc creates an image of sublimity that continually hypostasizes the eternality of human consciousness. Because even the ideas of the destructiveness and annihilation of mankind require human consciousness to give them force, they thus are testimony to the necessity of the continuation of the human" (Ferguson, "Shelley's 'Mont Blanc,'" 210). The poem seems to me to suggest that "the ideas of the destructiveness and annihilation of mankind" have force entirely independent of anthropocentric orientations

of the world. Granted, if a tree falls in the forest and no one hears it, then no one has heard, but if a tree falls in the forest on someone, then someone feels it.

49 Graham Harman, "On Landscape Ontology: An Interview with Graham Harman," 98, *faslanyc*, accessed 1 February 2014, http://faslanyc.blogspot.com/2012/07/on-landscape-ontology-interview-with.html.
50 Marjorie Levinson, *Wordsworth's Great Period Poems: Four Essays* (Cambridge: Cambridge University Press, 1986), 24.
51 Gottlieb, *Romantic Realities*, 178.
52 Wasserman, *Shelley*, 269–70. John Milton, *Paradise Lost*, ed. William Kerrigan, John Rumich, and Stephen M. Fallon (New York: Random House, 2007).
53 Shelley, "A Defence of Poetry," 528.
54 Keach, *Shelley's Style*.
55 Shelley, "A Defence of Poetry," 510–11.
56 Shelley, "A Defence of Poetry," 511.
57 Adam Smith, *A Theory of Moral Sentiments: The Glasgow Edition of the Works of Adam Smith* (New York: Liberty Fund, 2009). David Hume, *A Treatise of Human Nature: The Clarendon Edition of the Works of David Hume*, ed. David Fate Norton (Oxford: Oxford University Press, 2011).
58 Shelley, "A Defence of Poetry," 512.
59 Shelley, "A Defence of Poetry," 512.
60 Shelley, "A Defence of Poetry," 517.
61 Jacques Derrida, "White Mythology: Metaphor in the Text of Philosophy," in *Margins of Philosophy*, trans. Alan Bass (Chicago: University of Chicago Press, 1978), 207–72.
62 Shelley, "A Defence of Poetry," 535.
63 Carl Grabo recounts Shelley's knowledge of Newton. Grabo, *A Newton among Poets: Shelley's Use of Science in "Prometheus Unbound"* (New York: Cooper Square Publishers, 1968). More recent accounts by Sharon Ruston and Denise Gigante feature examinations of Shelley's poetic incorporation of the scientific vitalist and organicist theories of the time. Ruston, *Shelley and Vitality* (Houndmills, UK: Palgrave Macmillan, 2012). Gigante, *Life: Organic Form and Romanticism* (Ithaca, NY: Yale University Press, 2009).
64 Shelley, "A Defence of Poetry," 511.
65 Shelley, "A Defence of Poetry," 517.
66 Shelley, "A Defence of Poetry," 517.
67 Shelley, "A Defence of Poetry," 530.
68 Shelley, "A Defence of Poetry," 515.
69 Shelley, "A Defence of Poetry," 533.
70 Wasserman, *Shelley*, 269.

71 Newton's main preoccupation throughout his life was theological end-times exegesis. Much of this remains unpublished and unread.

72 Jacques Derrida, "Of an Apocalyptic Tone Newly Adopted in Philosophy," in *Derrida and Negative Theology*, ed. Harold Coward and Toby Foshay (Albany, NY: SUNY Press, 1992), 25–72. "Whoever takes on the apocalyptic tone comes to signify to, if not tell, you something. What? The truth, of course, and to signify to you that it reveals the truth to you: tone is revelatory of some unveiling in process. Unveiling or truth, apophantics of the imminence of the end, of whatever comes down, finally, to the end of the world. Not only truth as the revealed truth of a secret on the end of the secret of the end. Truth itself is the end, the destination, and that truth unveils itself is the advent of the end. Truth is the end and the instance of the last judgment. The structure of truth here would be apocalyptic. And that is why there not be any truth of the apocalypse that is not the truth of the truth" (53).

73 Shelley, "A Defence of Poetry," 513.

74 Shelley, "A Defence of Poetry," 535.

2. No More Cakes and Ale, Only Oil Slicks

1 Godwin, *An Enquiry Concerning Political Justice*, 53, 56.

2 Peter Melville's amazing book also offers a reading of hospitality in Mary Shelley's novel, but his reading takes a different path than my own and concerns how hospitality humanizes the human subject in any encounter with the nonhuman other. Melville, *Romantic Hospitality*, 139–74.

3 Shukin, *Animal Capital*. For a discussion of biopolitics in the novel, see Ranita Chatterjee, "Our Bodies, Our Catastrophies: Biopolitics in Mary Shelley's *The Last Man*," *European Romantic Review* 25, no. 1 (2014): 35–49.

4 Andrea Haslanger also examines animal life in *The Last Man*, although she does so within the frame of Cynic cosmopolitanism. According to her, the novel draws on this type of cosmopolitanism, which originated with Kant at the end of the previous century (although Haslanger does not see Shelley's cosmopolitanism as specifically Kantian), to show that humans should mimic animal life, living as "simply as possible, without any excess needs or desires" (661). This also gives the Cynic distance from their community in order to reflect on and critique it. On my reading, the novel wants us to live with, not like, animals and thereby to *respect* rather than collapse difference. Haslanger, "The Last Animal: Cosmopolitanism in *The Last Man*," *European Romantic Review* 27, no. 5 (2016): 659–78.

5 William and Nicholas Klingaman's *The Year without a Summer: 1816 and the Volcano That Darkened the World and Changed History* (New York: St Martin's, 2014).

6 D'Arcy Wood, *Tambora*, 2.
7 D'Arcy Wood, 10.
8 Of course, there had been a vogue for last-man texts before 1816, but the Shelleys and Byron contextualized the idea in terms of climate change.
9 Cormac McCarthy, *The Road* (New York: Vintage, 2006), 169.
10 Peter Melville also notes this problem of omniscience for Lionel, but he reads it in a colonial context: "Lionel essentially colonizes the world over once more: he claims to embody all of humanity. It would seem that, for Lionel, if the world is left with only one surviving Englishman, there is but one human – a kind of logic which, interestingly, reminds us of Kant's witty assessment of English hospitality: as far as Lionel's narrative is concerned, all other foreigners, all other human beings scattered across the globe in this plague-ridden world, will be left to 'die on the dunghill' not as men, and certainly not as last men, precisely because they are not 'Englishmen,' that is not 'human being[s].'" Melville, *Romantic Hospitality*, 145.
11 Barbara Johnson proposes a kind of deconstructive reading in which all systems of meaning are erased by the plague. Johnson, "The Last Man," in *A Life with Mary Shelley* (Stanford, CA: Stanford University Press, 2014), 10. Anne Mellor offers a reading similar to that of Johnson in that "the very concept of meaning is, finally, meaningless." Mellor, *Mary Shelley*, 166.
12 I have discussed the differences between de Man's notion of allegory and irony, and its implications for speculative realism, in "Romanticism and Speculative Realism."
13 Morton D. Paley's well-known essay on the novel argues that its unrelenting nihilism makes it a rejection of Romantic apocalyptic millenarianism but that the novel ends as a place from which nothing generative can emerge. In his words, the novel "is a cruel joke on the reader by the author." Paley, "Mary Shelley's *The Last Man*: Apocalypse without Millennium," *Keats-Shelley Review* 4 (1989): 1–25. Sandra Gilbert and Susan Gubar, however, find the novel's nihilism (though this is not the primary topic of their chapter on Shelley) recuperating the lost paradise sought by the creature in *Frankenstein*. Gilbert and Gubar, *The Madwoman in the Attic: The Woman Writer and the Nineteenth-Century Literary Imagination* (New Haven, CT: Yale University Press, 2000), 247.
14 I discuss Derrida's idea of "living on" in my introduction and chapter 1, and I take it up again later in more detail. Derrida, "Living On."
15 Hobbes, *Leviathan*, 76.
16 Rousseau, *The Social Contract*.
17 See Paley, "Apocalypse without Millennium," 1. Jonathan Bate nicely outlines some of the weather patterns in the poem while also reading it and Keats's "To Autumn" against McGann's charge of Romantic ideology

at work in both poems. Bate, "Living with the Weather," *Studies in Romanticism* 35, no. 3 (1996): 431–47.

18 Mary Shelley, *The Last Man*, ed. Morton D. Paley (Oxford: Oxford World's Classics, 2008).

19 Mary Wollstonecraft's *Vindication of the Rights of Men* (1790) and *Vindication of the Rights of Woman* (1792) are full to brimming with this trope, as is Rousseau's *Discourse on Inequality* (1755) and *The Social Contract* (1762).

20 Fuson Wang reads the novel as recuperating the Romantic imagination to form new communities across lines of gender, race, and species: "the central theme of *The Last Man* cannot be, as several critics have claimed in some form or another, the failure of the Romantic imagination in the face of natural disaster" (249). Instead, "Shelley's cosmopolitan politics reanimates the principles of a conventionally Romantic poetics in its belief in the vatic poet's infinite creativity" (249). Wang, "'We Must Live Elsewhere': The Social Construction of Natural Immunity in *The Last Man*," *European Romantic Review* 22, no. 2 (2011): 235–55. Paley, as Wang points out, argues that the failure of the imagination is the novel's defining theme. Paley, introduction to *The Last Man*, by Mary Shelley, ed. Morton D. Paley, vii–xxiii. Elizabeth Effinger, however, finds that the novel resuscitates humanistic disciplinarity and art that will survive beyond the human. Effinger, "A Clandestine Catastrophe: Disciplinary Dissolution in Mary Shelley's *The Last Man*," *European Romantic Review* 25, no. 1 (2014): 19–34.

21 For readings that deal with the politics of the novel see Lee Sterrenburg, "*The Last Man*: Anatomy of Failed Revolutions," *Nineteenth-Century Fiction* 33, no. 3 (1978): 324–47; Mark Canuel, "Acts, Rules, and the Last Man," *Nineteenth-Century Fiction* 53, no. 2 (1998): 147–70; and Hilary Strang, "Common Life, Animal Life, Equality: 'The Last Man,'" *ELH* 78, no. 2 (2011): 409–31. Anne K. Mellor has made a similar point that "[Shelley] reveals the failures of the dominant political ideologies of her day – both radical (republican or democratic) and conservative (monarchical)" (*Mary Shelley*, 159). Mellor offers a fine reading of Shelley's view of these ideologies, but Mellor's Shelley remains within these politics, whereas my own reading shows Shelley diverging from them and developing a replacement model.

22 This paradox is, of course, the classic conundrum of democracy: giving up individual liberty for societal liberty. For a thorough reading of this paradox see Roberto Esposito, *Bios: Biopolitics and Philosophy* (Minneapolis: University of Minnesota Press, 2008).

23 Joel Faflak and Richard C. Sha, introduction to *Romanticism and the Emotions* (Cambridge: Cambridge University Press, 2014), 3–4.

24 The point throughout this book has never been to privilege the nonhuman over the human or to suggest that this type of speculative critical reading

is more important than feminist, critical race, post-colonial, or other such readings. Rather, from their so-called marginal positions, all such critical forms can be and should be intersectionally dialogued as parallel allies. Goldsmith, *Unbuilding Jerusalem*, 261–313.

25 Percy Shelley, "Letter to Thomas Love Peacock, December 22nd, 1818."

26 William Wordsworth, "The World Is Too Much with Us," in *The Major Works*, ed. Stephen Gill (Oxford: Oxford University Press, 2008), 270.

27 Raymond Williams, *The Country and the City* (Oxford: Oxford University Press, 1975).

28 William Shakespeare, *Twelfth Night, or, As You Will* (New York: Penguin, 2000). Act II, scene 3, lines 106–7.

29 Tom Furniss makes a similar point regarding the way in which Wollstonecraft deconstructs Burke's aesthetics via his politics. Furniss, "Nasty Tricks and Tropes: Sexuality and Language in Mary Wollstonecraft's *Rights of Woman*," *Studies in Romanticism* 32, no. 2 (1993): 177–209.

30 Nietzsche contrasts the last man to the *Ubermensch*, in *Thus Spoke Zarathustra*, trans. R.J. Hollingdale (New York: Penguin, 2003), 39–52.

31 Rousseau, *The Social Contract*.

32 Derrida, *Of Hospitality*, 25.

33 For a much different look at reciprocity and politics see David Collings, *Monstrous Society: Reciprocity, Discipline, and the Political Uncanny at the End of the Early Modern England* (Lewisburg, PA: Bucknell University Press, 2009).

34 Derrida, *Of Hospitality*, 25.

35 Kate Singer, "It's the End of the World as We Know It and I Feel Posthuman: Mary Shelley's Queer Animacies and Affects," a paper presented at the International Conference on Romanticism in Colorado Springs, 2016.

36 Melville, *Romantic Hospitality*, 148.

37 Derrida, *Of Hospitality*, 25.

38 This argument about a god to come occurs in Meillassoux's unpublished magnum opus *L'inexistence divine*, excerpts of which have been translated and published by Graham Harman. Meillassoux, *L'inexistence divine*, *Quentin Meillassoux: Philosophy in the Making* (Edinburgh, UK: Edinburgh University Press, 2011), 224–87.

39 Haslanger ultimately sees Lionel becoming an animal, as he is when the novel opens, and part of animal communities; yet the novel, in separating Lionel from animal communities at the end, seems to indicate the exact opposite ("The Last Animal," 669).

40 Haslanger, "The Last Animal," 674.

41 Lee Edelman, *No Future: Queer Theory and the Death Drive* (Durham, NC: Duke University Press, 2004). Ray Brassier, *Nihil Unbound: Enlightenment and Extinction* (Houndmills: Palgrave Macmillon, 2007).

3. Byron's Speculative Turn

1 Lord Byron, *Byron's Letters and Journals*, vol. 2, ed. Leslie A. Marchand (Cambridge: Belknap Press, 1973), 88.
2 Byron, *Byron's Letters and Journals*, vol. 2, 97–8.
3 "One reason Byron could so vigorously resist posthumous consolation was that he never gave up his hope of the terrestrial paradise." E.D. Hirsch, "Byron and the Terrestrial Paradise," *Byron's Poetry*, 1st ed., ed. Frank D. McConnell (New York: Norton, 1978), 447.
4 Throughout his letters Byron writes of his admiration for Epicurus and Lucretius, often quoting passages from memory. See Byron, *Byron's Letters and Journals*, vol. 1, 216; vol. 3, 188, 210; vol. 6, 67; vol. 7, 192, 200; vol. 11, 126.
5 Byron, *Byron's Letters and Journals*, vol. 4, 78.
6 Percy Bysshe Shelley, letter to John Gisborne, 26 January 1822, in *The Letters of Percy Bysshe Shelley*, vol. 2, ed. Frederick L. Jones (Oxford: Clarendon University Press, 1964), 388.
7 Since its publication, *Cain* has been hotly debated. Truman Steffan offers a valuable collection of reviews of *Cain* by Byron's contemporaries. Steffan, *Lord Byron's "Cain": Twelve Essays and a Text with Variants and Annotations* (Austin: University of Texas Press, 1968). M.K. Joseph surveys Byron's historical materials for the poem, in his *Byron the Poet* (London: Victor Gollancz, 1966), 116–26. Robert F. Gleckner sees the poem as reflective of Byron's "full-blown nihilism," a judgment with which I disagree (as will be seen). Gleckner, *Byron and the Ruins of Paradise* (Baltimore, MD: Johns Hopkins University Press, 1967), 324. Jerome McGann traces the poem's "Satanic" connections to Byron's poetic corpus, in his *Don Juan in Context* (Chicago: Chicago University Press, 1976), 23–31. For more recent criticism see Stephen L. Goldstein, "Byron's 'Cain' and the Painites," *Studies in Romanticism* 14, no. 4 (1975): 391–410; Paul A. Cantor, "Byron's 'Cain': A Romantic Version of the Fall," *Kenyon Review* 2, no. 3 (1980), 50–71; Wolf Z. Hirst, "Byron's Lapse into Orthodoxy: An Unorthodox Reading of 'Cain,'" *Keats-Shelley Journal* 29 (1980): 151–72; Richardson, *A Mental Theater*, 59–83; Kerry Ellen McKeever, "Naming the Name of the Prophet: William Blake's Reading of Byron's 'Cain: A Mystery,'" *Studies in Romanticism* 34, no. 4 (1995): 615–36; Peter A. Schock, "The 'Satanism' of Cain in Context: Byron's Lucifer and the War against Blasphemy," *Keats-Shelley Journal* 44 (1995), 182–215; Ian Dennis, "'Cain': Lord Byron's Sincerity," *Studies*

in Romanticism 41, no. 4 (2002): 655–74; and Madaleine Callaghan, "The Struggle with Language in Byron's *Cain*," *Byron Journal* 38, no. 2 (2010): 125–34.

8 Lord Byron, preface to *Cain: A Mystery*, in *The Major Works*, ed. Jerome McGann (Oxford: Oxford University Press, 2008), 882. Hereafter cited by act, scene, and line number. I cite this version of the play because it is more readily available, though I have also consulted the variorum edition.

9 Byron describes the poem thusly in a letter to Thomas Moore: "I have gone upon the notion of Cuvier, that the world has been destroyed three or four times, and was inhabited by mammoths, behemoths, and what not; but not by man till the Mosaic period, as, indeed, it proved by the strata of bones found; – those of all unknown animals, and known being dug out, but none of mankind. I have, therefore, supposed Cain to be shown, in the *rational* Preadamites, beings endowed with a higher intelligence than man, but totally unlike him in form, and with much greater strength of mind and person. You may suppose the small talk which takes place between him and Lucifer upon these matters is not quite canonical" (*Byron's Letters and Journals*, vol. 7, 215–16).

10 Byron, *Cain*, 882.

11 Jose Saramago's recent retelling of the Cain-and-Abel story features Cain's action culminating in the death of the human species with the exception of Cain himself. Cain becomes a "last man." Saramago, *Cain* (New York: Houghton, Mifflin, 2011).

12 Byron seems to conceive of the life cycle of the human species after Cain's murder of Abel in terms that are sympathetic to Hobbes's famous assertion that life is "solitary, poor, nasty, brutish, and short" (Hobbes, *Leviathan*, ed. Curley, 76). Edwin Curley notes that Hobbes, in the expanded Latin version of his work published in Amsterdam in 1668, cites the Cain-and-Abel story as proof of "the war of all against all'" in the state of nature (77).

13 The book of Genesis offers little clue to God's preferential treatment of Abel's sacrifice as it does not say why God had "respect": "And Abel, he also brought of the firstlings of his flock and of the fat thereof. And the Lord had respect unto Abel and his offering: But unto Cain and to his offering he had not respect. And Cain was very wroth, and his countenance fell" (King James, Genesis 4:4–5).

14 Giorgio Agamben, *Homo Sacer: Sovereign Power and Bare Life*, trans. Daniel Heller-Roazen (Stanford, CA: Stanford University Press, 1998), 3. Alastair Hunt and Matthias Rudolf offer a lucid explanation of the critical relations between Foucault and Agamben's articulation of the stakes of biopolitics in their recent Romantic Circles Praxis edition. "Introduction: The Romantic Rhetoric of Life," in *Romanticism and Biopolitics*, Romantic Circles Praxis Series,

December 2012, accessed 1 March 2013, http://www.rc.umd.edu/praxis/biopolitics/index.html.

15 Agamben, *Homo Sacer*, 8.

16 Agamben, *Homo Sacer*, 7.

17 Agamben, *Homo Sacer*, 82. Cary Wolfe nimbly explains the terminological and conceptual status of sacrifice and murder in Agamben: "It is worth voicing a clarification here with regard to 'sacrifice.' Sacrifice in Agamben would appear to be opposed to, not a part of, Derrida's 'sacrificial symbolic economy' when Agamben asserts that *homo sacer* 'is a human victim who may be killed but not sacrificed' (*Homo Sacer*, 83). But what 'sacrificial' references here for Agamben is, additionally, an earlier religious order out of which the properly political emerges, which is assimilated in Derrida's reading to the same essential logic. 'The political sphere of sovereignty ... takes the form of a zone of indistinction between sacrifice and homicide,' Agamben writes (*Homo Sacer*, 83). In other words, *homo sacer* as he who may be 'killed but not sacrificed' means, as it does in Derrida, 'killable but not murderable' but retains in Agamben the earlier religious sense as well." Cary Wolfe, *Before the Law: Humans and Other Animals in a Biopolitical Frame* (Chicago: Chicago University Press, 2012), 110.

18 Agamben, *Homo Sacer*, 1.

19 Shukin, *Animal Capital*, 9. Tilottama Rajan makes a related point about Cain: "To speak of Cain as pushed into resentment by man's insignificance is to assume that he puts man at the center of things; but Cain (unlike Manfred) does not assume an anthropological perspective." Rajan, "'Something Not Yet Made Good'": Byron's *Cain*, Godwin, and Mary Shelley's *Falkner*," in *Byron and the Politics of Freedom and Terror*, ed. J.A. Green and Piya Pal-Lapinski (Houndmills, UK: Palgrave, 2011), 95.

20 Esposito, *Bios*, 194.

21 Byron, *Byron's Letters and Journals*, vol. 9, 53–4.

22 Jacques Derrida, "Eating Well: Or the Calculation of the Subject," in *Points ... Interviews, 1974–1994* (Stanford, CA: Stanford University Press, 1995), 279.

23 Wolfe, *Before the Law*, 9.

24 Byron, *Byron's Letters and Journals*, vol. 8, 216.

25 Wolfe, *Before the Law*, 9.

26 It seems clear that the Angel's comment on Abel, that "he / thou slew'st was gentler as the flocks he tended," is meant ironically as well since it was he who violently slew those same flocks (3.1.504–5). That Cain appears in agreement with the Angel – "I / have dried the fountain of a gentle race" – enforces the futility of killing Abel to abolish the sacrificial structure of

life (3.1.556–7). From the play's perspective, human extinction might be desirable, as will be discussed later, but not through violence that simply perpetuates violence and war.

27 G. Wilson Knight, *Lord Byron: Christian Virtues* (London: Routledge, 1953).
28 Richard Holmes, *Shelley: The Pursuit* (New York: New York Review Books Classics, 1994), 684–5.
29 Leslie Marchand, *Byron: A Biography*, vol. 3 (New York: Alfred A. Knopf, 1957), 1034.
30 Byron, *Byron's Letters and Journals*, vol. 3, 237.
31 Byron, *Byron's Letters and Journals* vol. 2, 42.
32 Byron, *Byron's Letters and Journals* vol. 2, 51.
33 Byron, *Byron's Letters and Journals* vol. 7, 39.
34 Paul Crutzen coined the term *Anthropocene Era* in his "Geology of Mankind," *Nature* 415 (2002): 23.
35 For the conflict between animal welfare, animal rights legislation, and industrialized slaughterhouses see Hilda Klein. *Animal Rights: Political and Social Change in Britain since 1800* (London: Reaktion Books, 1998), 113–35.
36 Derrida, "Eating Well," 278.
37 Derrida, *The Animal That Therefore I Am*, 28–9.
38 Meillassoux, *After Finitude*, 5.
39 Meillassoux, *After Finitude*, 10.
40 Meillassoux, *After Finitude*, 112.
41 Eugene Thacker, *In the Dust of this Planet*, vol. 1 of *Horror of Philosophy* (Washington, DC: Zero Books, 2012), 4–5.
42 Bill Mckibben, *Eaarth: Making a Life on a Tough New Planet* (New York: Henry Holt, 2010), 176–8. Jonathan Safran Foer, *Eating Animals* (New York: Little, Brown, 2009), 58, 81–115.
43 Slavoj Žižek, *Living in the End Times* (London: Verso, 2010), 334.
44 Lord Byron, *Don Juan*, in *The Major Works*, ed. Jerome McGann (Oxford: Oxford University Press, 2008), 373–879.
45 James K. Chandler, "'Man Fell with Apples': The Moral Mechanics of *Don Juan*," in *Byron's Poetry and Prose*, ed. Alice Levine (New York: Norton, 2010), 998.
46 The politics of paradise in this canto can be seen as a revision of Milton's *felix culpa* in *Paradise Lost*: the Fall was unfortunate and fortunate. Milton, *Paradise Lost*, 409.
47 Genesis 1:24.
48 For the affirmative version of biopolitics see Shukin, *Animal Capital*; and Michael Hardt and Antonio Negri, *Multitude: War and Democracy in the Age of Empire* (New York: Penguin, 2004).
49 Jacques Derrida, "Autoimmunity: Real and Symbolic Suicides," in *Philosophy in a Time of Terror: Dialogues with Jurgen Habermas and Jacques*

Derrida, ed. Giovanna Borradori (Chicago: University of Chicago Press, 2003). Roberto Esposito, *Immunitas: The Protection and Negation of Life*, trans. Zakiya Hanafi (Boston: Polity, 2011).

50 Jacques Derrida, *Specters of Marx: The State of the Debt, the Work of Mourning, and the New International* (New York: Routledge, 1994), xix.

4. Birds Do It, Bees Do It

1 Although written years ago, John Barrell's comment that "almost every critic who has written about John Clare has seen the importance of relating the enclosure of Helpston to Clare's development as a writer and to the content of his work" remains true today (189). Barrell, *The Idea of Landscape and the Sense of Place 1730–1840: An Approach to the Poetry of John Clare* (Cambridge: Cambridge UP, 1972). However, little focus has been placed on how enclosure affects human-animal relations in Clare's poetry. See for example Johanne Clare, *John Clare and the Bounds of Circumstances* (Kingston, ON: McGill-Queen's University Press, 1987); Bob Heyes, "John Clare and Enclosure," *John Clare Society Journal* 6 (1987): 10–19; John Goodridge, "Pastoral and Popular Modes in Clare's 'Enclosure Elegies,'" in *The Independent Spirit: John Clare and the Self-Taught Tradition*, ed. John Goodridge (Helpston, UK: John Clare Society and the Margaret Grainger Memorial Trust, 1994), 87–129; and Alan Bewell, "John Clare and the Ghosts of Natures Past," *Nineteenth-Century Literature* 65, no. 4 (2011): 548–78.

2 John Clare, "The Lamentations of Round-Oak Waters," in *Major Works*, ed. Eric Robinson and David Powell (Oxford: Oxford University Press, 2004), 18–23.

3 Clare describes the woodsman similarly in "May," from *The Shepherd's Calendar*, ed. Tim Chilcott (Manchester, UK: Carcanet Press, 2006):

> But woodmen still on spring intrude;
> and thin the shadow's solitude;
> with sharpen'd axes felling down
> the oak-trees budding into brown,
> which, as they crash upon the ground,
> a crowd of labourers gather round.
> these, mizing 'mong the shadows dark,
> rip off the crackling's staining bark;
> depriving yearly, when they come,
> the green woodpecker of his home …

("May," in *The Shepherd's Calendar*, lines 73–82)

4 There is a possible autobiographical impetus to this new emphasis. According to Jonathan Bate, "in December 1830 he was especially horrified by an arson attack on a large farm out in Deeping Fen. It chilled Clare's blood to think of what had happened, not least because his humanitarian instincts recoiled from the suffering of cows, pigs and horses burnt to death in the blaze. There had been many rick-burnings in the months before, but this event struck home because of the loss of animal life" (357). Bate, *John Clare: A Biography* (New York: Farrar, Straus & Giroux, 2003). In a letter to Frank Simpson in late December 1830, Clare, commenting on this episode, says that "it chills my blood almost into water to think of." Clare, *The Letters of John Clare*, ed. Mark Storey (Oxford: Clarendon Press, 1985), 523. However, such biographical explanations do not seem to fit the action of the poems – the barn fire, for instance – and they seem to require complete surrender to the notion that Clare's poems are merely nakedly autobiographical, for example, the idea that the wounded animals represent him trapped in the asylum. This latter idea is shared by Eric Robinson and Seamus Heaney. Robinson, introduction to *John Clare by Himself*, ed. Eric Robinson and David Powell (New York: Routledge, 2002), ix. Heaney, "John Clare: A Bi-Centenary Lecture," in *John Clare in Context*, ed. Hugh Haughton, Adam Phillips, and Geoffrey Summerfield (Cambridge: University of Cambridge Press, 2005), 139.

5 Jacob von Uexküll, *A Foray into the Worlds of Animals and Humans: With a Theory of Meaning*, trans. Joseph O'Neil (Minneapolis: University of Minnesota Press, 2010), 42.

6 John Clare, "The Fallen Elm," in *Selected Poems*, ed. Geoffrey Summerfield (New York: Penguin, 2000), 167–8.

7 Calling the late Northborough sonnets "a watershed" and as surprising in their appearance in Clare's poetic corpus as Wordsworth's Lucy poems were in his, Robinson, Powell, and Dawson write that they are "distinct from everything Clare had written before." John Clare, *Poems of the Middle Period*, vol. 5, *1822–1837*, ed. Eric Robinson, David Powell, and P.M.S. Dawson (Oxford: Oxford University Press, 2003) (hereafter cited as *PMP*), xxiii. They, along with Jonathan Bate in his biography of Clare, note the experimental nature of the poems: "from a technical perspective Clare is evidently engaged in a period of experimentation" (*PMP*, xxiii). Bate, *John Clare: A Biography* (New York: Farrar, Straus & Giroux, 2003), 404.

8 Johanne Clare, *Bounds of Circumstances*, 43.

9 John Fisher, "The Birds of John Clare," in *The First Fifty Years: A History of the Kettering and District Naturalists' Society and Field Club* (Kettering, UK, 1956). Quoted in *John Clare's Birds*, ed. Eric Robinson and Richard Fitter (Oxford: Oxford University Press, 1982), xxi.

10 Clare in fact expresses incredulity that London people and poets do not know about nightingales. As Margaret Grainger notes, he seems to be specifically objecting to Coleridge's "The Nightingale: A Conversation Poem," which is, apparently, wrong in its details about the nightingale (*The Natural History Prose Writings of John Clare*, 42). Other critics have charted how Clare's poetry differs from the Wordsworthian sublime: Sarah Houghton, "'Enkindling Ecstacy': The Sublime Vision of John Clare," *Romanticism* 9 (2003): 176–95; Scott Hess, "John Clare, William Wordsworth, and the (Un)Framing of Nature," *John Clare Society Journal* 27 (2008): 27–44.

11 Clare, "The Yellowhammer's Nest," in *Selected Poems*, ed. Geoffrey Summerfield, 104–5.

12 Contra John Barrell, Timothy Brownlow argues that Clare was not a picturesque poet who looked for unlimited horizons to depict; rather, he was interested in local contiguous life. Brownlow's idea that Clare focuses on "micropanoramas" is similar in some ways to what I am saying here. Brownlow, *Clare and Picturesque Landscape* (Oxford: Clarendon Press, 1983), 66. Adam White disagrees that Clare disregards the picturesque, arguing that he uses the technique throughout his later poetry. White, "John Clare: 'The Man of Taste,'" *John Clare Society Journal* 28 (2009): 38–54.

13 Alan Vardy has a related argument: "Clare insists that ethics and aesthetic are intertwined … In order to represent the intrinsic value of the objects of nature, the poet and the audience must recede as the ultimate centres of aesthetic value." Vardy, *John Clare, Politics and Poetry* (New York: Palgrave, 2003), 21.

14 Clare, "The Nightingale's Nest," in *Selected Poems*, ed. Geoffrey Summerfield, 108–11.

15 "I usd also to be very fond of poking about the hedges in spring to hunt pootys and I was no less fond of robbing the poor birds nests" (Clare, "Autobiographical Fragments," 43).

16 John Goodridge and Kelsey Thornton argue that, "trespass imagery, considered in the broad sense of boundaries, and those who break or challenge them, pervades the whole of John Clare's writings." Goodridge and Thornton, "John Clare: The Trespasser," in *John Clare in Context*, ed. Hugh Haughton, Adam Phillips, and Geoffrey Summerfield (Cambridge: Cambridge University Press, 1994), 90.

17 David Perkins notices something similar in the bird poems: "Clare's naturalist's stance supports his stance as a lover of nature but also undermines it. The reason is not merely the comparative objectivity I just mentioned. Some of the quasi-scientific information could only be obtained by intruding destructively on the creatures." Perkins, "Sweet Helpston! John Clare on Badger Baiting," *Studies in Romanticism* 38 (1999): 398.

18 The poems discussed here are all found in the Northborough manuscripts MS A61 and MS B9, collected in *PMP*.

19 *PMP*, 360.

20 *PMP*, 358.

21 *PMP*, 358.

22 *PMP*, 359.

23 *PMP*, 362.

24 *PMP*, 359.

25 *PMP*, 360–2.

26 Some critics suggest that these poems represent Clare's own removal from Helpston to Northborough in 1832. Perhaps they do, but "The Nightingale's Nest" was likely written once he moved to Northborough, too. What exactly Clare himself thought about these poems, or the formal experimentation they contain, we do not know, but his relocation to Northborough, and his subsequent depression and mental afflictions, certainly testify to his understanding of how geographical changes wreak havoc on the rhythms of individual lives.

27 Paul de Man, "Autobiography as De-facement," in *The Rhetoric of Romanticism* (New York: Columbia UP, 1984), 67–82. De Man, "Hypogram and Inscription," in *The Resistance to Theory* (Minneapolis: University of Minnesota Press, 1986), 27–53, 48.

28 Sara Guyer, *Romanticism after Auschwitz* (Stanford, CA: Stanford University Press, 2007), 223.

29 Clare was familiar with other famous poems that featured cruelty to animals. Robert Bloomfield's portrayal of humans' mistreatment of the post-horse in the "Winter" section (ll. 160–212) of *The Farmer's Boy*, and the lamentation over the docking of horse tails in the "Summer" section (ll. 193–252), notably differs from Clare in that neither passage experiments with prosopopoeia. Bloomfield, *The Farmer's Boy*, edited by Peter Cochran (Cambridge: Cambridge Scholars Publishing, 2014). Similarly, William Cowper's long description of the harm done to rural labouring animals in book 6 of *The Task* does so from the speaker's perspective and very specifically makes this cruelty the main argument of the book. For Cowper, human abuse of animals is even a matter for God's divine judgment: "and God, some future day / will reckon with us roundly for the abuse / of what He deems no mean or trivial trust" (ll. 605–7). In other words, both offer moral complaints about the treatment of animals, whereas "The Badger" refuses to do so. Cowper, *The Task and Selected Other Poems*, ed. James Sambrook (New York: Longman, 1994).

30 Stephanie Kuduk Weiner, "Listening with John Clare," *Studies in Romanticism* 48 (2009): 378.

31 Although it differs from my argument, David Simpson finds Clare doing similarly original things with personification as it relates to place in "Swordy Well": "I can find no simple genre or rhetorical category that prefigures what Clare is doing here." Simpson, "A Speaking Place: The Matter of Genre in *The Lament of Swordy Well*," *Wordsworth Circle* 34, no. 3 (Summer 2003): 131.
32 Weiner, "Listening with John Clare," 384–90.
33 Weiner, "Listening with John Clare," 380.
34 David Perkins sees the poem differently: "In the 'Badger' sonnets Clare viewed the baited animal with a somewhat affectionate realism and the villagers with a somewhat humorous distance. His strongest desire, it seems, was to keep both at an emotional distance" (Perkins, "Sweet Helpston!," 405). For my part I can find nothing humorous in the poem or in Clare's attitude to the villagers. In his essay Eric Miller reads (among other poems) Clare's badger sonnets as a reflection of Clare's resistance to the Linnaean taxonomic categorization of the natural world. Miller, "Enclosure and Taxonomy in John Clare," *Studies in English Literature, 1500–1900* 40, no. 4 (2000): 635–57.
35 M.H. Abrams, "Structure and Style in the Greater Romantic Lyric," in *Romanticism and Consciousness: Essays in Criticism*, ed. Harold Bloom (New York: Norton, 1970), 201.
36 "The Hedgehog" ends with a similar note of ambiguity content-wise, but its tonal bleakness suggests that someone should, in fact, care: "but still they hunt the hedges all about / and shepherd dogs are trained to hunt them out / they hurl with savage force the stick and stone / and no one cares and still the strife goes on" (ll. 25–8). Coleridge, "To a Young Ass," in *The Complete Poems*, ed. William Keach (New York: Penguin, 1997), 66.
37 Robinson and Powell provide a dictionary of Clare's dialect. *PMP*, 645–711.
38 By contrast, in the bird's-nest poems and in "The Lament of Swordy Well," "Helpstone," and *The Shepherd's Calendar*, Clare often takes great pains to individuate the various animals, trees, and natural formations that populate the countryside. However, as John Barrell remarks, Clare's poetry often features a robust lack of description when it comes to human beings in his poetry: "The people Clare writes about are what they do: if they were anything else – if they had, somehow, more character – then the sense of place they help create in Clare's poems would change, and would have engaged in some compromise with what it is designed to exclude – the spirit and values of agrarian capitalism" (Barrell, *The Idea of Landscape*, 172–3). Clare takes greater pains with nonhumans. Anne Barton charts Clare's biography of the cart-horse Dobbin across many of his poems. She

does not deal with "The Badger," other than to say: "Clare did later, during the Northborough period, write about badger baiting in one of his darkest and most powerful poems, but that sonnet sequence feels like something forced out of him at that particular point by the extremity of his own situation." Barton, "Clare's Animals: The Wild and the Tame," *John Clare Society Journal* 18 (1999): 17.

39 Miller, "Enclosure and Taxonomy in John Clare," 655.

40 Vardy, *John Clare, Politics and Poetry*, 41.

41 Alexander Regier offers an incisive reading of anthropomorphism that makes a different, but related, point to mine. Regier, *Fracture and Fragmentation in British Romanticism* (Cambridge: Cambridge University Press, 2010), 74.

42 Niklas Luhmann, *Art as a Social System* (Stanford, CA: Stanford University Press, 2000), 52–70. W. John Coletta has demonstrated how Clare's ecologies rely on cybernetic feedback loops of the kind Luhmann describes, remarking that "perception ... can decide *quickly*, whereas art aims to *retard* perception and render it *reflexive* – lingering upon the object in visual art ... and slowing down reading in literature, particularly in lyric poetry" (Luhamann, *Art*, 14, quoted in Coletta). Coletta, "Ecological Aesthetics and the Natural History Poetry of John Clare," *John Clare Society Journal* 14 (1995): 29–46.

43 Clare, "Birds' Nests," in *The Later Poems of John Clare*, vol. 2, ed. Eric Robinson and David Powell (Oxford: Oxford University Press, 1984), 1106.

44 Vardy, *John Clare, Politics and Poetry*, 21. Foucault, *The History of Sexuality*, vol. 1, 138.

45 According to Foucault, the monarch's sovereign power derived from his right to "take life or let live," whereas the dominant methods of institutional control in newfound democratic states was in "making live or letting die" (*The History of Sexuality*, 138).

46 Foucault further defines it in the next lectures: "By this I mean a number of phenomena that seem to me to be quite significant, namely, the set of mechanisms through which the basic biological features of the human species became the object of a political strategy, of a general strategy of power, or, in other words, how, starting from the 18th century, modern Western societies took on board the fundamental biological fact that human beings are a species. This is what I have called biopower." Foucault, *Security, Territory, and Population: Lectures at the College de France, 1977–1978* (New York: Vintage, 2009), 6.

47 Timothy Campbell, "*Bios*, Immunity, Life: The Thought of Roberto Esposito," in Esposito, *Bios*, xx. John Howlett, *Enclosure and Population: An Enquiry into the Influence Which Enclosures Have Had upon the Population of*

England, 1786 & Enclosures; A Cause of Improved Agriculture of Plenty and Cheapness Provisions (Gregg International Publishers, 1973), 74.

48 Foucault, *Security*, 238. Wolfe, *Before the Law*, 1–5.

49 See Esposito's *Bios*, 184–5.

50 Johanne Clare, *Bounds of Circumstances*, 165.

51 See, for instance, the final chapter of Hardt and Negri's *Multitude*, and Hardt's "Two Faces of Apocalypse," *Polygraph* 22 (2010), 265–74.

52 Hardt and Negri, *Multitude*.

53 Sara Guyer has recently discussed other implications of biopolitics in relation to Clare, more specifically how more theoretical readings of Clare would allow for a renewal of close reading. My own essay on Clare and biopolitics in *European Romantic Review*, which forms part of this chapter, was published in 2014 before her book and goes in a different direction in regard to biopolitics. Guyer, *Reading with John Clare: Biopoetics, Sovereignty, Romanticism* (New York: Fordham University Press, 2015).

54 Hardt and Negri, *Multitude*, 348–58.

55 Seth T. Reno has recently argued for a Clare that promotes his "ecophilia," his love of all things. As we will see, though, for Clare, love stems from the other rather than from the self, hence love cannot be one directional, flaring outward from the human subject to animals, trees, fields, and humans, etc. In short, it is not that Clare loves all things, as in Reno's reading of Clare's poetry, but that he theorizes how love works. Reno, "John Clare and Ecological Love," *John Clare Society Journal* 35 (2016): 59–76.

56 John Clare, "I Am," in *Major Works*, ed. Eric Robinson and David Powell (Oxford: Oxford University Press, 2008), 361.

57 Goodridge and Thornton, "John Clare: The Trespasser." John Goodridge, *John Clare and Community* (Cambridge: Cambridge University Press, 2015).

58 John Clare, "Sonnet: I Am," in *Major Works*, ed. Eric Robinson and David Powell (Oxford: Oxford University Press, 2008), 361.

59 Timothy Morton, "John Clare's Dark Ecology," *Studies in Romanticism* 47, no. 2 (2008): 179–93.

60 John Clare, "The Mores," in *Major Works*, ed. Eric Robinson and David Powell (Oxford: Oxford University Press, 2008), 167–8.

61 John Barrell, *The Idea of Landscape and the Sense of Place, 1730–1840: An Approach to the Poetry of John Clare* (Cambridge: Cambridge University Press, 1972). Erica McAlpine writes: "Clare hesitates to seek communion with the natural world, despite his obvious passion for its animals and scenes. Instead, Clare maintains a distance between himself and nature, usually by imbuing his natural descriptions with a sense of wonder rather than claiming any intimate or specialized knowledge of them." McAlpine, "Keeping Nature at Bay: John Clare's Poetry of Wonder," *Studies in Romanticism* 50 (2011): 79.

62 John Clare, "Sighing for Retirement," in *The Later Poems of John Clare*, vol. 1, ed. Eric Robinson and David Powell (Oxford: Oxford University Press, 1984), 19–20.
63 Clare, "The Progress of Rhyme," in *Major Works*, ed. Eric Robinson and David Powell (Oxford: Oxford University Press, 2008), 153–60.
64 Weiner, "Listening with John Clare," 387.
65 Karen Barad, *Meeting the Universe Halfway: Quantum Physics and the Entanglement of Matter and Meaning* (Durham, NC: Duke University Press, 2007).
66 Some versions of the poem lack these final two lines. For this version see: John Clare, *"I am": The selected Poetry of John Clare*, ed. Jonathan Bate (New York: Farrar, Straus and Giroux, 2003), 120–31.
67 Jonathan Bate, *John Clare: A Biography* (Farrer, Straus & Giroux, 2003).

5. The Best of All Possible End of the Worlds

1 Jane Austen, *Jane Austen's Letters*, 4th ed., ed. Deirdre Le Faye (New York: Oxford University Press, 2011), 211–12.
2 Mary Favret shows us how involved in wartime affairs Austen's novels actually are despite their home-front setting. This wartime context belies the novels' assumed pacific nature, just as, I argue here, the nonhuman other does. Favret, *War at a Distance: Romanticism and the Making of Modern Wartime* (Princeton, NJ: Princeton University Press, 2009), 45–7, 145–9, 161–72.
3 For other works that are also useful for considering the novel in this relation see Siobhan Carroll, *An Empire of Air and Water: Uncolonizable Space in the British Imagination, 1750–1850* (Philadelphia: University of Pennsylvania Press, 2015); and D'Arcy Wood, *Tambora*.
4 Few critics have read Austen and Shelley in conversation with each other. Mary Poovey does read Austen and Shelley together, arguing that "Austen did concern herself with many of the same issues as Wollstonecraft and Shelley – with the process of a young girl's maturation, for example, and, more important, with the complex relationship between a woman's desires and the imperatives of propriety." Poovey, *The Proper Lady and the Woman Writer: Ideology as Style in the Works of Mary Wollstonecraft, Mary Shelley, and Jane Austen* (Chicago: University of Chicago Press, 1984), 172. Poovey, in fact, reads Lady Susan's energy as the same as the energy of Shelley's "monster" (174). More recently, Clara Tuite has written the first study of Austen's place in Romantic traditions. Tuite, *Romantic Austen: Sexual Politics and the Literary Canon* (Cambridge: Cambridge University Press, 2002). The classic work of feminist literary criticism by Sandra Gilbert and Susan Gubar also finds commonalities between Austen and Shelley as part of a longer feminist tradition of writing that challenges the typical

patriarchical canon of Romanticism and literature in general. Gilbert and Gubar, *The Madwoman in the Attic.*

5 Austen, *Pride and Prejudice*, 58.

6 Cary Wolfe, *Animal Rites: American Culture, the Discourse of Species, and Posthumanist Theory* (Chicago: University of Chicago Press, 2003), 9.

7 Foucault, *Security, Territory, and Population*, 6.

8 Foucault, *Society Must Be Defended*, 254.

9 See also Esposito, *Bios*; Derrida, "Autoimmunity"; and Derrida, "Faith and Knowledge: The Two Sources of 'Religion' at the Limits of Reason Alone," in *Acts of Religion* (London: Routledge, 2002), 40–101.

10 Mary Shelley, *Frankenstein, or The Modern Prometheus*, ed. J. Paul Hunter (New York: Norton, 2012).

11 I am adding species to the discourse on monstrosity. For Jeffrey Jerome Cohen, the monster is primarily a way of framing difference: "Any kind of alterity can be inscribed across (and constructed through) the monstrous body, but for the most part monstrous difference tends to be cultural, political, racial, economic, sexual." Cohen, "Monster Culture (Seven Theses)," in *Monster Theory: Reading Theory*, ed. Jeffrey Jerome Cohen (Minneapolis: University of Minnesota Press, 1996), 7. Mary Poovey reads the monster in the novel as an analogue for the contrasting imperatives that Shelley felt towards defying normative conventionality and adhering to standards of what Poovey calls the "proper lady." Poovey builds on Ellen Moers, who read *Frankenstein* as Shelley's dramatization of her own autobiographical birthing travails. Moers's work is credited with initiating feminist readings of the novel. Moers, "Female Gothic: The Monster's Mother," in *Literary Women* (Garden City, NJ: Doubleday, 1976).

12 Niklas Luhmann, *Social Systems*, trans. John Bednarz Jr (Stanford, CA: Stanford University Press, 1996).

13 Niklas Luhmann, *Love as Passion: The Codification of Intimacy*, trans. Jeremy Gaines and Doris L. Jones (Stanford, CA: Stanford University Press, 1998), 137. Emphasis mine.

14 Other scholars have found an explicitly queered Austen. See Eva Kosofsky Sedgewick, "Jane Austen and the Masturbating Girl," *Critical Inquiry* 17 (1991): 818–37; Claudia L. Johnson, "The Divine Miss Jane: Jane Austen, Janeites, and the Discipline of Novel Studies," *Boundary 2* 23, no. 3 (1996): 143–63; D.A. Miller, *Jane Austen, or the Secret of Style* (Princeton, NJ: Princeton University Press, 2005), 1–30; and Devoney Looser, "Queering the Work of Jane Austen Is Nothing New," *The Atlantic*, 7 July 2017, https://www.theatlantic.com/entertainment/archive/2017/07/queering-the-work-of-jane-austen-is-nothing-new/533418/.

15 Lee Edelman, for instance, argues that queerness is tied to the death drive because queerness halts heteronormative reproductive futurity. A similar

death drive is at work with the creature, only he will, if he can, reproduce on his own to halt heteronormative reproductive futurity. Edelman, *No Future*, 1–32.

16 David Marshall, *The Surprising Effects of Sympathy: Marivoux, Diderot, Rousseau, and Mary Shelley* (Chicago: University of Chicago Press, 1988), 178–227.

17 Adam Smith, *A Theory of Moral Sentiments: The Glasgow Edition of the Works of Adam Smith* (New York: Liberty Fund, 2009), 9.

18 Thomas Pfau, "A Certain Mediocrity: Adam Smith's Moral Behaviorism," in *Romanticism and the Emotions*, ed. Joel Faflak and Richard C. Sha (Cambridge: Cambridge University Press, 2014), 67.

19 For McLane, the question becomes, "Is common species being a pre-requisite for sympathy, or is sympathy the precondition for what I am calling 'common species being'?" As I read it here, species being is conditional for sympathy, as *Frankenstein* bears out. McLane, *Romanticism and the Discourse of the Human Sciences: Poetry, Population, and the Discourse of Species* (Cambridge: Cambridge University Press, 2006), 100–1. See his book 2 wherein Hume discusses how sympathy operates when we recognize the other person as homologous with us. Although Hume bears some similarities with Smith's version of sympathy, Smith's much more influential conception instantiates species distinctions in ways that Hume's does not. Humean sympathy, in fact, allows for the conscious choice of what to do when confronted by the other. Hume, *A Treatise of Human Nature*, ed. David Fate Norton (Oxford: Oxford University Press, 2000), 179–255.

20 Emmanuel Levinas, *Otherwise Than Being or Beyond Essence*, trans. Alphonse Lingis (Pittsburgh, PA: Duquesne University Press, 1998).

21 Smith, *A Theory of Moral Sentiments*, 9.

22 Smith, *A Theory of Moral Sentiments*, 10.

23 Smith, *A Theory of Moral Sentiments*, 190.

24 For an account of a conversation between John Llewellyn and Levinas, in which Levinas says that he does not know if animals have a face and are subject to, and subjects of, ethics, see Llewellyn, *Appositions of Jacques Derrida and Emmanuel Levinas* (Bloomington: Indiana University Press, 2002). See also Derrida, *The Animal That Therefore I Am*.

25 Jeanne M. Britton argues that sympathy in the novel "ultimately depends on auditory, not just visual experience, and, second it is manifested most reliably not in the imaginative space between two individuals, but rather in the textual space of the novelistic page." Britton, "Novelistic Sympathy in Shelley's *Frankenstein*," *Studies in Romanticism* 48, no. 1 (2009): 3. The notion of face, per Levinas and de Man, also entails the verbal and the aural. For Levinas, face incorporates the ability of the face to be addressed.

For de Man, prosopopoeia, as a trope, means to give face, but it also entails apostrophe, addressability.

26 Irigaray, *This Sex Which Is Not One*, passim. For other readings of *Frankenstein* that look at the homosocial in the novel see James Holt McGavran, "Science, Gender and Otherness in Shelley's *Frankenstein* and Kenneth Branagh's Film Adaptation," *European Romantic Review* 9, no. 2 (1998): 253–70; James Holt McGavran, "Insurmountable Barriers to Our Union: Homosocial Male Bonding, Homosexual Panic, and Death on the Ice in *Frankenstein*," *European Romantic Review* 11, no. 1 (2000): 46–67; and Michael Eberle-Sinatra, "Readings of Homosexuality in Mary Shelley's *Frankenstein* and Four Film Adaptations," *Gothic Studies* 7, no. 2 (2005): 185–202.

27 Mary Shelley, *Frankenstein*, Edited by J. Paul Hunter (New York: Norton, 2013), 10.

28 Scott Juengel, "Face, Figure, Physiognomics: Mary Shelley's *Frankenstein* and the Moving Image," *Novel* 33, no. 2 (2000): 362.

29 Marshall, *The Surprising Effects of Sympathy*, 195, 208.

30 Thomas DuToit, "Re-specting the Face as the Moral (of) Fiction in Mary Shelley's *Frankenstein*," *Modern Language Notes* 109, no. 5 (1994): 850.

31 Ian Balfour, "Allegories of Origins: *Frankenstein* after the Enlightenment," *Studies in English Literature* 56, no. 4 (2016): 789.

32 Poovey, *The Proper Lady and the Woman Writer*, 347.

33 On Paul Cantor's reading, the novel is a revision of Rousseau's *Discourse on Inequality*. Cantor, *Creature and Creator: Myth-Making and English Romanticism* (Cambridge: Cambridge University Press, 1984). Lawrence Lipking argues that "it would be easy to read *Frankenstein* as an allegory of what went wrong with Rousseau, or more precisely of the Rousseau enigma." Lipking, "*Frankenstein*, the True Story; or, Rousseau Judges Jean-Jacques," in *Frankenstein*, ed. J. Paul Hunter (New York: Norton, 2013), 429. Jonathan Bate sees the creature as a representative of the state of nature, and Victor of society. As I try to show in this chapter, such neat divisions are not possible. Bate, *Song of the Earth*, 49–55. Zoe Beenstock also suggests that the social contract only applies to men and will therefore leave the female creature outside of any such collective body. Beenstock, "Lyrical Sociability: The Social Contract and Mary Shelley's *Frankenstein*," *Philosophy and Literature* 39, no. 2 (2015): 406–21. On Rousseauian education in the novel see Alan Richardson, "From *Emile* to *Frankenstein*: On the Education of Monsters," *European Romantic Review* 1, no. 2 (1991): 147–62.

34 James O'Rourke, "'Nothing More Unnatural': Mary Shelley's Revision of Rousseau," *ELH* 56, no. 3 (1989): 543–69.

35 The classic reading of Miltonic themes in the novel is Gilbert and Gubar. For them the monster is an Eve rather than an Adam figure because he

is associated with moral reprobation and physical deformity (Eve being a deformed version of Adam). While an astute reading, it is complicated by the fact that the creature never replicates – an Eve from his rib metaphorically – or reproduces offspring. Adam and Eve manage to do both and, after they exit Paradise, become apocalyptic figures in the state of nature, questing after its return. In this sense they also exit the biblical narrative and enter Rousseau's, a mirror of the creature's life. They become, in short, like the creature, abandoned in a post-apocalyptic modernity. Gilbert and Gubar, *The Madwoman in the Attic*, 213–47. It is possible, as well, to see with Poovey that Victor wants to exile women altogether from the reproductive process.

36 McLane, *Romanticism and the Discourse of the Human Sciences*, 107, 104.

37 In this way autopoiesis is similar to what Lacoue-Labarthe and Nancy call "the subject-work" that is, in their example of *Frankenstein*, the auto-reproduction of the romantic subject in the literary. Philippe Lacoue-Labarthe and Jean-Luc Nancy, trans. Philip Barnard and Cheryl Lester, *The Literary Absolute: The Theory of Literature in German Romanticism* (New York: SUNY Press, 1988).

38 Anne Mellor reads Victor's destruction of the female as his support for "a patriarchal denial of the value of women and sexuality." Mellor, "Possessing Nature: The Female in *Frankenstein*," in *Romanticism and Feminism*, ed. Mellor (Bloomington: Indiana University Press, 1988), 220.

39 *The Matrix*, dir. Lana Wachowski and Lili Wachowski, Warner Brothers, 1999. See for instance Carol J. Adams, "Frankenstein's Vegetarian Monster," in *The Sexual Politics of Meat: A Feminist-Vegetarian Critical Theory*, 2nd ed. (New York: Bloomsbury, 2015), 95–108; and Timothy Morton, "In the Face: The Poetics of Natural Diet," in *Shelley and the Revolution in Taste* (Cambridge: Cambridge University Press, 1995), 81–126.

40 Sara Guyer writes: "the monster explains his own impending disappearance as the loss of face and feeling; he has never had a face. To lose his face, to lose what he never will have had, will be to be heard, not as a subject, but as the interruption of an almost human voice." Guyer, "Testimony and Trope in *Frankenstein*," *Studies in Romanticism* 45, no. 1 (2006): 111.

41 Although is it unknown what Austen read beyond the novels and poetry she mentions, several recent works have argued for the influence of Enlightenment discourse on her work. Austen, writing to J.S. Clarke, librarian to the Prince Regent, and suggesting she might write a novel about a clergyman, claimed she knew little of such things: "Of science and philosophy … I know nothing. A classical education, or at any rate, a very extensive acquaintance with English literature, ancient and modern,

appears to me quite indispensible for the person who would do any justice to your clergyman; and I think I may boast myself to be, with all possible vanity, the most unlearned and uninformed female who ever dared to be an authoress." Although Austen undoubtedly did not have a classical education, her facetiousness in this letter precludes taking it at face value. Jane Austen, *Jane Austen's Letters*, ed. Deirdre Le Faye (New York: Oxford University Press, 2011), 125. Karen Valihora charts the influence of Hume and Smith in separate chapters. Valihora, *Austen's Oughts: Judgment after Locke and Shaftesbury* (Newark: University of Delaware Press, 2010). Knox-Shaw finds echoes of Smith's *Theory of Moral Sentiments* in both *Sense and Sensibility* and *Pride and Prejudice*. Peter Knox-Shaw, *Jane Austen and the Enlightenment* (Cambridge: Cambridge University Press, 2004). See also Peter Knox-Shaw, "Philosophy," in *Jane Austen in Context*, ed. Janet Todd (Cambridge: Cambridge University Press, 2005), 346–56. Kenneth Moler finds the same Smithian influence in Austen's work. Moler, "The Bennett Girls and Adam Smith on Vanity and Pride," *Philological Quarterly* 46 (1967): 567–9.

42 For the classic study of character in the period and in Austen see Deidre Lynch, *The Economy of Character: Novels, Market Culture, and the Business of Meaning* (Chicago: Chicago University Press, 1998).

43 David Sigler, *Sexual Enjoyment in British Romanticism: Gender and Psychoanalysis, 1753–1835* (Toronto: McGill-Queens University Press, 2015), 57.

44 Johann Caspar Lavater, *Essays on Physiognomy* (London: Ward, Lock, & Bowden, n.d.). For more on Shaftesbury and Hutcheson see Carsten Zelle, "Soul Semiology: On Lavater's Physiognomic Principles," in *The Faces of Physiognomy: Interdisciplinary Approaches to Johann Caspar Lavater* (Columbia, SC: Camden House, 1993), 57. It is in the Istanbul Polemon that one first finds the story of Zopyrus, an apparent, noted physiognomist, who, upon studying the face of Hippocrates, says that it is a face linked to a soul full of lust and other vices. Hippocrates agrees but says everyone is born with such things, but they can suppress such things. Moreover Hippocrates emphasizes that this suppression should have been apparent in his face too. See also George Boys-Stones, "Physiognomy and Ancient Psychological Theory," in *Seeing the Face, Seeing the Soul: Polemon's Physiognomy from Classical Antiquity to Medieval Islam*, ed. Simon Swain (Oxford: Oxford University Press, 2007), 94.

45 In what follows, my reading is in sympathy with Elizabeth A. Fay's argument. She shows how "portraits and life writing rendered the outside-in and the inside-out explorations that were transforming British society from one dependent on place to one focused on subjective

identity." Fay, *Fashioning Faces: The Portraitive Mode in British Romanticism* (Durham: University of New Hampshire Press, 2010), 9.

46 Ashley Tauchert suggests that romance in the novel "resists definitive closure," remaining a fluid concept. Tauchert, *Romancing Jane Austen: Narrative, Realism, and the Possibility of a Happy Ending* (New York: Palgrave Macmillan, 2005), xi.

47 My reading thus repudiates and modifies Charlotte Brontë's notorious dismissal of Austen: "No glance of a bright, vivid physiognomy" can be found in Austen's work, only "an accurate daguerreotyped portrait of a commonplace face." Brontë elaborates on this by saying that Austen is only concerned with the superficial outer surface of a person, not their inner character: "Her business is not half so much with the human heart as with the human eyes, mouth, hands, and feet; what sees deeply, speaks aptly, moves flexibly, it suits her to study, but what throbs fast and full, though hidden, what the blood rushes through, what is the unseen seat of Life and the sentient target of death – this Miss Austen ignores" (quoted in Wiltshire, 2). Wiltshire situates the body as the locus of anxieties about health in Austen's novels. This anxiety, he argues, obscures social and gender politics. John Wiltshire, *Jane Austen and the Body: "The Picture of Health"* (Cambridge: Cambridge University Press, 1992).

48 While William H. Galperin, too, argues that by Pemberley it is clear that Elizabeth and Darcy "deserve one another," he reads the portrait scene as demonstrating the parallel between mastery and what he calls "mistressy," their mutual gazes' circumscription of them within a society whose universal truths they embody. The "repressed world of possibility" with which the novel opens, Galperin writes, gets downplayed in this scene, and the rest of the novel works to affirm these truths. Given the clear mediation and remediation at work in this scene, however, it seems to me that rescription is just as important as circumscription. Galperin, *The Historical Austen* (Philadelphia: University of Pennsylvania Press, 2003), 130.

49 Susan Fraiman reads this scene as further evidence of Elizabeth's surrender to the paternal sway of Darcy: "As with Darcy's letter, which seizes the female reader and turns her into the object of its force and her own hatred, here is another striking inversion – one that by flipping the idiom sets up the moment as a problem, making the reader pause and consider. The result, I would say, is once more to phrase Elizabeth's humiliating loss of pride as an awkward disordering, to defamiliarize the clichés of female development." Susan Fraiman, *Unbecoming Women: British Women Writers and the Novel of Development* (New York: Columbia University Press, 1993), 85.

50 Kate Singer, "Austen Agitated: Feeling Emotions in Mixed Media," in *Jane Austen and Sciences of the Mind*, ed. Beth Lau (New York: Routledge, 2018), 95–114.

51 Nina Auerbach, *Communities of Women: An Idea in Fiction* (Cambridge, MA: Harvard University Press, 1978), 39–42.

52 Michel Serres, *The Parasite* (Minneapolis: University of Minnesota Press, 2007).

53 Mudrick's work owes much to D.W. Harding's influential evaluation of Austen as hating the society in which she lived and satirizing it to distance herself from it. Mudrick, *Jane Austen: Irony as Defense and Discovery* (Princeton, NJ: Princeton University Press, 1952). D.W. Harding, "Regulated Hatred: An Aspect of the Work of Jane Austen," *Scrutiny* 8 (March 1940): 346–62.

54 Marilyn Butler, *Jane Austen and the War of Ideas* (Oxford: Clarendon Press, 1975). Alistair Duckworth, *The Improvement of the Estate: A Study of Jane Austen's Novels* (Baltimore, MD: Johns Hopkins University Press, 1971). Claudia L. Johnson, *Jane Austen: Women, Politics, and the Novel* (Chicago: Chicago University Press, 1988). Poovey, *The Proper Lady and the Woman Writer*.

55 Sigler, *Sexual Enjoyment in British Romanticism*, 59.

56 Poovey, *The Proper Lady and the Woman Writer*, 205.

57 Nancy Yousef has recently argued that the novel works on a similar plane of unequal relations except for her affections between Darcy and Elizabeth turn on shame and abasement: "Far from being obstacles to intimacy in the novel, these uncomfortable feelings of being utterly, abjectly, unequal to the other seem to engender an intimacy that exceeds the bounds, and exposes the constraints, of mutuality." Nonetheless, the upshot for Yousef is that affection does not need to be equal, and instead this unequalness provides a basis for a fuller love. Yousef, *Romantic Intimacy* (Stanford, CA: Stanford University Press, 2013), 106–7.

58 As Bharat Tandon has pointed out, Austen offers little in the way of foretelling what will happen to her characters once her novels end, but in actuality Austen's artistry resides in precisely her ambiguous evasion of prolepsis that closes her novels. Tandon, *Jane Austen and the Morality of Conversation* (London: Anthem Press, 2003), 171.

59 Singer, "Austen Agitated," 109.

60 In-effacement works differently than de Man's effacement of face, then, in that it allows for the full force of the nonhuman of figuration and materiality to be felt.

61 Joel Faflak, "Jane Austen and the Desire for Happiness," in *Romanticism and the Emotions*, ed. Joel Faflak and Richard C. Sha (Cambridge: Cambridge University Press, 2014), 98–123.

62 Austen, *Jane Austen's Letters*, 211–12.
63 Derrida, *Of Hospitality*, 125.

Coda: After Extinctualism

1 Jane Austen, *Persuasion*, ed. James Kinsley and Deidre Shauna Lynch (Oxford: Oxford University Press, 2008), 89.

Bibliography

Abrams, M.H. "English Romanticism: The Spirit of the Age." In *Romanticism and Consciousness: Essays in Criticism*, edited by Harold Bloom, 90–119. New York: Norton, 1970.

– *Natural Supernaturalism: Tradition and Revolution in Romantic Literature*. New York: Norton, 1971.

– "Structure and Style in the Greater Romantic Lyric." In *Romanticism and Consciousness: Essays in Criticism*, edited by Harold Bloom. New York: Norton, 1970.

#*Accelerate: The Accelerationist Reader*. Edited by Robin Mackay and Armen Avanessian. Falmouth, UK: Urbanomic, 2014.

Adams, Carol J. "Frankenstein's Vegetarian Monster." In *The Sexual Politics of Meat: A Feminist-Vegetarian Critical Theory*, 2nd ed., 95–108. New York: Bloomsbury, 2015.

Agamben, Giorgio. *Homo Sacer: Sovereign Power and Bare Life*. Translated by Daniel Heller-Roazen. Stanford, CA: Stanford University Press, 1998.

Auerbach, Nina. *Communities of Women: An Idea in Fiction*. Cambridge, MA: Harvard University Press, 1978.

Austen, Jane. *Jane Austen's Letters*. 4th ed. Edited by Deirdre Le Faye. New York: Oxford University Press, 2011.

– *Pride and Prejudice*. 3rd ed. Edited by Donald Gray and Mary Favret. New York: Norton, 2016.

– *Persuasion*. Edited by James Kinsley and Deidre Shauna Lynch. Oxford: Oxford University Press, 2008.

Balfour, Ian. "Allegories of Origins: *Frankenstein* after the Enlightenment." *Studies in English Literature* 56, no. 4 (2016): 777–98.

– *The Rhetoric of Romantic Prophecy*. Stanford, CA: Stanford University Press, 2002.

Barrell, John. *The Idea of Landscape and the Sense of Place 1730–1840: An Approach to the Poetry of John Clare*. Cambridge, UK: Cambridge University Press, 1972.

Barad, Karen. *Meeting the Universe Halfway: Quantum Physics and the Entanglement of Matter and Meaning*. Durham, NC: Duke University Press, 2007.

Barton, Anne. "Clare's Animals: The Wild and the Tame." *John Clare Society Journal* 18 (1999): 5–21.

Bate, Jonathan. *John Clare: A Biography*. New York: Farrar, Straus & Giroux, 2003.

– "Living with the Weather." *Studies in Romanticism* 35, no. 3 (1996): 431–47.

– *The Song of the Earth*. Cambridge, MA: Harvard University Press, 2000.

Beenstock, Zoe. *The Politics of Romanticism: The Social Contract and Literature*. Edinburgh: Edinburgh University Press, 2016.

– "Lyrical Sociability: The Social Contract and Mary Shelley's *Frankenstein*." *Philosophy and Literature* 39, no. 2 (2015): 406–21.

Bewell, Alan. "John Clare and the Ghosts of Natures Past." *Nineteenth-Century Literature* 65, no. 4 (2011): 548–78.

– *Romanticism and Colonial Disease*. Baltimore, MD: Johns Hopkins University Press, 1999.

Blake, William. "And Did Those Feet in Ancient Times." In *Milton, A Poem*, edited by Robert N. Essek and Joseph Viscomi. Princeton, NJ: Princeton University Press, 1998.

Bloom, Harold. *Shelley's Mythmaking*. Ithaca, NY: Cornell University Press, 1969.

– *The Visionary Company*. New York: Norton, 1971.

Bloomfield, Robert. *The Farmer's Boy*. Edited by Peter Cochran. Cambridge, UK: Cambridge Scholars Publishing, 2014.

Borushko, Matthew C. "The Politics of Subreption: Resisting the Sublime in Shelley's 'Mont Blanc.'" *Studies in Romanticism* 52, no. 2 (2013): 225–52.

Boys-Stones, George. "Physiognomy and Ancient Psychological Theory," in *Seeing the Face, Seeing the Soul: Polemon's Physiognomy from Classical Antiquity to Medieval Islam*, ed. Simon Swain. Oxford: Oxford University Press, 2007.

Brassier, Ray. *Nihil Unbound: Enlightenment and Extinction*. Basingstoke, UK: Palgrave Macmillan, 2007.

Britton, Jeanne M. "Novelistic Sympathy in Shelley's *Frankenstein*." *Studies in Romanticism* 48, no. 1 (2009): 3–22.

Broglio, Ron. *Beasts of Burden: Biopolitics, Labor, and Animal Life in British Romanticism*. New York: SUNY, 2017.

Brownlow, Timothy. *Clare and Picturesque Landscape*. Oxford: Clarendon Press, 1983.

Burke, Edmund. *A Philosophical Enquiry into the Origin of Our Ideas of the Sublime and the Beautiful*. Oxford: Oxford University Press, 2015.

Butler, Marilyn. *Jane Austen and the War of Ideas*. Oxford: Clarendon Press, 1975.

Byron, Lord. *Byron's Letters and Journals*. 12 vols. Edited by Leslie A. Marchand. Cambridge, MA: Belknap Press, 1973–82.

– *Cain: A Mystery*. In *The Major Works*, edited by Jerome McGann, 881–938. Oxford: Oxford University Press, 2008.

– "Darkness." In *The Major Works*, edited by Jerome McGann, 272–3. Oxford: Oxford University Press, 2008.

– *Don Juan*. In *The Major Works*, edited by Jerome McGann, 373–879. Oxford: Oxford University Press, 2008.

Callaghan, Madaleine. "The Struggle with Language in Byron's *Cain*." *Byron Journal* 38, no. 2 (2010): 125–34.

Cantor, Paul A. "Byron's 'Cain': A Romantic Version of the Fall." *Kenyon Review* 2, no. 3 (1980): 50–71.

– *Creature and Creator: Myth-Making and English Romanticism*. Cambridge, UK: Cambridge University Press, 1984.

Canuel, Mark. "Acts, Rules, and the Last Man." *Nineteenth-Century Fiction* 53, no. 2 (1998): 147–70.

Carroll, Siobhan. *An Empire of Air and Water: Uncolonizable Space in the British Imagination, 1750–1850*. Philadelphia: University of Pennsylvania Press, 2015.

Castellanno, Katey. *The Ecological Roots of British Romantic Conservatism, 1790–1837*. Houndmills, UK: Palgrave Macmillan, 2013.

Chandler, James K. "'Man Fell with Apples': The Moral Mechanics of *Don Juan*." In *Byron's Poetry and Prose*, edited by Alice Levine, 993–1008. New York: Norton, 2010.

Chatterjee, Ranita. "Our Bodies, Our Catastrophies: Biopolitics in Mary Shelley's *The Last Man*." *European Romantic Review* 25, no. 1 (2014): 35–49.

Chernaik, Judith. *The Lyrics of Shelley*. Cleveland, OH: Press of Case Western Reserve University, 1972.

Christensen, Jerome. *Romanticism at the End of History*. Baltimore, MD: Johns Hopkins University Press, 2004.

Clare, Johanne. *John Clare and the Bounds of Circumstances*. Kingston, ON: McGill-Queen's University Press, 1987.

Clare, John. "Autobiographical Fragments." In *John Clare by Himself*, edited by Eric Robinson and David Powell, 34–165. New York: Routledge, 2002.

– "The Badger." In *Poems of the Middle Period, 1822–1837*, edited by Eric Robinson, David Powell, and P.M.S. Dawson, 360–2. Oxford: Oxford University Press, 2003.

– "Birds' Nests." In *The Later Poems of John Clare*, vol. 2, edited by Eric Robinson and David Powell, 1106. Oxford: Oxford University Press, 1984.

– "The Fallen Elm." In *Selected Poems*, edited by Geoffrey Summerfield, 167–8. New York: Penguin, 2000.

– "The Fox." In *Poems of the Middle Period, 1822–1837,* edited by Eric Robinson, David Powell, and P.M.S. Dawson, 359. Oxford: Oxford University Press, 2003.
– "The Hedgehog." In *Poems of the Middle Period, 1822–1837,* edited by Eric Robinson, David Powell, and P.M.S. Dawson, 359. Oxford: Oxford University Press, 2003.
– "Helpston Green." In *Major Works,* edited by Eric Robinson and David Powell, 62-3. Oxford: Oxford University Press, 2008.
– "I Am." In *Major Works,* edited by Eric Robinson and David Powell, 361. Oxford: Oxford University Press, 2008.
– "The Lamentations of Round-Oak Waters." In *Major Works,* edited by Eric Robinson and David Powell, 18–23. Oxford: Oxford University Press, 2008.
– *The Letters of John Clare,* edited by Mark Storey. Oxford: Clarendon Press, 1985.
– "The Martin." In *Poems of the Middle Period, 1822–1837,* edited by Eric Robinson, David Powell, and P.M.S. Dawson, 360–3. Oxford: Oxford University Press, 2003.
– "The Mores." In *Major Works,* edited by Eric Robinson and David Powell, 167–8. Oxford: Oxford University Press, 2008.
– *The Natural History Prose Writings of John Clare.* Edited by Margaret Grainger. Oxford: Oxford University Press, 1984.
– "The Nightingale's Nest." In *Selected Poems,* edited by Geoffrey Summerfield, 108–10. New York: Penguin, 2000.
– "The Progress of Rhyme." In *Major Works,* edited by Eric Robinson and David Powell, 153–60. Oxford: Oxford University Press, 2008.
– "Schoolboys in the Morning." In *Poems of the Middle Period, 1822–1837,* edited by Eric Robinson, David Powell, and P.M.S. Dawson, 358. Oxford: Oxford University Press, 2003.
– *The Shepherd's Calendar.* Edited by Tim Chilcott. Manchester, UK: Carcanet Press, 2006.
– "Sighing for Retirement." In *The Later Poems of John Clare,* vol. 1, edited by Eric Robinson and David Powell, 19–20. Oxford: Oxford University Press, 1984.
– "Sonnet: I Am." In *Major Works,* edited by Eric Robinson and David Powell, 361. Oxford: Oxford University Press, 2008.
– "The Starnel." In *Poems of the Middle Period, 1822–1837,* edited by Eric Robinson, David Powell, and P.M.S. Dawson, 358. Oxford: Oxford University Press, 2003.
– "The Tame Badger." In *Poems of the Middle Period, 1822–1837,* edited by Eric Robinson, David Powell, and P.M.S. Dawson, 362. Oxford: Oxford University Press, 2003.

– "The Yellowhammer's Nest." In *Selected Poems*, edited by Geoffrey Summerfield, 104–5. New York: Penguin, 2000.

Cohen, Jeffrey Jerome. "Monster Culture (Seven Theses)." In *Monster Theory: Reading Theory*, edited by Cohen, 3–25. Minneapolis: University of Minnesota Press, 1996.

Colebrook, Claire. *The Death of the Posthuman: Essays on Extinction*, vol. 1. Ann Arbor, MI: Open Humanities Press, 2014. https://quod.lib.umich.edu/o/ohp/12329362.0001.001/1:3/ – death-of-the-posthuman-essays-on-extinction-volume-one?rgn=div1;view=fulltext.

Coleridge, Samuel Taylor. "Kubla Khan." In *The Complete Poems*, edited by William Keach, 249–51. New York: Penguin, 1997.

– "To a Young Ass." In *The Complete Poems*, edited by William Keach, 66. New York: Penguin, 1997.

Coletta, W. John. "Ecological Aesthetics and the Natural History Poetry of John Clare." *John Clare Society Journal* 14 (1995): 29–46.

Collings, David. *Monstrous Society: Reciprocity, Discipline, and the Political Uncanny at the End of the Early Modern England*. Lewisburg, PA: Bucknell University Press, 2009.

– "After the Covenant: Romanticism, Secularization, and Disastrous Transcendence," *European Romantic Review* 21, no. 3 (2010): 345–61.

Cowper, William. *The Task and Selected Other Poems*. Edited by James Sambrook. New York: Longman, 1994.

Crutzen, Paul. "Geology of Mankind." *Nature* 415 (2002): 6867.

Curran, Stuart. *Shelley's Annus Mirabilis: The Maturing of an Epic Vision*. San Marino, CA: Huntington Library, 1975.

Cuvier, Georges. *An Essay on the Theory of the Earth*. 1813.

D'Arcy Wood, Gillen. *Tambora: The Eruption That Changed the World*. Princeton, NJ: Princeton University Press, 2015.

de Man, Paul. "Autobiography as De-facement." In *The Rhetoric of Romanticism*, 67–82. New York: Columbia University Press, 1984.

– "Hypogram and Inscription." In *The Resistance to Theory*, 27–52. Minneapolis: University of Minnesota Press, 1986.

Dennis, Ian. "'Cain': Lord Byron's Sincerity." *Studies in Romanticism* 41, no. 4 (2002): 655–74.

Derrida, Jacques. *Adieu to Emmanuel Levinas*. Translated by Pascale-Anne Brault. Stanford, CA: Stanford University Press, 1999.

– *The Animal That Therefore I Am*. Edited by Marie-Lousie Mallet. Translated by David Wills. New York: Fordham University Press, 2008.

– "Autoimmunity: Real and Symbolic Suicides." In *Philosophy in a Time of Terror: Dialogues with Jurgen Habermas and Jacques Derrida*, edited by Giovanna Borradori, 85–136. Chicago: University of Chicago Press, 2003.

– "Eating Well: Or the Calculation of the Subject." In *Points…Interviews, 1974–1994*, 255–87. Stanford, CA: Stanford University Press, 1995.
– "Faith and Knowledge: The Two Sources of 'Religion' at the Limits of Reason Alone." In *Acts of Religion*, 40–101. London: Routledge, 2002.
– "Living On." In *Deconstruction and Criticism*, 62–142. London: Bloomsbury, 2004.
– "Of an Apocalyptic Tone Newly Adopted in Philosophy." In *Derrida and Negative Theology*, edited by Harold Coward and Toby Foshay, 25–72. Albany, NY: SUNY Press, 1992.
– *Of Hospitality*. Translated by Rachel Bowlby. Stanford, CA: Stanford University Press, 2000.
– *Rogues: Two Essays on Reason*. Translated by Pascal-Anne Brault. Stanford, CA: Stanford University Press, 2005.
– *Specters of Marx: The State of the Debt, the Work of Mourning, and the New International*. Translated by Peggy Kamuf. New York: Routledge, 1994.
– "White Mythology: Metaphor in the Text of Philosophy." In *Margins of Philosophy*, translated by Alan Bass, 207–72. Chicago: University of Chicago Press, 1978.

Duckworth, Alistair. *The Improvement of the Estate: A Study of Jane Austen's Novels*. Baltimore, MD: Johns Hopkins University Press, 1971.

Duffy, Cian. *Shelley and the Revolutionary Sublime*. Cambridge, MA: Cambridge University Press, 2005.

DuToit, Thomas. "Re-specting the Face as the Moral (of) Fiction in Mary Shelley's *Frankenstein*." *Modern Language Notes* 109, no. 5 (1994): 847–71.

Eberle-Sinatra, Michael. "Readings of Homosexuality in Mary Shelley's *Frankenstein* and Four Film Adaptations." *Gothic Studies* 7, no. 2 (2005): 185–202.

Economides, Louise. "'Mont Blanc' and the Sublimity of Materiality." *Cultural Critique* 61 (2005): 87–114.

Edelman, Lee. *No Future: Queer Theory and the Death Drive*. Durham, NC: Duke University Press, 2004.

Effinger, Elizabeth. "A Clandestine Catastrophe: Disciplinary Dissolution in Mary Shelley's *The Last Man*." *European Romantic Review* 25, no. 1 (2014): 19–34.

Ellermann, Greg. "Speculative Romanticism." *SubStance* 44, no. 1 (2015): 154–74.

Esposito, Roberto. *Bios: Biopolitics and Philosophy*. Translated by Timothy Campbell. Minneapolis: University of Minnesota Press, 2008.
– *Immunitas: The Protection and Negation of Life*. Translated by Zakiya Hanafi. Boston: Polity, 2011.

Faflak, Joel. "Jane Austen and the Desire for Happiness." In *Romanticism and the Emotions*, edited by Joel Faflak and Richard C. Sha, 98–123. Cambridge, MA: Cambridge University Press, 2014.

Faflak, Joel, and Richard C. Sha. "Introduction." In *Romanticism and the Emotions*, edited by Joel Faflak and Richard C. Sha, 1–18. Cambridge, MA: Cambridge University Press, 2014.

Favret, Mary. *War at a Distance: Romanticism and the Making of Modern Wartime*. Princeton, NJ: Princeton University Press, 2009.

Fay, Elizabeth A. *Fashioning Faces: The Portraitive Mode in British Romanticism*. Durham: University of New Hampshire Press, 2010.

Ferguson, Frances. "Shelley's 'Mont Blanc': What the Mountain Said." In *Romanticism and Language*, edited by Arden Reed, 202–14. Ithaca, NY: Cornell University Press, 1984.

Fisher, John. "The Birds of John Clare." In *The First Fifty Years: A History of the Kettering and District Naturalists' Society and Field Club*. Kettering, UK, 1956. Quoted in *John Clare's Birds*, edited by Eric Robinson and Richard Fitter, xxi. Oxford: Oxford University Press, 1982.

Foer, Jonathan Safran. *Eating Animals*. New York: Little, Brown, 2009.

Foucault, Michel. *The History of Sexuality*. Vol. 1, *An Introduction*, translated by Richard Hurley. New York: Vintage, 1990.

– *Security, Territory, and Population: Lectures at the College de France, 1977–1978*. Translated by Graham Burchell. New York: Vintage, 2009.

– *"Society Must Be Defended": Lectures at the College de France, 1975–1976*. Translated by David Macey. New York: Picador, 2003.

Fraiman, Susan. *Unbecoming Women: British Women Writers and the Novel of Development*. New York: Columbia University Press, 1993.

François, Anne-Lise. *Open Secrets: The Literature of Uncounted Experience*. Stanford, CA: Stanford University Press, 2008.

Frye, Northup. *The Anatomy of Criticism: Four Essays*. Princeton, NJ: Princeton University Press, 2000.

– *Fearful Symmetry: A Study of William Blake*. Princeton, NJ: Princeton University Press, 1969.

Fulford, Tim, ed. *Romanticism and Millenarianism*. Houndmills, UK: Palgrave Macmillan, 2003.

Furniss, Tom. "Nasty Tricks and Tropes: Sexuality and Language in Mary Wollstonecraft's *Rights of Woman*." *Studies in Romanticism* 32, no. 2 (1993): 177–209.

Galperin, William. *The Historical Austen*. Philadelphia: University of Pennsylvania Press, 2003.

Gigante, Denise. *Life: Organic Form and Romanticism*. New Haven, CT: Yale University Press, 2009.

Gilbert, Sandra, and Susan Gubar. *The Madwoman in the Attic: The Woman Writer and the Nineteenth-Century Literary Imagination*. 2nd. ed. New Haven, CT: Yale University Press, 2000.

Gleckner, Robert F. *Byron and the Ruins of Paradise*. Baltimore, MD: Johns Hopkins University Press, 1967.

Godwin, William. *An Enquiry Concerning Political Justice*. Edited by Mark Philp. Oxford: Oxford University Press, 2013.

Goldsmith, Steven E. *Unbuilding Jerusalem: Apocalypse and Romantic Representation*. Ithaca, NY: Cornell University Press, 1993.

Goldstein, Stephen L. "Byron's 'Cain' and the Painites." *Studies in Romanticism* 14, no. 4 (1975): 391–410.

Goodridge, John. *John Clare and Community*. Cambridge, UK: Cambridge University Press, 2015.

– "Pastoral and Popular Modes in Clare's 'Enclosure Elegies.'" In *The Independent Spirit: John Clare and the Self-Taught Tradition*, edited by John Goodridge, 139–55. Helpston, UK: John Clare Society and the Margaret Grainger Memorial Trust, 1994.

Goodridge, John, and Kelsey Thornton. "John Clare: The Trespasser." In *John Clare in Context*, edited by Hugh Haughton, Adam Phillips, and Geoffrey Summerfield, 87–129. Cambridge, UK: Cambridge University Press, 1994.

Gottlieb, Evan. *Romantic Realities: Speculative Realism and British Romanticism*. Edinburgh: Edinburgh University Press, 2016.

Grabo, Carl. *A Newton among Poets: Shelley's Use of Science in "Prometheus Unbound."* New York: Cooper Square Publishers, 1968.

Guyer, Sara. *Reading with John Clare: Biopoetics, Sovereignty, Romanticism*. New York: Fordham University Press, 2015.

– *Romanticism after Auschwitz*. Stanford, CA: Stanford University Press, 2007.

– "Testimony and Trope in *Frankenstein*." *Studies in Romanticism* 45, no. 1 (2006): 77–115.

Harding, D.W. "Regulated Hatred: An Aspect of the Work of Jane Austen." *Scrutiny* 8 (March 1940): 346–62.

Hardt, Michael, and Antonio Negri. *Multitude: War and Democracy in the Age of Empire*. New York: Penguin, 2004.

Hardt, Michael. "Two Faces of Apocalypse." *Polygraph* 22 (2010), 265–74.

Harman, Graham. "On Landscape Ontology: An Interview with Graham Harman." *faslanyc*. http://faslanyc.blogspot.com/2012/07/on-landscape-ontology-interview-with.html. Accessed 1 February 2014.

– *Prince of Networks: Bruno Latour and Metaphysics*. New York: re:press, 2009.

– *The Quadruple Object*. Washington, DC: Zero Books, 2010.

– "The Well-Wrought Broken Hammer." *New Literary History* 43, no. 2 (2012): 183–203.

Hartman, Geoffrey. *Wordsworth's Poetry, 1787–1814*. Cambridge, MA: Harvard University Press, 1964.

Haslanger, Andrea. "The Last Animal: Cosmopolitanism in *The Last Man*." *European Romantic Review* 27, no. 5 (2016): 659–78.

Heaney, Seamus. "John Clare: A Bi-Centenary Lecture." In *John Clare in Context*, edited by Hugh Haughton, Adam Phillips, and Geoffrey Summerfield, 130–47. Cambridge, UK: University of Cambridge Press, 2005.

Heringman, Noah. *Romantic Rocks, Aesthetic Geology*. Ithaca, NY: Cornell University Press, 2010.

Hess, Scott. "John Clare, William Wordsworth, and the (Un)Framing of Nature." *John Clare Society Journal* 27 (2008): 27–44.

Heyes, Bob. "John Clare and Enclosure." *John Clare Society Journal* 6 (1987): 10–19.

Hirsch, E.D. "Byron and the Terrestrial Paradise." In Lord Byron, *Byron's Poetry*, 1st ed., edited by Frank D. McConnell, 442–58. New York: Norton, 1978.

Hirst, Wolf Z. "Byron's Lapse into Orthodoxy: An Unorthodox Reading of 'Cain.'" *Keats-Shelley Journal* 29 (1980): 151–72.

Hitt, Christopher. "Shelley's Unwriting of 'Mont Blanc.'" *Texas Studies in Literature & Language* 47, no. 2 (2005): 139–66.

Hobbes, Thomas. *Leviathan*. Edited by Edwin Curley. New York: Hackett, 1994.

Holmes, Richard. *Shelley: The Pursuit*. New York: New York Review Books Classics, 1994.

Howlett, John. *Enclosure and Population: An Enquiry into the Influence Which Enclosures Have Had upon the Population of England, 1786 & Enclosures; A Cause of Improved Agriculture of Plenty and Cheapness Provisions*. Farnborough, UK: Gregg International Publishers, 1973.

Houghton, Sarah. "'Enkindling Ecstacy': The Sublime Vision of John Clare." *Romanticism* 9 (2003): 176–95.

Hume, David. *A Treatise of Human Nature: The Clarendon Edition of the Works of David Hume*. Edited by David Fate Norton. Oxford: Oxford University Press, 2011.

Hunt, Alastair, and Matthias Rudolf. "Introduction: The Romantic Rhetoric of Life." In *Romanticism and Biopolitics*, Romantic Circles Praxis, December 2012, accessed 1 March 2013, http://www.rc.umd.edu/praxis/biopolitics/index.html.

Irigaray, Luce. *This Sex Which Is Not One*. Translated by Catherine Porter and Caroline Burke. Ithaca, NY: Cornell University Press, 1985.

Johnson, Barbara. "The Last Man." In *A Life with Mary Shelley*, 3–15. Stanford, CA: Stanford University Press, 2014.

Johnson, Claudia L. "The Divine Miss Jane: Jane Austen, Janeites, and the Discipline of Novel Studies." *Boundary 2* 23, no. 3 (1996): 143–63.

– *Jane Austen: Women, Politics, and the Novel*. Chicago: Chicago University Press, 1988.

Joseph, M.K. *Byron the Poet*. London: Victor Gollancz, 1966.

Juengel, Scott. "Face, Figure, Physiognomics: Mary Shelley's *Frankenstein* and the Moving Image." *Novel* 33, no. 3 (2000): 354–76.

Kapstein, I.J. "The Meaning of Shelley's 'Mont Blanc.'" *PMLA* 62, no. 4 (1974): 1046–60.

Keach, William. *Shelley's Style*. London: Methuen, 1984.

Keats, John. "Letter to Richard Woodhouse, October 27th, 1818." In *Selected Letters*, edited by Robert Gittings, 147. Oxford: Oxford University Press, 2009.

Kenyon-Jones, Christine. *Kindred Brutes: Animals in Romantic-Period Writing*. New York: Routledge, 2001.

Khalip, Jacques. *Anonymous Life: Romanticism and Dispossession*. Stanford, CA: Stanford University Press, 2008.

– "Contretemps: Of Extinction and Romanticism," *Literature Compass* 13, no. 10 (2016): 628–36.

Khalip, Jacques, and David Collings, eds. *Romanticism and Disaster*. Romantic Circles Praxis. https://www.rc.umd.edu/praxis/disaster/.

Klein, Hilda. *Animal Rights: Political and Social Change in Britain since 1800*. London: Reaktion Books, 1998.

Klingaman, William, and Nicholas Klingaman. *The Year without a Summer: 1816 and the Volcano That Darkened the World and Changed History*. New York: St Martin's, 2014.

Knight, G. Wilson. *Lord Byron: Christian Virtues*. London: Routledge, 1953.

Knox-Shaw, Peter. *Jane Austen and the Enlightenment*. Cambridge, UK: Cambridge University Press, 2004.

– "Philosophy." In *Jane Austen in Context*, edited by Janet Todd, 346–56. Cambridge, UK: Cambridge University Press, 2005.

Kuiken, Kir. *Imagined Sovereignties: Towards a New Political Romanticism*. Brooklyn, NY: Fordham University Press, 2013.

Lacoue-Labarthe, Philippe, and Jean-Luc Nancy. *The Literary Absolute: The Theory of Literature in German Romanticism*. Translated by Philip Barnard and Cheryl Lester. New York: SUNY Press, 1988.

Leask, Nigel. "Mont Blanc's Mysterious Voice: Shelley and Huttonian Earth Science." In *Third Culture: Literature and Science*, edited by Elinor S. Shaffer, 182–203. New York: Walter de Gruyter, 1998.

Levinas, Emmanuel. *Otherwise Than Being or Beyond Essence*. Translated by Alphonse Lingis. Pittsburgh, PA: Duquesne University Press, 1998.

Levinson, Marjorie. *Wordsworth's Great Period Poems: Four Essays*. Cambridge, UK: Cambridge University Press, 1986.

Lipking, Lawrence. "*Frankenstein*, the True Story; or, Rousseau Judges Jean-Jacques." In Mary Shelley, *Frankenstein*, edited by J. Paul Hunter, 416–33. New York: Norton, 2013.

Liu, Alan. *Wordsworth: The Sense of History*. Stanford, CA: Stanford University Press, 1991.

Llewellyn, John. *Appositions of Jacques Derrida and Emmanuel Levinas*. Bloomington: Indiana University Press, 2002.

Looser, Devoney. "Queering the Work of Jane Austen Is Nothing New." *The Atlantic*, 7 July 2017. https://www.theatlantic.com/entertainment/archive/2017/07/queering-the-work-of-jane-austen-is-nothing-new/533418/.

Luhmann, Niklas. *Art as a Social System*. Stanford, CA: Stanford University Press, 2000.

– *Social Systems*. Translated by John Bednarz Jr. Stanford, CA: Stanford University Press, 1996.

– *Love as Passion: The Codification of Intimacy*. Trans. Jeremy Gaines and Doris L. Jones. Stanford, CA: Stanford University Press, 1998.

Lynch, Deidre. *The Economy of Character: Novels, Market Culture, and the Business of Meaning*. Chicago: Chicago University Press, 1998.

Marchand, Leslie. *Byron: A Biography*. New York: Alfred A. Knopf, 1957.

Marshall, David. *The Surprising Effects of Sympathy: Marivoux, Diderot, Rousseau, and Mary Shelley*. Chicago: University of Chicago Press, 1988.

McAlpine, Erica. "Keeping Nature at Bay: John Clare's Poetry of Wonder." *Studies in Romanticism* 50 (2011): 79–104.

McCarthy, Anne. "The Aesthetics of Contingency in 'The Universe of Things,' or 'Mont Blanc' without Mont Blanc." *Studies in Romanticism* 54 (2015): 355–75.

– *Awful Parenthesis: Suspension and the Sublime in Romantic and Victorian Poetry*. Toronto: University of Toronto Press, 2018.

McCarthy, Cormac. *The Road*. New York: Vintage, 2006.

McGann, Jerome. *Don Juan in Context*. Chicago: Chicago University Press, 1976.

– *The Romantic Ideology*. Chicago: University of Chicago Press, 1983.

McGavran, James Holt. "Insurmountable Barriers to Our Union: Homosocial Male Bonding, Homosexual Panic, and Death on the Ice in *Frankenstein*." *European Romantic Review* 11, no. 1 (2000): 46–67.

– "Science, Gender and Otherness in Shelley's *Frankenstein* and Kenneth Branagh's Film Adaptation." *European Romantic Review* 9, no. 2 (1998): 253–70.

McGeough, Jared. "Romanticism after the Anarchist Turn." *Literature Compass* 13, no. 1 (2016): 3–12.

McKeever, Kerry Ellen. "Naming the Name of the Prophet: William Blake's Reading of Byron's 'Cain: A Mystery.'" *Studies in Romanticism* 34, no. 4 (1995): 615–36.

Mckibben, Bill. *Eaarth: Making a Life on a Tough New Planet*. New York: Henry Holt, 2010.

McKusick, James. *Green Writing: Romanticism and Ecology*. Houndmills, UK: Palgrave Macmillan, 2010.

McLane, Maureen. *Romanticism and the Discourse of the Human Sciences: Poetry, Population, and the Discourse of Species*. Cambridge, UK: Cambridge University Press, 2006.

Meillassoux, Quentin. *After Finitude: An Essay on the Necessity of Contingency*. Translated by Ray Brassier. New York: Continuum, 2010.

– *Time without Becoming*. Edited by Anna Longo. Havertown, PA: Mimesis International, 2014.

– *L'inexistence divine, Quentin Meillassoux: Philosophy in the Making*. Edinburgh: Edinburgh University Press, 2011. 224–87.

Mellor, Anne. *Mary Shelley: Her Life, Her Fictions, Her Monsters*. New York: Routledge, 1989.

– "Possessing Nature: The Female in *Frankenstein*." In *Romanticism and Feminism*, edited by Anne Mellor, 220–32. Bloomington: Indiana University Press, 1988.

Melville, Peter. *Romantic Hospitality and the Resistance to Accommodation*. Waterloo, ON: Wilfrid Laurier University Press, 2007.

Miller, D.A. *Jane Austen, or the Secret of Style*. Princeton, NJ: Princeton University Press, 2005.

Miller, Eric. "Enclosure and Taxonomy in John Clare." *Studies in English Literature, 1500–1900* 40, no. 4 (2000): 635–57.

Milton, John. *Paradise Lost*. Edited by William Kerrigan, John Rumich, and Stephen M. Fallon. New York: Random House, 2007.

Moers, Ellen. "Female Gothic: The Monster's Mother," 90–8. In *Literary Women: The Great Writers*. New York: Doubleday, 1976.

Moler, Kenneth. "The Bennett Girls and Adam Smith on Vanity and Pride." *Philological Quarterly* 46 (1967): 567–9.

Morton, Timothy. *Ecology without Nature*. Cambridge, MA: Harvard University Press, 2007.

– *Hyperobjects: Philosophy and Ecology after the End of the World*. Minneapolis: University of Minnesota Press, 2013.

– "In the Face: The Poetics of Natural Diet." In *Shelley and the Revolution in Taste*, 81–126. Cambridge, UK: Cambridge University Press, 1995.

– "John Clare's Dark Ecology." *Studies in Romanticism* 47, no. 2 (2008): 179–93.

Mudrick, Marvin. *Jane Austen: Irony as Defense and Discovery*. Princeton, NJ: Princeton University Press, 1952.

Nersessian, Anahid. *Utopia, Limited: Romanticism and Adjustment*. Cambridge, MA: Harvard University Press, 2015.

Nietzsche, Friedrich. *Thus Spoke Zarathustra*. Translated by R.J. Hollingdale. New York: Penguin, 2003.

Oerlemans, Onno. *Romanticism and the Materiality of Nature*. Toronto: University of Toronto Press, 2002.

O'Neill, Michael. *The Human Mind's Imaginings: Conflict and Achievement in Shelley's Poetry*. Oxford: Clarendon Press, 1989.

O'Rourke, James. "'Nothing More Unnatural': Mary Shelley's Revision of Rousseau." *ELH* 56, no. 3 (1989): 543–69.

Paley, Morton D. *Apocalypse and Millennium in English Romantic Poetry*. Oxford: Clarendon Press, 1999.

– "Mary Shelley's *The Last Man*: Apocalypse without Millennium." *Keats-Shelley Review* 4 (1989): 1–25. https://www.rc.umd.edu/editions/mws/lastman/paley.htm.

Perkins, David. *Romanticism and Animal Rights*. Cambridge, UK: Cambridge University Press, 2007.

– "Sweet Helpston! John Clare on Badger Baiting." *Studies in Romanticism* 38 (1999): 387–408.

Pfau, Thomas. "A Certain Mediocrity: Adam Smith's Moral Behaviorism." In *Romanticism and the Emotions*, edited by Joel Faflak and Richard C. Sha, 48–75. Cambridge, UK: Cambridge University Press, 2014.

Poovey, Mary. *The Proper Lady and the Woman Writer: Ideology as Style in the Works of Mary Wollstonecraft, Mary Shelley, and Jane Austen*. Chicago: University of Chicago Press, 1984.

Rajan, Tilottama. "'Something Not Yet Made Good': Byron's *Cain*, Godwin, and Mary Shelley's *Falkner*." In *Byron and the Politics of Freedom and Terror*, edited by J.A. Green and Piya Pal-Lapinski, 84–101. Houndmills, UK: Palgrave Macmillan, 2011.

Regier, Alexander. *Fracture and Fragmentation in British Romanticism*. Cambridge, UK: Cambridge University Press, 2010.

Reno, Seth T. "John Clare and Ecological Love." *John Clare Society Journal* 35 (2016): 59–76.

Richardson, Alan. "From *Emile* to *Frankenstein*: On the Education of Monsters." *European Romantic Review* 1, no. 2 (1991): 147–62.

– *A Mental Theater: Poetic Drama and Consciousness in the Romantic Age*. University Park: Pennsylvania State University Press, 1988.

Roberts, Hugh. *Shelley and the Chaos of History*. University Park: Pennsylvania State University Press, 1997.

Rousseau, Jean-Jacques. *Discourse on Inequality*. Translated by Franklin Philip. Oxford: Oxford University Press, 1994.

– *The Social Contract*. Translated by Christopher Betts. Oxford: Oxford University Press, 1994.

Ruston, Sharon. *Shelley and Vitality*. Houndmills, UK: Palgrave Macmillan, 2012.

Saramago, Jose. *Cain*. New York: Houghton Mifflin, 2011.

Schock, Peter A. "The 'Satanism' of Cain in Context: Byron's Lucifer and the War against Blasphemy." *Keats-Shelley Journal* 44 (1995): 182–215.

Scott, Heidi C. *Chaos and Cosmos: Literary Roots of Modern Ecology in the British Nineteenth Century*. University Park: Pennsylvania State University Press, 2015.

Scrivener, Michael Henry. *Radical Shelley: The Philosophical and Utopian Thought of Percy Bysshe Shelley*. Princeton, NJ: Princeton University Press, 1982.

Sedgewick, Eva Kosofsky. "Jane Austen and the Masturbating Girl." *Critical Inquiry* 17 (1991): 818–37.

Serres, Michel. *The Natural Contract*. Translated by Elizabeth MacArthur and William Paulson. Ann Arbor: University of Michigan Press, 1995.

– *The Parasite*. Minneapolis: University of Minnesota Press, 2007.

Shaviro, Steven. *No Speed Limit: Four Essays on Accelerationism*. Minneapolis: University of Minnesota Press, 2015.

– *The Universe of Things: On Speculative Realism*. Minneapolis: University of Minnesota Press, 2014.

Shelley, Mary. *Frankenstein*. Edited by J. Paul Hunter. New York: Norton, 2013.

– *The Last Man*. Edited by Morton D. Paley. Oxford: Oxford World's Classics, 2008.

Shelley, Percy Bysshe. "A Defence of Poetry." In *Shelley's Poetry and Prose*, edited by Donald Reiman and Neil Fraistat, 509–35. New York: Norton, 2002.

– *Epipsychidion*. In *Shelley's Poetry and Prose*, edited by Donald Reiman and Neil Fraistat, 390–406. New York: Norton, 2002.

– "Essay on a Future State." In *Shelley's Prose: The Trumpet of a Prophecy*, edited by David Lee Clark, 175–8. Albuquerque: University of New Mexico Press, 1954.

– *The Letters of Percy Bysshe Shelley*, vol. 1. Edited by Frederick L. Jones. Oxford: Clarendon Press, 1964.

– "Letter to John Gisborne, Jan. 26, 1822." In *The Letters of Percy Bysshe Shelley*, vol. 2, edited by Frederick L. Jones, 388. Oxford: Clarendon University Press, 1964.

– "Letter to Thomas Love Peacock, December 22nd, 1818." In *The Letters of Percy Bysshe Shelley*, vol. 2, edited by Frederick L. Jones. Oxford: Clarendon University Press, 1964.

– "Lines Written in the Bay of Lerici." In *Shelley's Poetry and Prose*, edited by Donald Reiman and Neil Fraistat, 480–1. New York: Norton, 2002.

– "Mont Blanc." In *The Complete Poetry of Percy Bysshe Shelley*, vol. 3, edited by Donald H. Reiman, Neil Fraistat, and Nora Crook, 79–90. Baltimore, MD: Johns Hopkins University Press, 2012.

– "On Life." In *Shelley's Poetry and Prose*, edited by Donald Reiman and Neil Fraistat, 505–9. New York: Norton, 2002.
– "Ozymandius." In *Shelley's Poetry and Prose*, edited by Donald Reiman and Neil Fraistat, 109. New York: Norton, 2002.
– *Prometheus Unbound*. In *Shelley's Poetry and Prose*, edited by Donald Reiman and Neil Fraistat, 202–85. New York: Norton, 2002.
– *The Triumph of Life*. In *Shelley's Poetry and Prose*, edited by Donald Reiman and Neil Fraistat, 481–502. New York: Norton, 2002.
– "Speculations on Metaphysics and Morals." In *Shelley's Prose: The Trumpet of a Prophecy*, edited by David Lee Clark, 181–94. Albuquerque: University of New Mexico Press, 1954.
Shukin, Nicole. *Animal Capital: Rendering Life in Biopolitical Times*. Minneapolis: University of Minnesota Press, 2009.
Sigler, David. *Sexual Enjoyment in British Romanticism: Gender and Psychoanalysis, 1753–1835*. Montreal: McGill-Queens University Press, 2015.
Simpson, David. "A Speaking Place: The Matter of Genre in *The Lament of Swordy Well*." *Wordsworth Circle* 34, no. 3 (2003): 131–6.
Singer, Kate. "Austen Agitated: Feeling Emotions in Mixed Media." In *Jane Austen and Sciences of the Mind*, edited by Beth Lau, 95–114. New York: Routledge, 2018.
– *Romantic Vacancy: The Poetics of Gender, Affect, and Radical Speculation*. New York: SUNY, 2019.
– "It's the End of the World as We Know It and I Feel Posthuman: Mary Shelley's Queer Animacies and Affects." Paper presented at the International Conference on Romanticism, Colorado Springs, Colorado, 2016.
Smith, Adam. *A Theory of Moral Sentiments*: *The Glasgow Edition of the Works of Adam Smith*. New York: Liberty Fund, 2009.
Steffan, Truman. *Lord Byron's "Cain": Twelve Essays and a Text with Variants and Annotations*. Austin: University of Texas Press, 1968.
Sterrenburg, Lee. "*The Last Man*: Anatomy of Failed Revolutions." *Nineteenth-Century Fiction* 33, no. 3 (1978): 324–47.
Strang, Hilary. "Common Life, Animal Life, Equality: 'The Last Man.'" *ELH* 78, no. 2 (2011): 409–31.
Tandon, Bharat. *Jane Austen and the Morality of Conversation*. London: Anthem Press, 2003.
Tauchert, Ashley. *Romancing Jane Austen: Narrative, Realism, and the Possibility of a Happy Ending*. New York: Palgrave Macmillan, 2005.
Thacker, Eugene. *After Life*. Chicago: University of Chicago Press, 2010.
– *In the Dust of this Planet*. Vol. 1 of *Horror of Philosophy*. Washington, DC: Zero Books, 2012.
Tuite, Claire. *Romantic Austen: Sexual Politics and the Literary Canon*. Cambridge, UK: Cambridge University Press, 2002.

Valihora, Karen. *Austen's Oughts: Judgment after Locke and Shaftesbury*. Newark: University of Delaware Press, 2010.

Vardy, Alan. *John Clare, Politics and Poetry*. Houndmills: Palgrave Macmillon, 2003.

von Uexküll, Jacob. *A Foray into the Worlds of Animals and Humans: With a Theory of Meaning*. Translated by Joseph O'Neil. Minneapolis: University of Minnesota Press, 2010.

Wang, Fuson. "'We Must Live Elsewhere': The Social Construction of Natural Immunity in *The Last Man*." *European Romantic Review* 22, no. 2 (2011): 235–55.

Wang, Orrin. *Romantic Sobriety: Sensation, Revolution, Commodification, History*. Baltimore, MD: Johns Hopkins University Press, 2011.

Washington, Chris. "Romanticism and Speculative Realism." *Literature Compass* 12, no. 9 (2015): 448–60.

Washington, Chris, and Anne C. McCarthy, eds. *Romanticism and Speculative Realism*. New York: Bloomsbury, 2019.

Wasserman, Earl. *Shelley: A Critical Reading*. Baltimore, MD: Johns Hopkins University Press, 1977.

Weiner, Stephanie Kuduk. "Listening with John Clare." *Studies in Romanticism* 48 (2009): 371–90.

Weiskal, Thomas. *The Romantic Sublime: Studies in the Structure and Psychology of Transcendence*. Baltimore, MD: Johns Hopkins University Press, 1976.

White, Adam. "John Clare: 'The Man of Taste.'" *John Clare Society Journal* 28 (2009): 38–54.

Williams, Raymond. *The Country and the City*. Oxford: Oxford University Press, 1975.

Wilson, Ross. *Shelley and the Apprehension of Life*. Cambridge, UK: Cambridge University Press, 2013.

Wiltshire, John. *Jane Austen and the Body:"The Picture of Health"* Cambridge, UK: Cambridge University Press, 1992.

Wolfe, Cary. *Animal Rites: American Culture, the Discourse of Species, and Posthumanist Theory*. Chicago: University of Chicago Press, 2003.

– *Before the Law: Humans and Other Animals in a Biopolitical Frame*. Chicago: Chicago University Press, 2012.

Wollstonecraft, Mary. *A Vindication of the Rights of Woman and A Vindication of the Rights of Men*. Oxford: Oxford University Press, 2008.

Woodman, Ross Greig. *The Apocalyptic Vision in the Poetry of Shelley*. Toronto: University of Toronto Press, 1964.

Wordsworth, William. *The Prelude, 1799, 1805, 1850*. Edited by Jonathan Wordsworth, M.H. Abrams, and Stephen Gill. New York: Norton, 1979.

– "The Prospectus." *The Excursion*. Edited by Sally Bushell, James A. Butler, Michael C. Jaye, and David Garcia. Ithaca, NY: Cornell University Press, 2007.
– "The World Is Too Much with Us." In *The Major Works*, edited by Stephen Gill, 270. Oxford: Oxford University Press, 2008.
Wroe, Ann. "Resolutions, Destinations: Shelley's Last Year." In *The Oxford Handbook of Percy Bysshe Shelley*, edited by Michael O'Neill, Anthony Howe, and Madeleine Callaghan, 48–64. Oxford: Oxford University Press, 2013.
Yousef, Nancy. *Romantic Intimacy*. Stanford, CA: Stanford University Press, 2013.
Žižek, Slavoj. *Living in the End Times*. London: Verso, 2010.

Index